The Freedmen's Bureau and Black Texans

The Freedmen's Bureau and Black Texans

by Barry A. Crouch

UNIVERSITY OF TEXAS PRESS, AUSTIN

First Edition, 1992

Requests for permission to reproduce material from this
work should be sent to Permissions, University of Texas
Press, Box 7819, Austin, Texas 78713-7819.

⊗ The paper used in this publication meets the
minimum requirements of American National Standard
for Information Sciences—Permanence of Paper for
Printed Library Materials, ANSI Z39.48-1984.

Library of Congress Cataloging-in-Publication Data

Crouch, Barry A., 1941–
    The Freedmen's Bureau and black Texans / by Barry A.
Crouch. — 1st ed.
        p.   cm.
    Includes bibliographical references and index.
    ISBN 0-292-72475-6
    1. Afro-Americans—Texas—History—19th century.
2. United States. Bureau of Refugees, Freedmen, and
Abandoned Lands—History.   3. Freedmen—Texas—
History—19th century.   4. Texas—Race relations.
I. Title.
E185.93.T4C76   1992
976.4'00496073—dc20   91-29138
                                              CIP

for Patsy and Larry

Contents

Preface

THIS BOOK HAS had a long gestation period, but throughout the many years needed to bring the work to fruition, the Texas Freedmen's Bureau and its agents have never ceased to amaze me. However one views the attempts of the Freedmen's Bureau to initiate the former slaves into the mysteries of freedom, its agents certainly, at least in the Lone Star State, acquitted themselves rather remarkably. Life in the South during the turbulent early years of Reconstruction, when all classes of people had to make readjustments, could not have been easy. Old institutions had been destroyed, and new ones were designed to bring equality, citizenship, and a different form of race and labor relations. The Bureau found itself at the very heart of the transition.

Reconstruction, it seems, still fascinates historians because it focuses upon the freeing of four million people from bondage and their subsequent attempts to build a life for themselves. Although referring to the Bureau agents who served the Texas black community as guardians of the freedpeople may seem like a misnomer, in a sense they did attempt to perform this role. Lacking the resources to protect freedpeople against the incredible amount of violence that occurred in the state, they did encourage efforts to establish organizations and schools, ensure legal rights, and promote community solidarity in the hope that black Texans could begin to experience freedom fully.

Bureau agents did not view black Texans with an open mind. Imbued with the racial attitudes of the nineteenth century, when most white Americans believed that blacks were inferior, the agents seem to have performed in a manner that is nonetheless quite surprising. Indeed, they made mistakes, occasionally viewed the black community as backward, believed their work rhythm did not always coincide with a free labor ideology, and saw their morals as suspect at times. More often than not, however, they blamed these "deficiencies" upon slavery. Considering the agents' background and the social and racial milieu within which they functioned, their collective efforts in behalf of the legal rights, education, and social problems of the former slaves appear to be of a sincere nature. On the whole, they demonstrated honesty and perseverance in the face of incredible odds.

Over the years many people have assisted me in a variety of ways in attempting to understand Reconstruction and the Freedmen's Bureau. LaWanda Cox always provided encouragement as did Donald G. Nieman, Stanley L. Engerman, and Eric Foner. Joseph S. Kelley, Jr., gave me a computer education. In the past Donald A. MacKendrick and Gene M. Gressley stirred my interest in history and supplied me with a solid foundation. The staff at the National Archives, to my mind, is the best. From Elaine C. Everly to Michael T. Meier and William S. Lind, they have always been generous in sharing their knowledge and time. In Texas, Donaly A. Brice of the Texas State Library has answered numerous questions and been unfailing in pointing me to sources that I may have missed.

A research grant from the Penrose Fund of the American Philosophical Society provided some necessary funds for exploring resources beyond the National Archives. The Gallaudet University Research Institute, under the able direction of Michael A. Karchmer, awarded me various stipends to allow trips to Texas and the Southern Historical Collection at the University of North Carolina. Members of the Gallaudet University history department have been supportive and encouraged completion of this work, especially John V. Van Cleve. In Texas, Cecil Harper has exchanged ideas with me and helped me to refine my interpretation. Carl M. Moneyhon at the University of Arkansas at Little Rock, who paved the way for a different perspective on Reconstruction in Texas, shared information that made this a better book.

Friends and family are important sources of support when doing a book. Patrick, Denise, "Bear," and Jennifer all supported me. Naomi was wonderful. My wife Joan is a constant inspiration. Helen B. Mitchell has been a tireless critic and has saved me from numerous errors. Arnoldo De León has inspired by example and has been a steadying influence over the years. When this book reached its latter stages, I assumed care of my granddaughter, Katherina, for a time. A delightful and energetic child, she helped me realize how to put everything into perspective. This book is dedicated to my sister, Patsy, who has tolerated a historian in the family with graciousness, wit, and charm. Her unfailing confidence has aided in difficult times.

Larry Madaras, my dear friend, critic, and supporter over the years, originally suggested the idea for this book. He has had to live with it ever since. Without either one of them, it would never have been completed. Their faith that I would eventually finish the book never wavered. I cannot thank them enough.

Introduction

IN 1864 the final report of the American Freedmen's Inquiry Commission justified the establishment of an interim governmental agency to assist former slaves in their transition from bondage to freedom. "For a time we need a freedmen's bureau, but not because these people are negroes," the commissioners determined, "only because they are men who have been, for generations, despoiled of their rights." Any assistance "given to these people should be regarded as a temporary necessity," and "all supervision over them should be provisional only, and advisory in its character." Essentially, the commissioners contended, the nation should "secure to them the means of making their own way; that we give them, to use the familiar phrase, 'a fair chance.'"[1]

From its inception through most of the twentieth century, the Bureau of Refugees, Freedmen, and Abandoned Lands, commonly referred to as the Freedmen's Bureau, has been at the center of many historical and institutional debates. From the commissioner to the assistant commissioners to the local agents, and the implementation of policy, the Bureau has been subjected to wide-ranging and conflicting assessments. J. G. De Roulhac Hamilton realized the problems in analyzing this unique post–Civil War agency when he wrote in 1909 that "no more difficult task can confront the historical investigator than an attempt to form a just estimate of the work, character, and general influence of the Freedmen's Bureau."[2] This dictum still holds true today.

Almost nine decades ago, W. E. B. Du Bois fired the opening salvo over how historians would view the creation and operation of the Freedmen's Bureau. In the first modern assessment of the agency from a trained academic perspective, Du Bois perceived the Bureau "as one of the most singular and interesting of the attempts made by a great nation to grapple with vast problems of race and social condition." No "correct history of civilization can ever be written which does not throw out in bold relief, as one of the great landmarks of political and social progress," Du Bois magnanimously concluded, without discussing the "organization and administration of the Freedmen's Bureau." A "great work of social reform," he observed.[3]

Although Du Bois did not have access to the original Bureau records, he became its first astute scholarly observer. Viewing the Bureau as "an attempt to establish a government guardianship over the negroes and insure their economic and civil rights," Du Bois saw its mission as a "herculean task both physically and socially, and it not only met the solid opposition of the white South, but even the North looked at the new thing as socialistic and ever-paternal." The Bureau "accomplished a great task but it was repudiated." Du Bois capsulized the Bureau's image when he wrote that "above all, nothing is more convenient than to heap on the Freedmen's Bureau all the evils of that evil day, and damn it utterly for every mistake and blunder that was made."[4]

After Du Bois, the historical career of the Freedmen's Bureau has been checkered. This anomalous institution has posed, in many ways, an enigma for historians. Damned by white Southerners for unwarranted interference with the former slaves and local folkways, the Bureau is now castigated by historians for not providing more help (or the wrong kind, generally paternalistic) to Southern blacks in the early years of freedom. Within this general circle of condemnation, the Bureau's interpretative fortunes have indeed been mixed, partially depending upon the status of the larger field of which it is a part, Reconstruction history. In no state is this more evident or revisionism more overdue than in Texas, where the Bureau's ordeal continues and is yet unfinished.

Among historians of Texas, the Bureau has not been well served. Generally seen as interfering in state affairs, it has never received a full-scale treatment. Following the negative interpretation of the agency found in the work of Charles W. Ramsdell, other historians accepted his perception until the 1970s. At the time that Ramsdell wrote, Bureau manuscripts were not available, so he apparently selected conservative sources with the idea of showing the Bureau in the worst possible light. Two decades ago, scholars began to do in-depth research in the Texas Freedmen's Bureau records in the National Archives. This research encouraged additional efforts, and collectively a different perspective has now been cast upon the Bureau's activities.

Whatever the current direction of the history of the Texas Freedmen's Bureau, praise for its efforts has hardly been universal. The

Bureau, like many other facets of the Texas Reconstruction era, has been only partially reevaluated in the past two decades. The process has been piecemeal because much of the emphasis in consulting Bureau records has been upon a way to understand the responses of black Texans to freedom. In many of the writings about postwar Texas, the Bureau is a secondary consideration, for little is known about its operations or functions. Continued reliance upon older published works paints an unflattering portrait of what the Bureau attempted to do at all levels of Texas society.

The Bureau papers "provide valuable data on Texans' attitudes and actions toward blacks," writes Nora E. Owens. "Except those [Bureau records] dealing specifically with blacks or the agency itself," she continues, the "historians of Reconstruction in Texas have made scant or no use of the papers." Bureau personnel may have occasionally been "misinformed, or incompetent, or self-serving," but the reports of the local agents "provide an enormous reservoir of social, political, and economic information which is difficult to obtain elsewhere." Precisely because it was a "pioneer social welfare agency" dealing with sensitive Reconstruction issues, the agency becomes "an essential element in any study of the period."[5]

The approach here is different. At the outset it must be made clear that this is not a full-scale history of the rise and demise of the Texas Freedmen's Bureau. It is selective in what it discusses, with the focus primarily upon the local level, and thus attempts a different tack than other works about the Freedmen's Bureau. The discussion begins with an overview of what has been written about the Bureau from the late nineteenth century to the present day. Until recently, the agency records were often ignored by Texas historians, and numerous negative interpretations of the organization emerged. Actually, little was known about what the Bureau did, how it performed, or what obstacles it encountered.

Two overarching interpretations are the themes of this book. First, by exploring the historiography of the Texas Freedmen's Bureau, we understand where we have been, what is the current status of the Bureau in Texas Reconstruction history, and where we might be going. When we look at the historiographical background of the Texas Bureau and the sources which make up this composite of Texas Bureau history, the limited perspectives of past writings become evident. Second, the Texas Bureau is explored from the top down and from the bottom up, based upon the extensive papers in the National Archives. This exploration suggests the many facets of its relationship to the white and black communities.

It is important to understand what the Bureau assistant commissioners believed, how they went about implementing their policies, and what effect their ideas and administration had upon agents throughout the Lone Star State. Although they have been studied as army men, they seldom have been investigated as Bureau men. Their collective commissionerships cannot be counted a rousing success. Many factors arose that curtailed what they could or could not do, not to mention their own personal limitations. They each emphasized certain aspects of the Bureau's program, but generally economics and labor relations came to the forefront. A reevaluation of these individuals suggests a new interpretation is in order.

Directly below the assistant commissioners' jurisdiction in the Bureau's organizational chart was an area designated as a subdistrict. Although these units were not strictly defined until 1867, they are important in understanding the workings of the Texas Bureau on the regional and local level. Within these geographical confines, an agent interacted with headquarters, responded to the respective black and white communities that he served, and performed a myriad of tasks. The region that a Bureau agent supervised was much too large for one man, and as a result, even within an individual subdistrict, an agent's coverage was limited. Lack of financial and institutional resources hampered an agent at every turn.

The Thirtieth Subdistrict, which included Smith County and those counties surrounding it, exemplifies this approach. The Thirtieth was not unique, for all the problems and difficulties that Bureau agents encountered in this region were similar to problems in every other subdistrict across the state. Overweening white hostility, a harassed black population, uncooperative civil and judicial officials, too many duties to perform, little protection, and clashes with undesirable elements—all characterized the Thirtieth Subdistrict as it did many other subdistricts in the Lone Star State. Politics and economics exacerbated an already tense situation, and agents had to steer a delicate course to ensure that the freedpeople received some equal consideration.

In some ways chapters 3 and 4 overlap. Obviously, an individual agent worked within his own subdistrict, but some subdistricts had more changes in personnel than did others. It is important to see how Bureau policy was implemented by various agents in a particular region and also what the policy was like under one agent who served for a relatively extended time in a specific area. Moreover, this approach demonstrates the diverse personalities of the individuals, what attitudes they brought with them, how they approached their Bureau duties, and the response of Texas blacks to their efforts.

Understanding some of the difficulties these agents encountered during their Bureau service is crucial.

In chapters 3, 4, and 5, extensive use has been made of local agents' records in the National Archives. These are important sources because they are not duplicated in the microfilm edition of Record Group 105 distributed by the archives. There is some duplication between the agents' files and those of the Texas assistant commissioner, which have been microfilmed. For whatever reason, a large portion of this material did not make its way into the central files and thus is available only in the National Archives. This group includes letters to local black and white citizens, contractual relations between employer and employee, numerous complaints, and agent commentary upon relations with the surrounding community, plus much more.

One example should suffice: An agent who is the subject of chapter 4. In the Texas assistant commissioner's files on microfilm, there are about fifty letters from William G. Kirkham, plus his monthly operations report. Unquestionably, these are significant records that demonstrate many of Kirkman's problems and his relationship with headquarters. His local records comprise five volumes, not including letters he sent to local officials that also are not on microfilm. When a historian fails to research an agent's files, the impression is that a subassistant commissioner was not doing as much as he could. Consulting the agent's own copies presents an entirely different picture and a more complete record of his activities.

Kirkman was probably typical of a Texas Bureau agent and characterized many of the agent's best attributes. Dedicated, honest, and hardworking, he experienced the frustrations and small victories that every other agent across the state felt. Also he died in the line of duty while most agents did not. He was chosen for intensive investigation for three reasons. First, Kirkman left extensive records, although headquarters complained about his filing forms in the "proper manner." Second, he served in a subdistrict that was particularly violent and far removed from state headquarters. Third, his handwriting is truly distinctive and can be recognized immediately.

Finally, in chapter 5, the interaction of whites, blacks, the Bureau, economics, politics, and race relations comes into play during the first significant racial confrontation in the summer of 1868. Once again, a microcosmic approach: in this case one county and one town serve as a springboard to view what happened when a black community leader emerged, the freedmen became active in Republican politics through the organization of a Union League, and the Ku Klux Klan began to harass black organizational activities, and what role economics and race played at this time. The Freedmen's Bureau, at the center of much that occurred in Brazos County and the small village of Millican, could not prevent a clash between blacks and whites.

In summary, a different outlook on the Texas Bureau is set forth, first, by considering where we are (historiographically, chapter 1); second, how the assistant commissioners approached their job, what they thought, and how they implemented their ideas based on the sources (chapter 2); third, how Bureau operations functioned at the level directly below the assistant commissioners by tracing the life of a subdistrict from its creation to its demise (chapter 3); fourth, how an individual agent who stayed in one area for a considerable time met the challenges of Reconstruction (chapter 4); fifth, how the Bureau dealt with the important topics of labor, politics, and race relations in one country (chapter 5). Finally, a conclusion.

Bureau historiography has magnified the ideals of its inspirers but has belittled the performance of its field agents. This is unfortunate because more often than not they attempted to be equitable in their treatment of both blacks and whites. Indeed, this may suggest that the Bureau was more successful than past historians have realized. This book does not attempt the task of completely reevaluating the Texas Bureau, but through a series of case studies on the subdistrict and local level that are clearly typical and representative of the Texas Bureau effort, it sheds light on numerous aspects of Bureau activities and provides an intensive look at the Texas Bureau from various institutional, regional, individual, and social levels.

The various historical interpretations surrounding the post–Civil War years have created challenging debates for those involved in writing Reconstruction history. The Bureau, in the words of William S. McFeely, was designed to assist blacks "to struggle, with some hope of success, for the social, economic, and political rewards in a community offering equal opportunities to its citizens." Perhaps Du Bois, almost ninety years ago, expressed best what the Freedmen's Bureau exemplified when he wrote that the "very name of the Bureau stood for a thing in the South which for two centuries and better men had refused even to argue,—that life amid free Negroes was simply unthinkable, the *maddest of experiments.*"[6]

This is only the fourth published state study of the Bureau in the twentieth century. The last one, on Louisiana, appeared over two decades ago. Although the assistant commissioners are discussed, they are but a small part of the overall picture. Their backgrounds, policies, and problems are highlighted to provide a summary overview of the origins and development of the Texas Bureau. Moreover, the emphasis here is not upon administrative history, which does play a part, but on the Bureau and its functions as they related to certain select communities. A social perspective has been adopted, with an analysis of other elements as they impinged on the activities of the Bureau agents. Thus, the agent is viewed as interacting with the community.

Historians continue to view the Bureau as part of the problem in the failure of national policy, instead of its aiding in a deeper understanding of black and white responses to the Reconstruction process. Because of past negative descriptions of the Bureau, and their continued reiteration, no one takes seriously what the Bureau attempted to do. It was a delicate situation for field agents, as they were the individuals to whom the freedpeople pled their cases or demanded satisfaction and resolution to a host of difficulties. A study focusing upon one state and concentrating upon these issues should begin to clarify some of the confusion and to fill in some important gaps in the Reconstruction story.

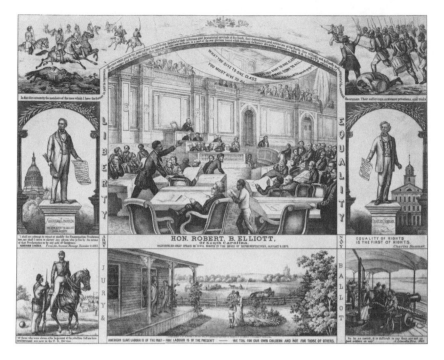

The transition from slave to free labor. Courtesy Library of Congress.

The horrors of slavery and its eradication. Courtesy Library of Congress.

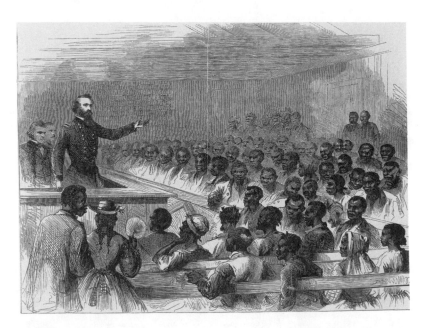

President Andrew Johnson selected General James B. Steedman and Brevet Brigadier General Joseph S. Fullerton to investigate the Bureau and hopefully discredit the agency. Courtesy Library of Congress.

This could have been a Freedmen's Bureau agent's office anyplace in Texas. Courtesy Library of Congress.

Joseph J. Reynolds. Courtesy Library of Congress.

Brevet Major General Charles Griffin was the controversial third assistant commissioner of the Texas Freedmen's Bureau. Courtesy National Archives.

Brevet Major General Gordon Granger. Granger, commander of the
District of Texas, issued the famous June 19, 1865, proclamation
that formally freed the Texas slaves. Courtesy National Archives.

Many Southerners believed that the former slaves should not be allowed to participate in government. Courtesy Library of Congress.

Planters threatened their laborers with dismissal if they voted the Republican ticket. Courtesy Library of Congress.

Both white and black Southerners suffered in the aftermath of war.
Courtesy Library of Congress.

"THE POPULAR IDEA OF THE FREEDMEN'S BUREAU—PLENTY TO EAT AND NOTHING TO DO."

A popular Texas misconception and lie perpetuated by many was that the Bureau encouraged the idleness of the freedpeople. Courtesy Library of Congress.

1. The Freedmen's Bureau in Texas: A Historiographical Appraisal

Origins

With the establishment of the Bureau of Refugees, Freedmen, and Abandoned Lands, the United States Congress determined that the work of overseeing the transition from slavery to freedom of the South's emancipated slaves could be performed only by the government. Originally proposed by Massachusetts Congressman Thomas D. Eliot in 1863, the Freedmen's Bureau found itself at the center of debate over what emancipation portended. Once the Bureau began to function in the conquered states, the white South began an unceasing critical barrage of this unique and controversial governmental institution. Throughout the Bureau's existence, and for long afterward, contentiousness and criticism plagued the organization.[1]

Eliot's idea for an emancipation bureau led to a prolonged conflict between the Treasury and War departments over which would control the agency. The organization finally came under the aegis of the latter. The Freedmen's Bureau became an adjunct of the military, and many of its agents were former Union army veterans. Ironically, one of the most conservative institutions in American society was chosen to direct the immediate postwar course of Southern affairs and the readjustment of the former slaves into that region's social, economic, and political realm. As its wartime genesis suggests, from its very commencement the Freedmen's Bureau and the policies it attempted to implement became intertwined with the progress of Southern blacks.

The Bureau had two beginnings that accounted for the dual obligations in its title. First, in 1863 the War Department conceived the American Freedmen's Inquiry Commission (AFIC). Its task was to explore the best method to aid emancipated slaves. The AFIC emphasized that the assistance required by blacks was "no different from that which southern whites fleeing from the Confederacy would need."[2] Second, a year later, the American Union Commission (AUC) was established by antislavery advocates, who were also instrumental in framing the final Bureau law. Focusing its attention upon Southern white refugees, the AUC aimed to remold Southern attitudes into those of the North.

Although not as well known as the Freedmen's Bureau, the AUC's efforts in behalf of Southern whites included obtaining "seed and equipment for farming; transport[ing] refugees to their homes or re-locat[ing] them in new ones; operat[ing] schools and industrial training homes; advocat[ing] temporary occupation of abandoned lands for immediate sustenance and recommend[ing] changes in land tenure; and urg[ing] emigration, new industry, and a free press in the South." Both the AUC and the AFIC, as part of their underlying philosophy and pressure from Northern public opinion, expected the white refugees and the freedpeople to remain in the South. Economic competition and a free labor ideology had to be introduced into the conquered states.[3]

The AFIC had a different agenda. The three-member committee's final report ambivalently concluded that any agency established by the government should "exercise a benevolent guardianship" over the former slaves and that blacks be "placed on the road to self-reliance as quickly as possible." Also the committee insisted that the Bureau never should become a "permanent institution." And so the Freedmen's Bureau became the AFIC's "child." The Bureau was committed to "legal equality [for blacks] in a laissez faire social context."[4] Congressional support, Eric Foner writes, "symbolized the widespread belief among Republicans that the federal government must shoulder broad responsibility for the emancipated slaves, including offering them some kind of access to land."[5]

Following the AFIC's recommendations, Congress wished to avoid "overlegislating for the former slaves." The statute that created the Bureau had a quite radical aspect and paradoxically, the AUC and its work with white refugees contributed this feature. It was not until the Ohioan, Robert C. Schenck, introduced the concept of "no discrimination on account of color" into the anticipated legislation that its passage became a certainty. A "favorite phrase" among congressional members, according to Schenck, it was "well understood" to mean legal equality. The inclusion of white refugees in the Bureau's purview, a "decisive consideration" in the political maneuvering, made the agency's existence possible.[6]

On March 3, 1865, the Bureau of Refugees, Freedmen, and Abandoned Lands became a reality. Its tenure was limited to the end of the conflict and "for one year thereafter." The Bureau's legal aura was, in the words of Donald G. Nieman, "extremely vague." This vagueness was essential, however, as Congress had never before encountered such an unusual social and economic upheaval. Congress conferred upon the Bureau "control of all subjects relating to refugees and freedmen in the rebel States." The law, Nieman continues, "did not explicitly authorize them" to become involved in educating blacks, treating them medically, supervising labor relations, or affording freedmen legal protection. Yet the Bureau performed all these functions and more.[7]

Many of the deficiencies in the original law were rectified in July 1866, when Congress, over President Andrew Johnson's veto, extended the Bureau's existence for two more years and funded it separately. The second Bureau bill provided that all citizens "without respect to race or color, or previous condition of slavery" could enter into contracts, sue, give evidence in court, and deal in real estate. Blacks received "full and equal benefit of all laws and proceedings," including the "constitutional right to bear arms." No penalties imposed upon the former slaves could be "greater than the penalty or punishment to which white persons may be liable by law for the like offence." Congress simultaneously enacted the 1866 Civil Rights Bill.[8]

Even though the Civil War unquestionably wrought a significant change in the status of the former slaves (citizenship, voting, and legal rights) and the nation's constitutional structure, Southerners were determined that any alteration would be minimal.[9] A storm of abuse descended upon the Freedmen's Bureau from the white South. Their "aggressive self-assertions of being the 'Negroes best friends,'" Willie Lee Rose observes, "alternate[d] with an almost irrational denunciation of blacks' new friends, namely northern teachers and the Freedmen's Bureau." Whites "resented the Bureau as a symbol of Confederate defeat and a barrier to the authority reminiscent of slavery that planters hoped to impose upon the freedmen."[10]

National Perspectives

To comprehend the Bureau's role in Texas, it is necessary to survey the ways past historians have perceived the agency. Condemning the Bureau and the philosophy that nurtured the organization, writers viewed the Bureau as a gross interference with state's rights and the evolution of a "natural order." Many historians seemed to imply an admiration for such an incredible undertaking, but had difficulty in overcoming the racial milieu in which they wrote. Nonetheless, a very brief revolution occurred in the early 1900s and again in the 1950s. In the latter decade, the Bureau was seen as a "qualified failure" because the situation it encountered (race and class) was simply too complex for this short-lived institution to overcome.

The last survey of the Freedmen's Bureau appeared in 1955. George R. Bentley accused it of being a tool of the Radical Republicans and of seeking "too much for the Negro too soon—and not so much for his own sake as for the benefit of a faction of a party bent on the economic and political exploitation of the states where the Negroes lived."[11] In the most recent study of the Bureau, William S. McFeely contends that Oliver Otis Howard's commissionership was one of "naivete and misunderstanding, timidity, misplaced faith, disloyalty to subordinates who were loyal to the freedmen, and an attempt to diminish the Negroes' aspirations." Subtle charges of racism against Howard also surfaced. Reconstruction failed due to a lack of commitment to its original ideals.[12]

Howard and the Bureau have had few defenders. John A. Carpenter, Howard's biographer, states that, considering all the obstacles that the Bureau faced during its brief existence, it "performed near miracles." John and LaWanda Cox conclude that "even the most friendly studies of the Bureau have exaggerated its weaknesses and minimized its strength." It was the "symbol and substance of military occupation, a hateful or at best an unwelcome power of restraint to those under its shadow and to all men who believe in liberty." Eric Foner's recent assessment is significant: "Perhaps the greatest failing of the Freedmen's Bureau was that it never quite comprehended the depths of racial antagonism and class conflict in the postwar South."[13]

Only three book-length state studies have been published about the Freedmen's Bureau; two on South Carolina and one on Louisiana. The most recent appeared two decades ago. Martin Abbott finds the South Carolina Bureau a "qualified failure" because of "its anomalous position in American society of the mid-nineteenth century." Through its "very presence and concern," Abbott concludes, "it made an intangible yet important contribution towards helping the Negro to walk in greater dignity as a free man." Faced with manpower and financial shortages, and an awkward relationship with the military, the Bureau "could do little more than approximate the potential that lay within it for advancing the general welfare of the freedmen."[14]

The Louisiana Freedmen's Bureau, according to Howard A. White, served successfully "as a pressure group which exercised power and influence on behalf of the freedmen." Perhaps the Bureau's "greatest accomplishment," he writes, came from its "distorted and imperfect" impressions given to the freedpeople of the "practical meaning of freedom." He finds the Bureau "inefficient, and at times corrupt," but it planted the "concept of freedom and dignity in the hearts" of the former slaves and gave them hope for the future. White believes that the Bureau successfully implemented programs that provided relief, medical services, and to a lesser extent, education. His tone, however, suggests that the Bureau hindered more than it helped.[15]

Abbott and White basically view the Bureau from the top down, in short from the perspective of the assistant commissioner. Although one does get an occasional sense of what the local agents encountered in the field, basically both writers emphasize an administrative approach. How the agents interacted with the freedmen and their communities, the most significant aspect of the Bureau's functions and responsibilities, however, is missing. Written before social history came into vogue, they present divergent opinions about the successes and failures of the Bureau. Abbott tends to side with the Coxes and Carpenter, whereas White is more attuned to the old Dunning tradition and in some ways presages McFeely's arguments.

Donald G. Nieman approaches the Freedmen's Bureau from the legal aspects of its operations. Unfortunately, he argues, federal policy rested on the faulty assumption that by guaranteeing the freedmen equal rights in state law and in participation in the election of state officials, they would be able to protect themselves. Throughout its existence, however, the "Bureau lacked the ability to provide blacks with the legal protection necessary to support their freedom." A fiscally conservative Republican policy, and one adverse to expanding the federal bureaucracy, meant that the Bureau never received the "adequate manpower and military support" it so desperately needed. Finally, it possessed "insufficient authority."[16]

Although Nieman does not judge the Bureau a failure, he states that the "fact that Bureau officials, at the conclusion of their work, were able to boast of little success resulted not only from their own attitudes and assumptions, but also from the political, economic, and institutional constraints under which they had labored." In disagreeing with McFeely about the importance of racism, which Nieman does not deny, he finds that "Bureau officials' fear of social disorder and their faith in human rationality and the inevitability of progress led them to act in ways that were sometimes detrimental to the interests of the freedmen."[17] In short, the goals established for the Bureau exceeded the authority and money that Congress was willing to expend.

Texas

In the early historiography of the Texas Bureau, the writers were those who had observed the agency in action or heard tales about its performance. In 1898 Oran M. Roberts, strong secessionist and former Texas governor, wrote that the agency "took no cognizance of injuries done by negroes to white people" and that black complaints "amounted to an almost continual harassment of the citizens of the country."[18] Charles William Ramsdell, the first professional historian to write about the Texas Freedmen's Bureau, believed strongly in black inferiority (he refers to blacks as "too ignorant," their "incapacity" to learn, and their "immunity from work") and claimed that the Bureau became involved in politics, usurped the jurisdiction of civil officials, and hindered Texas' restoration attempts.[19]

In the 1930s, 1940s, and 1950s, historians continued to parrot Ramsdell. S. S. McKay believed the former slaves "expected support from the government," their former masters being "shouldered aside" by the Freedmen's Bureau, who "taught" blacks to "distrust" them.[20] In 1952 Claude Elliott demonstrated the burden under which the agency operated but adopted the Ramsdell stance. "Whatever the bureau accomplished in Texas," wrote Elliott, "it achieved in the face of a withering, vicious, and scurrilous barrage of editorial comment from the Texas press."[21] Edgar M. Gregory, the first Texas assistant commissioner, demonstrated a "pathetic ignorance of his wards" with conceptions that were "completely without foundation."[22]

Later writers neither significantly deviated from Ramsdell's basic assumptions nor did they perform the original research required to present a more balanced viewpoint. W. C. Nunn believes the agency "did not prove satisfactory because the organization, through its Bureau agents, interfered with the relations between the employer and his Negro employees, to the detriment of the workers' dependability." It was "an obvious failure."[23] Ernest Wallace finds the Bureau's actions and its choice of personnel unpraiseworthy.[24] Into the 1960s and 1970s, the same negative themes continue to appear. T. H. Fehrenbach, following other writers, claims that because of its interference in labor relations "it was fiercely resented by whites."[25]

Before revisionism began to modify standard interpretations about the Bureau, specific themes had emerged. Blacks were unprepared for freedom, and although the agency allegedly assisted the planters to keep the former slaves bound to the plantation it eventually turned against the landlords by overprotecting laborers and ignoring state regulations. The Bureau interfered with the local and state judicial system, made decisions largely prejudicial to black Texans, and ignored civil officials. Agents encouraged freedmen to arm themselves, to form military companies, to embrace the Republican party, to establish Union Leagues, and to accept unequivocally black protestations about unfair treatment without considering white attitudes.

Although numerous works appeared in the 1970s and 1980s, still no general history of the state Bureau appeared. Historians have focused upon particular aspects of the organization or have used the Bureau papers for other purposes than writing the Bureau's history. In recent works the Bureau's activities are generally presented much more positively, but it is still accused of failing to avert circumstances over which it had little or no control. Edgar P. Sneed observes that "frequently the Freedmen's Bureau is blamed for much of the violence and disorder during military rule," but in many instances it "had justice, if not local law, on its side." Two constant themes emerge from Bureau reports: "white duplicity and maltreatment."[26]

Unquestionably the Bureau was a military organization, but being a Bureau agent had a different connotation even before the merger of the U. S. army and Bureau command structure in 1867. Throughout its existence, relations between Bureau personnel and the army never were consistently good, even when one man held the dual position of assistant commissioner and district commander. The only two writers to deal extensively with Bureau-military affairs are Robert W. Shook and William L. Richter. At opposite ends of the historiographical spectrum on general matters relating to Texas Reconstruction, they are more closely aligned where the Bureau is concerned, although Richter is more critical of national interference in state affairs (whether army or Bureau).

As Shook perceives the Bureau-military nexus, Texas was "perhaps the most hostile of the ex-Confederate states in regard to Bureau action." The state's size "made the military's task virtually impossible given the variety of responsibilities and local hostility to the Bureau's presence." Bureau activities "provoked the most specific, if poorly documented, criticism of military rule; it was the Bureau agent who touched the vital source of discontent—the freedmen—and who often enlisted by necessity the support of troops." Shook maintains that the agents were "vanguards of a frontier as surely as were soldiers who performed defense and engineering chores long accepted on the frontier."[27]

Richter, the major interpreter of the Union army's presence in Reconstruction Texas, is critical of its influence, but he writes more sympathetically about the Freedmen's Bureau.[28] In fact, the two were symbiotic. Richter evaluates the assistant commissioners of the Lone Star State negatively. Edgar M. Gregory felt himself superior to the former slaves. He "did little more than encourage blacks to stay at home, sign a contract, and work for their former master." Joseph B. Kiddoo was a tool of the planters "issuing tough labor regulations" but did strengthen Bureau courts. Charles Griffin is viewed as a tyrant because he ignored the state's civil administration, and Joseph J. Reynolds was nothing more than a political opportunist (see chapter 2).[29]

Few studies have been undertaken of Bureau administrative divisions, such as a subdistrict, an area that comprised from two to five counties. For Ross N. Dudney, Smith County and Tyler had "no special significance for the purpose of [his] study, except as a focal point." This subdistrict was a "typical headquarters" and the "activities of the agents assigned to this area and the activities of the citizens, both black and white, appear to be illustrative of similar activities throughout the state." White attitudes toward the Bureau did not deviate "appreciably from one area of the state to another," so an investigation of a concentrated geographical area should tell us something about the success or failure of the Texas Bureau.[30]

In redirecting interpretations about the Bureau, James M. Smallwood "suggests that a reanalysis of the local agents should be made." Focusing upon two agents, William G. Kirkman and Charles E. Culver, he finds them to be "interlopers who upset the 'Southern way of life.'" Both agents "tried as best they could to perform the duties of their offices" through "honesty and fairness" and "personified the best attributes of the agents of the Freedmen's Bureau." In short, Smallwood concludes, "if future findings prove their cases typical," then the "old depiction of local bureau agents stands in need of revision." And I arrive at similar conclusions for the agents who served in the Thirtieth subdistrict.[31]

Clearly, not all Texas agents had the interests of the agency of the former slaves at heart. Richter, focusing upon the career of DeWitt C. Brown, concludes that Brown's tenure reveals some "disturbing aspects about bureau operations in northeastern Texas," perhaps the scene of more violence than any other area in the state. These included "lack of commitment," a "pervasive racism," the "absence of cooperation between the army and bureau," and the "organized attack of outlaw gangs." Partial blame for lack of greater Bureau effectiveness, Richter surmises, "lay with the support officers in the army's Texas command, the unimaginative staff members of the state's Freedmen's Bureau headquarters, and disgruntled, abandoned bureau field agents."[32]

Additional scholarship has seriously revised the negative portrait of the Texas Freedmen's Bureau agents. Cecil Harper, Jr., finds that a total of 202 men served as subassistant commissioners during the Bureau's Texas tenure. "Those who served as assistant commissioners in Texas made every attempt to secure men of ability and proven loyalty to serve as local agents," writes Harper, "but clearly, they were not always successful." Some agents, Harper notes, were drunks, functionally illiterate, or criminally dishonest, but cannot be labeled as "typical." In general, the agent's commitment was real, and overall they can be characterized as men of ability, integrity, and honesty "who did the best they could."[33]

Intimately involved in the economic reconstruction of agriculture, the Bureau became a labor clearinghouse and a regulator of employer-employee relations. As most blacks continued to work the land, part of the agency's responsibility was to implement a new, or different, system of labor. A definitive discussion of Bureau efforts in relation to black farm workers has not been written, but numerous individuals have commented upon the agency's efforts to restructure the plantation system. The "early policies of the army" and later the Bureau, Smallwood believes, "restricted blacks." Bureau labor pronouncements were strict, but emphasized contractual obligations on the part of both blacks and planters.[34]

A differentiation existed "between bureau contracts which subagents approved and the legislature's code which, if followed," would have given "landlords predominate power in law." Local "law enforcement officers and courts often defied" Bureau regulations, supported the planters, and "obeyed their legislature." What developed revealed a "nebulous situation" wherein both military agencies "worked to enforce the congressional civil rights act and to protect freedmen while whites in many areas continued to behave as though the South had won the war." At the close of 1868, "federal labor supervision" ceased when the Bureau was withdrawn from the state and the "precarious condition of black labor became even worse."[35]

Randolph B. Campbell writes that the Bureau "sought to help blacks economically primarily by urging them to sign contracts and labor faithfully and by attempting to see that landowners respected those contracts." When the Bureau was withdrawn, black farmers "moved into the 'no-win' cycle of sharecropping," thus the agency's previous "limited form of economic assistance was removed." In the final analysis, writes Smallwood, whites reintroduced "as many economic restrictions on freedmen as they could. They wanted to ensure the perpetuation of caste." Nora Owens suggests that "much of the credit for whatever success freed black labor enjoyed belongs to the untiring efforts of the Bureau which was nevertheless extremely unpopular."[36]

The most damning critical study of the Texas agency focuses upon its social-welfare functions. Painting a harsh picture, Ira C. Colby asserts that Bureau efforts were "doomed to defeat from the onset." It was a "loosely knit organization without any consistent direction" or program because each assistant commissioner had his own "private concerns." Its response to state antiblack legislation was "negligible beyond the ineffective admonition of such" laws. By regulating black welfare to the "local white community," the Bureau "helped to reaffirm the state's structure of white supremacy." What Colby fails to mention is that the Bureau, severely restrained financially and legally, did not have the resources to do more.[37]

Every writer, except Colby, concedes that, in providing an educational beginning for the black populace, the Bureau and its agents performed exemplary work. Even Elliott admits that its educational activities achieved some success. Between 1865 and 1870, according to Alton S. Hornsby, the expert on Bureau educational endeavors, the agency "under almost impossible circumstances" conducted a "unique mission." Characterized literally by a series of up and downs, the "federal government terminated the Bureau's schools, but the agency left behind a legacy which included more than 20,000 literate blacks in the state and, perhaps more important, a sound foundation for Negro education in Texas."[38]

Controversy does exist among scholars as to what degree educational strides were due to black self-help or to the assistance which the Bureau provided. I argue that in the Thirtieth Subdistrict (the Smith County area) "blacks did not have the means to aid their own cause in any major way," but others have challenged this assertion. Self-help's "exact extent" or "effectiveness," says Smallwood, are difficult to measure. Unquestionably, he observes, "black self-help programs were extremely important, but self-help alone could not bring about satisfactory progress." Black Texans, quite limited in their financial resources, found outside aid "necessary if not imperative." The Bureau provided many of the necessary funds.[39]

Even into the early 1990s, the Bureau's accomplishments are still belittled and its purposes distorted. Two historians have recently concluded that "even though the Bureau intervened actively in the affairs of the planters and the freedmen, its success in labor relations, like that in legal matters, amounted to little." Agents did not have a "working knowledge of the technical points of law," thus colliding with civil authorities. Even if they "lacked legal training and occasionally acted too harshly towards whites, they represented the only hope for justice in legal matters involving black Texans." Recent historians conclude that the Bureau, encountering many obstacles in Texas, "did well to accomplish the little it did."[40]

Texas history textbooks have perpetuated many of the same biases. In *Texas: The Lone Star State*: "bureau officials gave the state government scant consideration," and thus "its accomplishments were rather disappointing." Later editions modified this stance.[41] The newest textbook by Robert A. Calvert and Arnoldo De Leon states that Texans believed agents "wanted to render the South powerless, as intruders bent on interfering with race relations, and as opportunists working only for the money they derived from their offices." However perceived, "they pursued a moderate course." Gregory, a "pragmatist," contended for freedmen's equal rights and had a "sympathetic attitude toward their aspirations."[42]

Historians have increasingly presented a much revised perspective from the older views of the agency as deleterious to Texas Reconstruction. But even some of the newer accounts still fail to grasp what the Bureau was attempting, or they find it a nuisance during the early years of Reconstruction. Owens summarizes white Texans' attitude toward the Bureau, writing that they criticized the Bureau for its "unwarranted interference with state authorities and rights, with stirring up trouble between white and black, with serving as a coercive arm of the Republican party, and with being corrupt and inefficient."[43] The Bureau was probably "guilty" of all these charges but not in the sense that historians of Texas have suggested.

Reevaluating the Texas Bureau is now necessary. A good place to begin is through the thoughts and actions of assistant commissioners. Although varying in attitudes, ability, and implementing various aspects of Bureau policy, they encountered similar difficulties in introducing a different labor system, providing for the welfare and protection of the freedmen, establishing schools, assuring black equality before the law, and dealing with the violence that so plagued Texas in the aftermath of the Civil War. That they were only partially successful can be attributed to many factors. As a guardian of the freedpeople, and limited protector, what the Bureau accomplished was the initiation of blacks into the mysteries and burdens of freedom.

2. The Texas Assistant Commissioners: Labor, Justice, Education, and Violence under the Bureau

Antecedents and Beginnings of the Bureau

Texas, the last Confederate state in which the Bureau of Refugees, Freedmen, and Abandoned Lands was organized, posed special problems for Bureau personnel. Relatively untouched by the ravages of war and unscarred by the psychology of defeat, Texans carried into the post–Civil War era the idea that their state had never been subdued. A Northern traveler observed that the citizens did not feel "whipped in spirit" but "only nominally whipped in being surrendered by the official act of General E. Kirby Smith." Texans claimed they had not been "conquered and that they would renew the fight at some future date." The immensity of the state and the scattered population compounded the unique difficulties confronted by the Texas Freedmen's Bureau.[1]

In late May 1865, General E. Kirby Smith surrendered the remaining Southern armies. E. R. S. Canby optimistically wrote Ulysses S. Grant that the "Confederate military authorities will use their influence and authority to see that public property in the hands of the agents of the late Rebel government are duly surrendered to the U.S. authorities." Occupation began almost immediately. Two pressing concerns instantly arose: to prevent any "complication on the Mexican frontier" and to make arrangements for emancipating the slaves. The social and economic implications of this revolution led to an outburst of violence that deeply influenced the future of Bureau relations with the Texas populace.[2]

Disturbing reports emanated from the Lone Star State. Canby asserted that while the Texas Confederate troops had generally disbanded, they had "gone to their homes plundering public stores." With an estimated thirty-eight thousand soldiers paroled in the Trans-Mississippi Department, the adjustment to peacetime conditions would not be smooth. Before order could be fully restored, the state treasury at Austin fell victim to the marauding former Confederate soldiers. Canby, "limited virtually to the determining of questions that are purely military in character," found that civil, social, and political problems had to be ignored. Determining the categorization of these postwar questions became impossible. Where did one stop and the other begin?

The Bureau and Its Personnel

If the fighting did not bloody Texas soil, the peace unquestionably brought a new type of conflict into the Lone Star State. In early June, General Gordon Granger assumed command of all federal troops. On June 19 he issued an order that informed the people of Texas that their slaves were now free. Black freedom meant "an absolute equality of personal rights and rights of property between former masters and slaves." As for labor, the connection now "existing between" former slave and former master "becomes that between employer and hired labor." Granger advised former slaves to "remain quietly at their present homes and work for wages." They neither would be allowed to congregate at military posts nor would they be supported in idleness.[3]

Lieutenant Colonel R. G. Laughlin, the provost marshal general, subsequently enlarged on Granger's original order. Declaring that the freedpeople should work under such contracts as currently could be negotiated—mainly because their own interest and that of their former masters rendered it necessary—these temporary measures were to endure until permanent arrangements could be introduced by the Freedmen's Bureau. Cruel treatment would not be allowed. The former slaves could not travel on public roads or assemble without passes from their employers. These regulations continued in force until the Bureau became organized in Texas, but two more months would pass before that occurred.[4]

Between the time of Kirby Smith's surrender in late May and early September 1865, the Freedmen's Bureau did not exist in Texas. The delay caused numerous hardships for Thomas W. Conway, the Louisiana assistant commissioner. In the first week of June, Conway confirmed Canby's previous assessment, writing to Commissioner Oliver Otis Howard that the "adjoining states are scenes of untold difficulty." The freedmen "are terribly persecuted by the returned rebel soldiers." Conway attempted to assist Texas blacks by suggesting to the National Freedmen's Relief Association that it establish schools in the Lone Star State. The Louisiana Bureau also aided Texas refugees, if possible, whenever they desired to return home.[5]

By July, Conway was desperate. He telegraphed Howard: "Matters in Texas are bad. Has any Assistant Commissioner been appointed for that State? My assistant at Shreveport is taking charge of several counties but in the state generally there is a bad condition of affairs." Howard replied that Edgar M. Gregory had been assigned to the state and would "soon be in [the] field." Howard's optimism of Gregory's "soon" assuming his duties as chief of Texas Bureau operations did not immediately come to pass. Numerous postponements ensued, and Gregory, prevented from reaching his destination, did not arrive until the summer had dwindled away. Bureaucracy functioned slowly. In August, Commissioner Howard still made the same promise.[6]

The Texas situation continued to deteriorate during the summer. Two reports from Hempstead indicated that blacks were ill treated and that the army afforded them little or no protection. A Texan wrote that blacks still remained enslaved, and a Hubodaux, Louisiana, agent exclaimed: "'How long Oh Lord, how long?'" The Galveston provost marshal concluded that not much could be done for blacks or whites as the "state of affairs being at present so unsettled here, and in the absence of any charitable institutions." The former slaves suffered the most from the lack of Bureau organization. The army's mission simply did not envision that soldiers should become involved in the social and economic ramifications of emancipation.[7]

Louisiana Bureau agents assisted the provost marshals and also assumed jurisdiction over certain Texas counties close to the Louisiana border. In July, W. B. Stickney, the Shreveport agent, reported 206 contracts signed in Marion County, Texas, and he awaited the returns from Harrison County. His final totals suggested that for both Marion and Harrison counties, 872 contracts had been signed, covering 6,461 laborers. According to the 1870 census, Stickney had induced nearly half the black population in these two Texas counties to enter into contracts. Considering the volatile nature of circumstances in the aftermath of war and the upheaval caused by the freeing of the slaves, this could be considered a remarkable feat.[8]

Edgar M. Gregory

In late August, Edgar M. Gregory finally arrived in New Orleans. Delayed for a week in the Crescent City, he awaited transportation to Galveston. Gregory visited Conway and "carefully examined" all his "orders, circulars, records, etc., and took copies" to "assist him." Conway wrote Howard that Gregory manifested a "cordial interest in the work, and I think he is adapted to the field to which you have assigned him." Eager to assume his Texas responsibilities, by early

September Gregory left for the Lone Star State. Conway ordered his Shreveport agent to make no more appointments for Texas as "no portion of that State is [now] considered within the jurisdiction of this Bureau."[9]

The *Houston Daily Telegraph* suggested what the future might hold for the Texas Bureau. In Texas, slavery had remained relatively intact during the course of the war. The *Daily Telegraph* summarized the tenor of prevailing white Texans attitudes: "The relationship between master and servant is one rendered sacred in the hearts of the people of the South, by long-maintained political conviction; by domestic philosophies, sentiments and associations." The newspaper maintained that these ties had "given the blacks the relation of members of the family; and by the memories of a long and bloody war, in which, according to the Southern mind, they fought equally for the rights, homes and happiness of both blacks and whites."[10]

On September 19 Howard officially announced the appointments of the assistant commissioners for Georgia, Alabama, and Texas. Gregory had arrived in Galveston two weeks earlier. The oldest of all state Bureau chiefs, he had neither served with Howard in the army nor previously worked with blacks. Although McFeely labels Gregory a "radical Abolitionist," this appellation is questionable. In his autobiography Howard wrote that Gregory was "well reputed for the stand he always took in the army in favor of clear-cut uprightness of conduct. He was so fearless of opposition or danger" that Howard sent him to Texas, "which seemed at the time of his appointment to be the post of greatest peril." The word often used to describe his character. "zealous."[11]

Little is known about Gregory's background. Originally from New York, which possibly was his birthplace, he was a civilian before the outbreak of the war. A volunteer, he received a commission as colonel of the Ninety-first Pennsylvania Infantry in August 1861. Noted for his "bravery and energy," Gregory was breveted brigadier general for gallantry and distinguished service in the battle of Poplar Spring Church near Petersburg, Virginia, in September 1864. He added another brevet, to major general, for his bravery at the Battle of Five Forks in April 1865. Although described as lacking the "amenity of manner" and the "savoir faire" necessary to deal with planters, he did believe in the "discipline of law" to protect the freedpeople.[12]

Gregory perceived the Bureau and his purpose as a fourfold duty: to organize and superintend the labor system, to defend black rights, to "inculcate" in the freedpeople "their duties," and to "give" black Texans "control of themselves subject only to the common law." He would interfere in judicial matters only when the state refused to act or when it became "manifest" that "injustice was done." Gregory insisted that "no distinction against one race" would be allowed "in favor of the other." County and local officials had the "stern discipline of justice" and the "apparatus of the law" to meet all contingencies. "Class legislation" aimed at blacks, he deemed uncalled for and "unwise."[13]

Gregory immediately attempted to foster a workable and stable economic relationship between the freedpeople and their employers. His task of ensuring fair treatment for blacks and the harvesting of the crops had to be initiated as soon as possible. Gregory, a pragmatist, understood that radically changing the social and economic system could never be achieved in the time allotted to the Bureau, but reinventing agricultural relations after the war proved to be a wrenching experience for all concerned. The planters professed a willingness to cooperate, but they loudly complained that the freedmen did not do as much work as they had under slavery. "And yet," Gregory reported, "most of the present crops will be saved to the country."[14]

Gregory's initial appraisal indicated a willingness on the part of planters to cooperate with the Bureau. Although they reluctantly agreed to "try" blacks as free laborers, Gregory also instructed the owners about their new obligations. After giving planters every encouragement to adapt to the new state of affairs, Gregory also counseled them to treat their laborers "with liberality and on a basis of justice." Give them a "chance," Gregory wrote one planter, "to secure themselves from fraud and inequality before the law." This should be done "not with any attempts at serfdom under a new form," but to "permit" the former slaves "to run without a load the race of life." The freedpeople would be "fully protected in their rights."[15]

The assistant commissioner contended that the former slaves should be able to contract to work where and for whom they pleased. Gregory found it necessary to repeat what the army had already pronounced because planters continued to believe that black freedom, unwise and arbitrary, should be severely constrained. "In no case will freedmen be forced to contract with or work for obnoxious employers," he announced in his first circular, but a "life of idleness will not be encouraged or allowed." Gregory found blacks to be working "as well as could be expected" in "commencing the transition state [which] to them [is] almost a new world" and to be conducting themselves in the proper spirit of a free people.[16]

A month after Gregory had assumed his duties as Texas Bureau chief, the Shreveport agent still supervised parts of eastern Texas. Thomas Calahan reported that Smith County had a total of 62,128 acres under cultivation, including the following divisions: corn, 29,423; wheat, 7,888; cotton, 2,005; rye, 861; oats, 512.5; potatoes, 396; barley, 47; sorghum, 22; tobacco, 5; and rice, 1. By this time, 684 contracts, which included 2,993 laborers, had been signed. There were 188 employers who had "neither lands nor crops," yet had contracted with 680 freedmen. In his analysis of these figures, the Shreveport agent saw an ominous sign for the emerging social structure: class and race simultaneously began to surface.[17]

"Making due allowance for persons living in villages," the Louisiana agent wrote, he feared that Texas would encounter the similar "serious difficulty" that had also plagued his state. "Many of the Freedmen have fallen into the hands of '*the poor white trash*,'" he continued, "who being destitute both of moral principle and money swindle the Freedmen outrageously." Before the war these lower-class whites "could not have bought and kept one negro baby if such a commodity had been sold at the rate of five dollars per dozen," but they now had three or four blacks working for them. "They are unsparing in their exactions of work and never pay." Coupled with planter recalcitrance, blacks found themselves in a precarious position.[18]

The tremendous strain and pressure upon Gregory and his limited resources continued to mount. A particularly vexing problem, the persistence of slavery and the mentality that had supported the institution, concerned everyone. Provisional Governor Andrew J. Hamilton told President Johnson that the planters hastened to take the amnesty oath but continually discussed the "*gradual emancipation* of the slaves as the proper policy for Texas." Blacks continued to be sold. Gregory, cognizant of the treatment of blacks, complained that, with no available military assistance, "freedmen are restrained from their liberty, and slavery virtually exists the same as though the old system of oppression was still in force."[19]

Gregory commenced a seven-hundred-mile journey (Elliott called it a "twenty-one day whirlwind trip") through the cotton-growing portions of Texas. The freedmen "when under the influence of the excitement incident to their transition from bondage to freedom," he wrote Howard, and "while they were more or less unsettled and undecided in their purposes" had produced a cotton crop that would "bring more wealth into the State than any ever marketed." Significantly, the freedpeople understood the "value of their labor" and refused "to be imposed upon by employers." They had not and "will not commit any act of lawlessness," Gregory wrote, "but will settle down in the enjoyment of life, liberty, and the pursuit of happiness."[20]

Black Texans did relatively well while Gregory directed the state Bureau. With labor arrangements still in a transition process, the 1865 crop proved better than expected despite complaints by various newspapers. The *Houston Telegraph* editorialized that the former "slaves proved unfaithful and deserted [at] the first opportunity" but reported that "every station on the Central and Washington Railcounty railroads are crowded with cotton bales" and could not be shipped off "as fast as it comes for want of sufficient rolling stock." The future looked promising as nine-tenths of the former slave population, under contract for 1866, worked "steadily and soberly in the fields."[21]

Gregory, by no means "pathetically ignorant" of previous events or of the obstacles he faced in making black freedom a reality, had a keen sense of history. He wrote that the "governing classes are today what the past has made them, and they cannot cut loose at a single blow from their past traditions, beliefs, hatreds and hopes." Even after the "rough schooling of this war they have still a lesson and a hard one to learn, it is to be just to the black man." Gregory realized that "long after the oppressed race shall rise into rights, duties and capacities so haughtily denied[,] the dominant class will not have overcome their contempt for the negro." Into the future the "roots" of this contempt would "exist and trouble the land."[22]

Assessing black Texans, Gregory wrote that "in general the Freedmen of Texas present a record which, for service and order, is most commendable." Turned "head long into freedom," he informed a Panola County resident, "without reparation, without premonition, by men at war with their masters, and told that they have been wronged and have a heritage of vengeance, they exhibit in their industry, docility and patience, an example beyond the expectation of man. No people had ever been so tried. None ever so stood trial." If the former slaves had responded to freedom like the "poor toilers of any European state," they would have taken their rulers "by the throat and carried carnage into every homestead in the South."[23]

Gregory frequently buttressed his decisions through intelligent observation. He visited the lower Brazos, Oyster Creek, Old Caney, and Colorado districts, an area that "comprised the most productive and influential cotton and sugar growing portion of the state." Formerly "crowded with slaves," these bottomlands characterized by their "inexhaustible fertility" demonstrated the "great variety of contracts" with "much vagueness of terms" that blacks had negotiated. Freedmen "*only* requested that the promises made by the planters be enforced by the government." Modern times, he wrote, "cannot furnish a parallel to the high inducements held out to labor" in Texas, and most "social disruptions" had all but disappeared.[24]

Less than a month before being relieved, Gregory again embarked upon a tour. (One must certainly give him credit for his perseverance in viewing for himself the social and economic condition of Texas blacks.) The freedmen, "steadily at work" and "well and profitably employed," had ambitions to become "landowners" or "small proprietors," which kept them "from idleness and excess." Except for the continuing violence against them, their future prospects seemed bright. If the freedmen could go "faultlessly through the excitement and temptations" of contract time, Gregory wrote, "there need be but little doubt of their doing good service during the year." But outrages increased proportionately as the number of troops decreased.[25]

Believing in self-sustaining schools, Gregory did not stress black education. The schools should "conform in discipline and instruction to the best common school system of the North," and he hoped the state government would "continue them on a stable foundation." By spring 1866, ninety schools came under Bureau supervision, including forty-two day, twenty-nine night, and nineteen Sunday schools, with an additional eighteen to twenty private schools taught by blacks. They comprised 4,590 students (2,830 children and 1,760 adults) with forty-three teachers: sixteen white males, thirteen white females, and fourteen blacks (who were not categorized by gender). Animosity against educating blacks had decreased in the larger towns and in the "more settled and intelligent portions" of Texas.[26]

By the end of Gregory's Texas Bureau service, he had only begun to formalize and expand the agency's organization. The statistics do not appear particularly impressive. Along with the regular headquarters staff, he had appointed only seventeen subassistant commissioners, including two civilians serving without pay. With an aggregate territory as large as New York and New England, his entire force, combining troops, comprised only 251 men, 10 of whom fell into the civilian category. Consequently, he sadly concluded, "much the larger portion" of Texas had no Bureau agent or representative. When one agent requested troops, headquarters told him that "they are so scarce that it is difficult to say whether we shall succeed or not."[27]

Gregory, detested by the planters because of his promotion of black rights, finally fell prey to their machinations. Cyrus B. Comstock, an aide to Ulysses S. Grant, confided to his diary that Gregory was "well hated by the Rebs." He talked "too harsh" to them, but the "negroes [were] doing well under him." Horatio G. Wright, the district commander, believed Gregory to be "very unpopular and is not the best fitted by nature, education, or prejudice for getting along harmoniously [with the planters]; but he is zealous and energetic." From "confidential inquiries," Wright believed Gregory "labored zealously and unremittingly." If Johnson decided a Bureau chief obstructed his "conservative friends in the South," writes McFeely, removal soon followed.[28]

Howard and President Johnson received numerous complaints about Gregory's manner of dealing with the planters and his strong support in behalf of freedpeople's rights. In fact, he was accused of being so friendly to blacks "as to overlook the interests of the whites." Howard respected Gregory's "zest and energy" but warned him to be "exceedingly cautious" and "to be as wise as a serpent as well as harmless." But Gregory could not change his character and continued to exert as much effort as possible in behalf of the freedpeople and their economic rights. Planters, who marshaled their collective political influence, gained control of the state administration and forced the hand of President Johnson, who subsequently removed him.[29]

Gregory was recalled to Washington because of the planters' dislike of him for his efforts in behalf of the freedpeople and because of his failure to convince the Texas populace that blacks should have equality before the law. With limited funds, Gregory attempted to stabilize the labor system, emphasized freedpeople's civil rights, and made brief beginnings in the educational field. He was not, however, the most efficient administrator, and this outlook carried over to the field agents or subassistant commissioners. This fault may also have partially provided the rationale for his removal, since much remained unfinished when he departed from Texas. Four months later Howard appointed him assistant commissioner of Maryland, where he remained for fifteen months.[30]

William L. Richter writes that Gregory "felt he personally was superior to any black."[31] Like McFeely's "radical abolitionist" assertion," or Elliott's "naive" statement, a precise definition of Gregory becomes an elusive task. One might read the "superiority" complex into his pronouncements. But even if Gregory did view himself as "superior" to blacks, the fact would tell us little about his performance that, from the evidence, seems much better than past historical accounts would suggest. His attitude in the light of nineteenth-century racial beliefs did not seem uncommon or unusual. Gregory is misunderstood and therefore dismissed as "pathetically ignorant" of the freedpeople because he made considerable efforts in their behalf.

Consistently portrayed as a failure by Texas historians who have surveyed the Reconstruction era, Gregory's record suggests otherwise. (Because they neglected to investigate primary sources, other historians have made gross mistakes about Gregory's background, ability, and administration of the Texas Freedmen's Bureau.) His deficiencies had nothing to do with his mental capabilities or perception of the Texas dilemma. These can be directly tied to finances, separate commands for the Bureau and the army, deciding which sections of the state to concentrate upon, general white opposition, and how much support the army could provide. Gregory, quite perspicacious about what slavery had wrought and what the future held, knew his limitations.

Gregory had his failings. He did not create a widespread Bureau presence in Texas or appoint local agents for areas beyond the coastal section. Several civilians applied for positions as agents, but Gregory, even if they could have taken the required amnesty oath, had to decline their applications, as no funds existed to pay them. Gregory focused upon labor relations and the former slaves' economic rights. He did not carefully nurture Bureau justice; physical protection for blacks remained minimal; and black education largely fended for itself. His "greatest sin," writes Richter, was that he was "much too conscientious" in "trying to make the ex-slave free in fact, not just on paper."[32] Gregory made modest but important beginnings for the Bureau.

Joseph B. Kiddoo

Arriving in Galveston on May 11, 1866, and relieving Gregory on May 14, General Joseph B. Kiddoo assumed control of the Texas Bureau. Although war wounds bothered him, Kiddoo believed that he would be able to discharge his duties without "inconvenience." He observed that the "present aspect of affairs of the Bureau" in Texas seemed to be "very encouraging." Gregory had been "helpful and kind" but had not emphasized the education of the freedpeople. Kiddoo did not wish to "intimate" that schools had been "neglected," but he "desired to make the educational interests of the state a *specialty*." He also had an "earnest desire" to establish a "vigorous system of labor," demonstrating the "superiority of free over slave labor," which was also Gregory's objective.[33]

Kiddoo, born in Pennsylvania about 1840, enlisted in April 1861 in the Twelfth Pennsylvania Infantry. He served only briefly, being discharged in August. Kiddoo joined the Sixty-third Pennsylvania Infantry and participated in the Peninsular Campaign, seeing action at Yorktown, Williamsburg, Fair Oaks, and Malvern Hill. Discharged in August 1862, he was commissioned a lieutenant colonel, later promoted to colonel, in the 137th Pennsylvania and fought at South Mountain, Antietam, Fredericksburg, and Chancellorsville. Resigning his commission, Kiddoo became a major in the Sixth U.S. Colored Infantry and at Petersburg, received severe leg and spinal wounds which never healed and later caused him incredible pain.[34]

Kiddoo immediately stressed the necessity for more agents with army background, as he believed civilians could not be trusted and did not have the freedpeople's best interests at heart. Instead, a controversy erupted over the powers bestowed upon military commissions and Bureau courts. Kiddoo argued that the "prejudices of this people are so strong against" the equality of the freedpeople "before the laws, that in criminal cases their trial before Civil courts is *worse than a farce*." He needed the "power to arrest a white man for the wilful felonious murder of a freedman, when I have the best of reasons for believing that the Civil Courts will make a farce of a trial, and ask for a commission to try him."[35]

Immediately after Kiddoo settled into his duties as Bureau chief, he reported to the investigation by Joseph S. Fullerton and James B. Steedman, two men picked by President Andrew Johnson to evaluate Bureau performance.[36] After filing his account, which naturally portrayed the Texas Bureau in a favorable light, Kiddoo left on a tour of Fort Bend, Colorado, and Wharton counties. Cautiously optimistic about the status of the crops, Kiddoo conversed with both former slaves and planters. Though the growing season had been abnormal with untimely rains and the appearance of the army worm, some of the experienced planters expressed a positive outlook. Most freedpeople worked for a portion of the crop but had problems with a certain class of employers in gaining their "just wages."[37]

These individuals, whom Kiddoo described as a "dyspeptic" group of lower-class planters, viewed blacks as "lazy, indolent, and insolent" and reasoned that "no harm" came in "cheating" blacks because the government had "unconstitutional[ly]" confiscated whites' property. According to them, slavery was the only form of labor that blacks understood, thus from previous experience they had become "constitutional thieves and constitutional liars." Even those planters who expressed surprise over the "commendable propriety" of black work habits would again institute slavery if they had the power to do so. Kiddoo considered such an acknowledgment by planters an admission of the "superiority of free over slave labor," but only from a "pecuniary point of view."[38]

Kiddoo's program aimed to vindicate the government's wisdom in emancipating the slaves, thus proving to everyone that the war resulted in a "moral, social, and financial blessing." He encouraged a "commonality of interest" between employee and employer. The shortage of black laborers throughout Texas briefly benefitted the former slaves. Kiddoo estimated that an additional seventy-five thousand workers could immediately procure contracts if they "landed on the wharf at Galveston." The "scarcity of labor was due to a scarcity of freedmen and not to the fact that they will not work." Some "disaffected" whites refused to believe that blacks would ever work to their capacity and thus formed an immigration company to attract white foreigners.[39]

In addition to planters hindering the implementation of a free labor system, freedpeople violated contracts. Demand became so great that employers "dishonorably" took "advantage" of the blacks' "ignorance." They enticed laborers away from other planters by offering higher wages, or they claimed the previous contract to be "unjust" or "illegal" (although Bureau approved). Attempting to compensate for former slaves' lack of experience, their alleged "shiftlessness," and the fact that they were the "weaker party" in the transition from "compulsory to voluntary labor," Kiddoo freely admitted that he "heavily discriminated against the employer in the matter of fines" and tightened labor regulations by issuing a revised labor circular.[40]

Although Kiddoo observed that blacks "worked too hard and got too little for it," he found it necessary to restrain a portion of the freedpeople "from shifting from one employer to another" on "flimsy pretexts, thus demoralizing the vigorous system of labor" that Gregory had established. Kiddoo's pronouncements concentrated upon the planters' contractual obligations pertaining to "wages, rations, and treatment." The Bureau needed to become a "moral party" to the negotiating process, thus combining economics and morality. Through the "medium of personal finance," he wrote Howard, Southerners would become "morally convinced" sooner than by any other method of the "justice of freedom and the injustice of slavery."[41]

Kiddoo may have been paternalistic, but this does not mean he failed to consider the former slaves' economic interests. When the state legislature enacted labor laws in late 1866 as part of the Black Codes, he immediately consulted with Howard. The "whole purpose" of the labor laws, only a "gloss for the injustice in the rest,"

was to "re-enslave the Negro." He recommended that the objection-
able labor sections be ignored and that Bureau agents be ordered to
disallow any contracts based solely on the 1866 law. Kiddoo realized
that interfering with state legislation, particularly of a *"new* State
Government," was a "delicate matter." If necessary, however, he
would take *"absolute"* control of the cotton crop and designate certain merchant houses to accept cotton shipments.[42]

Kiddoo viewed the Bureau as the "Freedman's guardian and protector." He thus believed that contracts should be annual because of
the important periods in the growth of crops. The seasonal nature of
such work demanded a ready labor force, especially at harvesttime.
The laborers should have an opportunity to negotiate their terms, as
he felt that free labor should naturally go to the "highest bidder."
Once a contract was signed "by both parties in good faith" and accepted by a Bureau agent, then all its requirements should be ful-
filled, especially the length of time involved. According to Kiddoo's
philosophy, the Bureau was the "guardian of the freedman to see
that he gets a fair and equitable bargain."[43]

Kiddoo cooperated with religious, benevolent, ecclesiastical societies and freedmen's organizations which desired to buy land to
erect churches and schools. It was his *"strong desire"* that titles be
in *"fee simple"* to land and buildings, invested in a designated group
from the black community so that the "influence of the Bureau may
be felt among freedmen beyond its legal existence by act of Congress." The Bureau intended for the freedpeople to acquire land titles
themselves. For Kiddoo, the "salvation of the liberated slaves from
degradation, oppression, and perhaps *extinction* depend[ed] essentially on their being educated." At least blacks should be taught that
freedom meant "industry, economy, and patience."[44]

Although Gregory and his superintendent of education, Edwin M.
Wheelock, had made "vigorous and useful" educational beginnings,
he had been forced to depend upon "self-sustaining" schools. Thus,
a "large amount" of poor blacks deprived of school privileges needed
access to schooling. The newspapers and the "better class" of citizens, according to Kiddoo, "advocated" limited education to make
blacks more "profitable laborers," but this remained the extent of
their commitment. In some areas, schools for blacks could not be
maintained because there were no soldiers to protect the teachers.
This attitude he attributed to the "vulgar and uncommendable
prejudice" among whites "whose own moral and intellectual interests had been sadly neglected."[45]

Besides general violence directed at blacks, one of Kiddoo's "deepest provocation[s]" during his tenure involved the "virulent abuse of female school teachers." It had become quite common for the newspapers to insinuate that women teachers could not be looked upon in any "other light than Common Prostitutes." Kiddoo considered it a primary duty to protect these women who had displayed so "true a missionary spirit as to expose themselves to such barbarity in order to elevate the negro children of the South." Because of troop limitations, he "could do little more" for blacks than to "give assistance of the Bureau in procuring for them the elements of an English education and would give that branch of duties special attention."[46]

The promotion of black education occupied much of the focus of Kiddoo's assistant commissionership, and his efforts in behalf of the bureau's educational program exceeded those of Gregory. He worked closely with the American Missionary Association in procuring teachers, although he encountered difficulties in protecting them from abuse and violence. He also attempted to aid Texas black communities in acquiring land on which to build educational and religious establishments. The school system, reinvigorated by Kiddoo's efforts, experienced setbacks, but a solid organizational base was established, though it would rise and fall with the economic fortunes of the freedpeople and of whomever controlled state politics.[47]

Just as Gregory had become frustrated and finally had despaired of attempting to protect Texas blacks against white outrages, Kiddoo expressed the same sentiments. Reports suggested that violence and murder directed at the freedpeople continued to *"increase."* Killed "from one to five at a time," blacks had been left "powerless" because of a "want of troops" to sustain local agents. Kiddoo grew "sick at heart" and wondered about the powers of a government that left an "unfortunate race of people, whom it had liberated by force, exposed to the violence of chagrined and life long enemies." As the evidence of murder and abuse of freedpeople mounted, Kiddoo begged for assistance "as will make my duties here a *reality* instead of a *farce.*"[48]

Using agents' reports, Kiddoo wrote Governor James W. Throckmorton that the brutality inflicted upon blacks could not be considered *"half the truth."* The acts were committed by a "class of men who never owned slaves," Kiddoo stated, "who have been their competitors in labor to some extent and consequently been their lifelong enemies," and who were enraged by emancipation. He recommended legislation that would require civil tribunals to give blacks "adequate civil protection" from these individuals. When this occurred, Kiddoo would *"most cheerfully* withdraw from them the supervision" of the Bureau. Until Kiddoo left the Texas Bureau, he and Throckmorton clashed over the protection of black rights and the abuse endured by blacks at the hands of Texas whites.[49]

In the last months of his assistant commissionership, Kiddoo experienced five problems. First, he was absent from the state on an extended trip to Washington, D.C. Second, a rumor circulated throughout the state that he had prohibited freedpeople from entering into contracts for 1867. Third, Ulysses S. Grant reportedly had issued an order forbidding the military to arrest any person accused of murder or of committing an outrage upon the freedpeople. Fourth, a personal difficulty ensued between Bureau headquarters officials and those of the U.S. army. Finally, tension between Kiddoo and the new District of Texas commander, Charles Griffin, over their precise division of power and responsibilities led to Kiddoo's resignation.[50]

In late January 1867, Kiddoo, tired of the conflict between the authority of the Bureau and the army, requested that he be relieved. Kiddoo also informed Charles Griffin that as arrangements were made for the "future conduct of the Bureau," Kiddoo himself had no "desire to be further connected with it in any capacity." Kiddoo explained to Howard that "there are so many officers who rank me and whose troops are serving in the State, available for such duty that I do not consider my services longer needed." He wanted to relieve Griffin of any embarrassment "on account of my present connection with the Bureau." Kiddoo wished to remain long enough to set into operation a free school system and in this task he had been "partially successful."[51]

Kiddoo encountered problems similar to Gregory's in encouraging the former slaves to sign contracts, but perhaps handled the planters more deftly and with more diplomacy. That Kiddoo's policy "favored" the planters is a distortion of the evidence. Although he did not manifest the disdain for the former owners that Gregory had been accused of openly demonstrating, Kiddoo negated the 1866 labor laws and attempted to establish a contract system that would bring some stability to the agricultural sector. To Kiddoo, labor safeguarded through a proper contract seemed the only viable economic pattern that could be utilized in Texas. Bureau intervention made it possible for the freedpeople to receive more equitable treatment though far short of what they desired.[52]

Serving less than a year, Kiddoo, one of the two Texas assistant commissioners who did not also double as military commander, became frustrated over the limitations of the position. He brought more organization and efficiency to the agency than had Gregory, but the Bureau remained understaffed and inadequately financed.

But under Kiddoo, it had made some strides. His relentless concern for the labor rights of the freedpeople did provide the former slaves with protection they otherwise would not have received. Kiddoo's desire to assist black education through expanded schooling made inroads against illiteracy. Although not as zealous as Gregory, Kiddoo made the services of the Bureau available to a wider array of freedpeople.[53]

Charles Griffin

Charles Griffin relieved Kiddoo on January 24, 1867. Griffin, the third Texas assistant commissioner, may have been as controversial as was Gregory, and he frequently clashed with the conservatives, headed by Governor James W. Throckmorton. He supervised the Texas Freedmen's Bureau at a critical point in national Reconstruction, as the U.S. Congress assumed control. Griffin also angered many Texas whites by enhancing the responsibilities of the local Bureau courts and by centralizing the organization and increasing the number of agents. Characterized as "bluff, bellicose, outspoken, and quick to take offense," Griffin, the first Texas chief to combine military and Bureau duties, rapidly expanded the agency.[54]

Griffin, Ohio born, a former Kenyon College student, and an 1847 artillery graduate of West Point, served in the Mexican War, on the southwestern frontier, and then became an instructor in artillery tactics at his alma mater. In January 1861, he organized a field battery composed of the regulars stationed at West Point. Griffin, who was idolized by his men, saw action at First and Second Manassas, the Peninsular Campaign, Antietam, Fredericksburg, Chancellorsville, Gettysburg, the Wilderness, Spotsylvania, Cold Harbor, and Petersburg, and was one of the surrender commissioners at Appomattox. Appointed a colonel in the Thirty-fifth U.S. Infantry and District of Texas commander when the Regular Army reorganized in 1866, he was known as a "hard case."[55]

Griffin found twenty-nine agents, fourteen military officers, and fifteen civilians on duty in the Texas Bureau when he assumed the assistant commissionership. All twenty-nine agents, with one exception, were stationed in the "Southern part of the state." The remotest subassistant commissioner served only 180 miles from Galveston. Even in this confined region, agents were "powerless unless in the vicinity of troops." Griffin estimated that the Texas Bureau encompassed hardly one-third of the area and one-half the population of the state. Reports of violence perpetrated against the freedpeople "poured in unremittingly from remote parts" of the Lone Star

State. Clearly, the Bureau needed to expand its coverage of the state to avoid "wanton outrages, robbery and murder."[56]

Griffin immediately ordered all post commanders to assume the duties of Bureau agents. As of June 1, 1867, he had established fifty-seven subdistricts with sixty-nine agents, made up of thirty-eight officers and thirty-one civilians. This organizational maneuver dramatically increased the Bureau's influence and extended "protection and redress" for the freedpeople to the remotest parts of Texas. By combining the military and Bureau and using post commanders as agents, Griffin extended the Bureau's geographical limits to areas that previously had been ignored. Before his arrival, the friction and separate spheres of the two institutions left many black Texans without assistance. Now all Bureau and army power resided in one man.[57]

Griffin quickly focused upon agriculture. A majority of the former slaves labored in the cotton-raising counties along the Colorado and Brazos rivers, with a significant minority working near the Nueces, Guadalupe, and Red rivers. Others could be found "scattered" over the grain-raising counties in the eastern, central and northern portion of the state. Without means to "plant on their own account," Griffin wrote, blacks found themselves compelled to work as laborers or to contract for one-third, planters furnishing "horses, tools, and provisions." Nearly one-half the blacks labored for shares in the cotton counties. Planters "prefer[red] this way to payment of wages—the incentive to care and industry being greater."[58]

Griffin realized that blacks desired more opportunities. He believed that as they accumulated property the contract system would be replaced by their direct renting of the land, "which is preferable but still above the means of the mass of freedmen." The number renting and farming lands on their "own account was largely in excess" of the previous year and constantly increasing, but still comparably small. Griffin observed that farms operated by blacks appeared to be as "well-managed and successful as those of their white neighbors." In the grain-raising, lumbering, and grazing counties of the state, the former slaves, mostly employed as monthly wage laborers, received $14 specie for adult males and $10 for females.[59]

The problem of freedpeople receiving equitable proceeds from their labor became a focal point of Griffin's administration. He recommended that an agent be assigned to whom blacks could voluntarily consign their cotton so they would be assured of receiving "full market price." The previous year, blacks, unable to market their crop for "want of means" or the "knowledge of what to do," had been swindled. To assist them an individual, recommended by local Bureau agents and under bond, could be referred to the freed-people. The former slaves would not be "forced" or "under any obligation" to market their crop this way, but could determine how to dispose of it themselves. Every man could arrange for his "earnings as he saw fit."[60]

Undoubtedly, a "large number" of blacks sold their product to the planter instead of marketing it themselves. To avoid dishonesty, Griffin issued an order forbidding planters' accounts to constitute a lien upon the freedmen's portion of the crop. But if blacks could not get their cotton to market, the order was useless. Griffin's proposed plan did not "divest things from the regular channel of trade," but tended to "place freedmen in the same position he must fall into in the course of time and after the Bureau ceased to exist." If only three men in a county could market their crop themselves and "realize its value," then the "work is accomplished." In the next year "all will know the value of their crops."[61]

Griffin found the 1866 state contract laws the "most vicious" statutes and "in violation of every principle of sound sense and justice." They allowed the planter to fine the employee and deduct the amount from wages of the laborer. Fines could be imposed for a host of enumerated transgressions. The planter, also empowered to send a laborer to jail if he or she refused to work for whatever reason, had enormous discretion under the law. If sent to jail, freedpeople could be compelled to toil on the public roads "until willing to return to the employer." If the laborer, regardless of the circumstances, decided to seek other employment, no one else would be allowed to employ the individual under penalty of "a ruinous fine."[62]

If allowed to be enforced, these laws would result in the reduction of the laborers to peonage, Griffin concluded. Although the Bureau had previously attempted to negate them, they still had a most "demoralizing effect." The planters, instead of "discharging lazy or worthless laborers," tenaciously clung to the idea of making up the loss of time through fines, stoppages, and other necessary means, which the Bureau refused to accept. Employer and employee relations could be improved through the elimination of "antiquated and unwise legislative attempts to regulate" labor conditions. Through the natural workings of the system, the "parties interested" could thus secure "personal independence of the laborers and employer from pecuniary loss."[63]

By mid-1867 the agricultural scene had begun to change perceptibly. Although not as much land had been cultivated as the previous year, it was "better worked, and will produce more," Griffin wrote. Nature did not cooperate, however. Prolonged heavy rains far into the summer had destroyed crops on many of the river plantations. Those on higher ground, particularly under cotton cultivation, encountered problems with grass. Because of the heavy rains, grass had a good start. Coupled with the scarcity of labor, it would take a considerable effort on the part of the planters to regain this land. The wheat and corn crops in the central and northern portion of Texas, described as in a "very fine" condition, would have a good yield.[64]

The blacks, "almost universally working well," despite all the previous complaints of the planters, found the demand for their services "astonishing." Wages, because of the competition for labor, according to Griffin, remained high. Employer treatment of labor appeared "much better than usual," he stated, "owing perhaps to the reason that they must treat them well to secure their labor." A new attitude in relation to black Texans, especially in their laboring capacity, finally seemed to be emerging two years after the end of the war. "Among the first classes of the people," Griffin observed, the estrangement between whites and blacks that had arisen at the moment of emancipation had been replaced by a "more kindly feeling."[65]

But white violence directed at blacks continued to be a subject of major concern, and public opinion condoned atrocities committed upon the freedpeople. Griffin perceived that the civil and judicial system had collapsed. The number of soldiers, never large enough to spread over the state and overawe the people, could not compel enforcement of the laws. He believed that in many counties of the state "little lawlessness" occurred and "in many more" the life of a freedman could be considered "as safe as that of a white." Nevertheless, large parts of the Lone Star State continued to be dangerous, "where murder is bold and unchecked—in those parts the life of a white man is worth but little, the life of a freedman is worth nothing."[66]

Among other reasons, violence troubled the Griffin commissionership because of uncooperative officials who "thwart the ends of justice." It is "utterly impossible to stem the tide of murder and disorder" without "wholesale removal" of county officers, he wrote Howard. Among governmental responsibilities owed to its citizens, Griffin declared, the "very highest duty" had to be "physical protection." With an "effective force" of only 3,465 troops, Griffin found it difficult to force state officials to respect black rights. Public sentiment had improved in "some of the most advanced parts of the state," but where "ruffians" and "desperadoes" controlled public opinion, citizens evinced an open hostility to the freedmen.[67]

Griffin also set about reforming the educational system and directly linking it to his division of the state into subdistricts. All agents became mini-superintendents of education and, at least once a month, were required to visit every school located in their area. The agents would "use every means" to obtain "plots of ground" for black schools, to contract with individuals for the completion of buildings, the placing of desks, and other physical requirements. Agents, according to headquarters, also had to visit private schools and "encourage" their "self sustaining basis." Located in small villages and on plantations where Sunday and night sessions for the adults were often held, these private schools were to be assisted in whatever way possible.[68]

In December 1865, when a majority of the schools remained in the category of self-sustaining, there were approximately 5,000 scholars. At the end of the first quarter in 1866, attendance had slightly decreased to 4,804 pupils in a total of 93 schools, with 106 teachers. Of this number of teachers, the American Missionary Association (AMA) only furnished 16 of the total. By the middle of 1867, Griffin estimated that the aggregate number of blacks attending day, night, and Sunday schools had increased to nearly 6,000, and 17 additional teachers had been sent by the AMA. Griffin, impressed by their dedication, wrote that they labored for the "mental and moral improvement" of their students with "a zeal and devotion" he had "never seen surpassed."[69]

During the summer of 1867, a yellow fever epidemic occurred in Galveston and began to move into the hinterland. Griffin, concerned about black suffering, sought to discover whether private associations established by the freedpeople could provide assistance. Although he was encouraged to remove Bureau headquarters out of Galveston, he steadfastly refused. Griffin became infected, and on Sunday, September 15, it was the "painful and melancholy duty" of the clerk to report that Griffin had died at 12:57 A.M. With Griffin's death, the state office, temporarily in disarray, could do little. In addition, curtailing expenses substantially reduced the number of local agents. At a critical point, the Bureau's effectiveness was being diminished.[70]

Yellow fever swept along the Gulf Coast and "far into the interior." It held "few terrors" for the blacks, wrote Joseph J. Reynolds, who were "almost entirely exempt from its ravages." The epidemic that infested Texas in mid and late 1867, devastated the Bureau and its staff. Papers and records were thrown "into confusion." Sickness and death among Bureau officials and their families "paralyzed" the agency's operations for nearly three months. The number of deaths from the "ravages of this terrible scourge" could not be definitely ascertained but included an assistant commissioner, two medical officers, six agents, one inspector, three clerks, and three teachers. Other enlisted men, clerks, and orderlies also succumbed.[71]

Griffin, although his assistant commissionership lasted only seven months, significantly expanded the Bureau's influence. Combining army post commander's duties with those of a subassistant commissioner, he made it possible for the agency to serve the freedpeople in remote areas by organizing the Bureau into subdistricts, which had specific geographical limits. In this way, the Bureau's responsibilities became more efficiently managed and the agency strengthened. Griffin brought the Texas Bureau to its peak in manpower and coverage. Through his strength of personality and policy implementation, he perhaps assisted the former slaves in their transition to freedom and assured their rights more successfully than any other assistant commissioner.

Joseph J. Reynolds

Griffin's successor, Joseph J. Reynolds, immediately transferred Bureau headquarters from coastal Galveston to Austin, far removed from the ravages of the yellow fever epidemic. Kentucky born but raised in Indiana, Reynolds attended Wabash College, then graduated from West Point in 1843. He served on the frontier, taught at West Point for eight years, and, in 1857, resigned and became a professor at St. Louis' Washington University and a grocery merchant. Commissioned a colonel in the Tenth Indiana, later a brigadier and major general in the U.S. Volunteers, he fought at Cheat Mountain. Resigning in 1862, Reynolds helped recruit and train Indiana regiments. He finished as a corps commander in Louisiana and Arkansas.[72]

Reynolds commanded the Subdistrict of the Rio Grande when appointed assistant commissioner. Harvest season and contract negotiations were under way when Reynolds assumed his Bureau duties. The freedpeople, cheated out of "commissions" and other "proceeds" because they had no means to ship their crops, frequently had to sell it "on ground." Reynolds claimed "it was simply impossible to execute" previous Bureau pronouncements, so he devised a different method, which he hoped would provide some protection for the former slaves in the division of the crops. One of an agent's prime responsibilities to freedpeople, Reynolds informed his subalterns, was to make certain that they received a "fair share of the crop" and "advise them of disposal."[73]

Employers declared that the "nigger will not work," which Reynolds believed, "to state it mildly, an error." That blacks had done so well surprised everyone "after the fraud, cruelty, and deceit that has been and is yet being continually practiced upon them." Opposed to the "share wages" system (paying blacks a fraction of the crop), they viewed it as a "surrogate for the slave plantation." Freedpeople were induced to enter into new contracts for 1868 only by the "advice and exertions" of the Bureau agents. "It seems almost impossible," Reynolds observed, "to disabuse their minds of the conviction that it is a species of slavery." As a system it had "eventually [to] pass away," with blacks gaining more control over their labor and the land.[74]

Another problem with the new class of planters was that they endeavored to farm the old plantations with "gangs of hands as of old." Reynolds believed that "necessity compelled," and "habit permitted," gang labor "to continue." Like share wages, it too had to "pass away." Meanwhile, blacks would "gain experience" and "become enlightened" through these methods. More and more their feelings against this system would increase, and the "liberty to choose their vocations will break it up," and in its place many small farms would arise. Blacks, adamantly opposed to gang labor, resisted contracts that contained such a provision. This may have been another reason why they had not labored as intensively as the assistant commissioner desired.[75]

If black labor caused concern, employers evinced the most difficulty. During the previous two years, the "unreliable" and "irresponsible" character of the planters "as a class" had been a continual "source of annoyance" to the Bureau and a pecuniary loss to the former slaves. Although not a general pattern, Reynolds said, plantation owners and "old owners of slaves" had not attempted the experiment of "working free labor but leased places instead to their old overseers" and "other irresponsible parties." Those who had previously depended upon black labor, "much their best friends," had abandoned farming. Reynolds believed a different class now controlled the agricultural scene, a class that demonstrated an overt hostility to freedpeople.[76]

By the end of 1868, when the Bureau removed most of its local agents, the crops had not been "fully harvested" but had "progressed far enough to yield far more than any year since emancipation." There would be about one-half a cotton crop; the corn looked "very fine"; and sugar cane, "equally good." A fairer settlement, and with less trouble, would be made by Bureau agents than in previous years. Reynolds' optimistic tone resulted from two factors: the greater yield of the harvest, leaving the planter more profits after division, and the planters' realization from past experience that if they did not divide the crop fairly agents "would step in and compel it." The former slaves seemed to be almost "entirely self supporting."[77]

In education, Reynolds had to mediate a conflict between the Texas Bureau and the AMA. To reduce tensions and to gain additional teachers, he negotiated with the AMA's New York secretary, George Whipple, instead of the Chicago office. Nevertheless, Howard, disappointed in the "diminished" attendance in Texas black schools, queried Reynolds about the decline, and Reynolds attempted to explain. In 1865 and 1866, schools largely supported themselves, but this "debarred many of the poorer class from school privileges." Meanwhile, a considerable fund accrued from the rents of confiscated property, so the Bureau channeled the money into education. They hired teachers, reduced tuition to a "nominal sum," and made the schools "substantially free."[78]

Throughout the early spring and summer of 1867, schools grew in numbers and improved in quality. Then the yellow fever epidemic "wasted the seaboard from July until November, paralyzing all educational activity." By the latter month, scarcely 10 percent of the schools continued in operation, teachers had died, and others had left the state, adamantly refusing to return. The fund previously used to pay teachers, now almost exhausted, had no available means of "replenishment." Resuming the self-supporting schools (of which there had always been a large number due to black initiative) and charging instructional fees seemed to be the only solution. With tuition reestablished, many pupils withdrew.[79]

Finding and maintaining "competent and efficient" teachers for freedpeople proved to be a major obstacle, hindering the "influence and success" of Bureau educational endeavors. Texas was a brutal and cruel place for a teacher, whether white or black, male or female. Securing room and board for Northern women sent to the state by the missionary societies proved nearly impossible. People refused to accept these "nigger teachers." Local officials provided no civil or military protection against the "cowardly insults" to which teachers found themselves constantly subjected. The "bitterness of prejudice" still ran deep. Surprisingly, "little difference" in sentiment for black education existed between Unionists and Confederates.[80]

Reports and "information from every source" indicated "no such thing as civil law justly and fairly administered." Reynolds claimed that "hundreds of freedmen had been murdered" and "thousands mutilated" since the war's close, yet the "perpetrators of these deeds go unpunished." Although "many cases" came to the notice of the civil authorities, no action appeared to be taken under state law. No consequences followed these actions, "save in acquitting the offender or putting a bar to further action in the case through a manipulation of the law." The court's behavior proved to be "farcical and productive of no result whatever" except to demonstrate the premise that no effective law enforcement existed.[81]

Civil courts prosecuted blacks "rigorously, cruelly and unjustly—having no charity for them in their weakness and ignorance and ignoring their early education which taught them that the sum of all punishments was a whipping." They had been "prosecuted for offenses of all sorts, many real but crimes of law degree—others having no foundation save in the breasts of those who originated them—the result is that the States prison is filled to overflowing." Governor E. M. Pease had begun an investigation of each case, and "under it no doubt many will be pardoned." Injustices had surely been committed against "these victims of the rebellion that reflects to the dishonor of those in whose hands their freedom found them."[82]

Reynolds also dealt with other matters. (According to Richter's interpretation Texas Republican politics became Reynolds' special interest. But he did have time to ferret out dishonest agents (the transgression: bribery), and to concern himself with the deteriorating state of race relations in Brazos County (see chapter 5), where economics, race, and politics led to open conflict between blacks and whites. Troops needed to be moved to make them available to protect some agents, and he attempted to relieve those subassistant commissioners in the most dangerous areas. As blacks entered the political arena, agents' lives were threatened. Before the Bureau could fully withdraw, one agent was assassinated (see chapter 4), and others made hasty exits.[83]

Reynolds' problems, similar in scope to those of the previous Bureau chief's, continued to bedevil his assistant commissionership. Politics consumed more of his time because Congress had assumed direction of Reconstruction, but the "greatest difficulty," Reynolds recorded, was "securing justice to the freedmen in cases of criminal nature." He had exhausted his patience and had used "every means" he could employ to "educate and force" civil authorities into "doing something near their duty, but the sentiment of the entire people is as demoralized and they are specially averse to recognizing the equality of the Negro before the law, that I cannot report any very great amount of progress in that direction."[84]

Although Reynolds issued few orders in administering the Bureau, his "constant aim" was to give the freedpeople "all the protection possible with the means at his disposal" and simultaneously to "leave them free to act for themselves in all things pertaining to their material welfare." In contract matters, whether involving wages or shares, the Bureau "exercised" little control over black Texans save "in so far as they would be guided by the advice and counsel" of the agents. Because of the condition of affairs in the state, Reynolds had been compelled in many instances to authorize agents to arrest, try, and punish "certain classes of offenses committed upon the freedpeople."[85]

Reynolds summarized many of the problems the Texas Bureau encountered in seeking to reconstruct the Lone Star State. "The demoralized condition of the sentiment of the whole people—their total disregard for law and order, their intolerance of opinions differing from their own, and the light value they place upon human life" had been constant themes in all the Texas assistant commissioner's correspondence. To say more upon a "subject that has already become so notorious through the length and breadth of the land seems like idle repetition," Reynolds wrote Howard. The violence, so appalling in its "circumstances of cruelty and torture" that attended many of the outrages, pointed to acts "of a most revolting and fiendish character."[86]

Although violence and upheaval still blanketed the state, the feeling among the planters and the freedpeople in the southern portion of Texas, where the Bureau and the army concentrated their activities, had slightly improved and appeared "much better than heretofore." In northern and eastern Texas, the exact reverse of this situation prevailed. In that area outlaws and guerrillas had taken control, creating havoc among numerous communities in Texas and Arkansas. Union men and blacks, "if not killed, [had been] driven from their homes by acts of violence and warnings as to their fate if they did not leave." Desperadoes intimidated black voters, as did the Ku Klux Klan, which now made its appearance.[87]

Reynolds, castigated and despised by historians of Texas Reconstruction because he allegedly made it possible for the Radicals to assume state power in 1870, oversaw the dismantling of the Bureau before his political involvement. He has been portrayed as a kind of "master politician" who, after returning to command the District of Texas in 1869, became a wily politico. Not only is he credited with being responsible for the E. J. Davis accession to the governorship, but some newspapers and private correspondents touted him for one of the two senatorships the Lone Star State had to offer. There remains much controversy over precisely which political role Reynolds played in Texas Reconstruction.

Reynolds tended to focus more attention upon army business and, to a certain extent, politics than he did upon the Bureau. During his tenure, violence and politics intertwined, creating upheaval, disruption, and political instability. Once again, Texas proceeded through voter registration (which now included blacks), and elections had to be scheduled for delegates to a new constitutional convention. Bureau agents, at the heart of this process and conflict, needed assistance at the same time the army began to reduce the number of men. Reynolds had difficulties in determining where to station his meager numbers. His tenure as Bureau chief cannot be rated as highly successful, but he did manage to provide some help to the black community.

Conclusion

As the Texas Freedmen's Bureau began its withdrawal from the state, except in the educational arena, a former Bureau inspector, William H. Sinclair, suggested to Governor Pease that the agency "be continued" until the "vote upon the adoption of the [1869] Constitution is had." Sinclair declared that Union sympathizers had to "use every means we can command to carry a majority of the voters and the most powerful medium is the influence the agents have over the freedpeople and their—the freedpeoples—confidence in the agents." Without the "protection and advice of the agents," black Texans would be "left at the mercy of the rebels with little or no influence to counteract and guide them in the right course."[88]

Sinclair exaggerated the power of the Bureau to influence blacks and Unionists who already knew which course to pursue. It is true, however, that once the Bureau left the state, no buffer remained to deflect the attitudes of those who refused to accept the results of the Civil War and who steadfastly rejected Reconstruction. Sinclair may have been closer to the mark when he observed that the freedpeople had much confidence in Bureau personnel. Indeed, at times blacks became dissatisfied with Bureau decisions or its slowness to act, but overall those who could avail themselves of the agency's assistance did so. Texas blacks understood that the Bureau could provide some aid but that its resources and manpower were limited.

The problems that Texas and Texans posed for the Freedmen's Bureau in terms of space, time, and control were beyond what the agency could do in so short a period. The Bureau did not become operational until September 1865 and was all but phased out by January 1, 1869. Only the education division continued in existence, ceasing to function in 1872. In urban areas, such as they were, freedpeople did much better in terms of education, civil rights, economic security, and general welfare than their counterparts in rural regions.

The Bureau provided little material relief for black Texans, but as a labor moderator, it was moderately successful. The one area where it failed miserably was in protecting blacks against violence.

The Texas assistant commissioners pursued and emphasized different policies. Gregory attempted to stabilize the labor system and to extend full citizenship rights to the freedpeople. Educational efforts were left to the black community. Kiddoo focused upon education and justice but never ignored economics, negating the Black Codes. Griffin's strength was organization. He brought the Bureau to its peak in manpower and area supervision. Reynolds found politics to be his strong point and moved in that direction, but that was essentially after the Bureau ceased to exist. He tried to provide freedpeople with more economic rights and continued to stress education. All assistant commissioners despaired over the violence committed upon Texas blacks.

All the assistant commissioners in Texas—Gregory, Kiddoo, Griffin, and Reynolds—tried to give the freedpeople as much protection as possible.[89] As in the rest of the South, complete freedom for blacks in the individual or economic sphere was never realized, no matter what policies the assistant commissioners followed or how diligent they attempted to be in assisting the former slaves in their relations with employers or in their grievances against civil authorities. Every assistant commissioner noted and consistently complained about the gross mistreatment of black Texans but never had sufficient troops nor financial resources to even begin to protect the black community through a sustained commitment.

Neither the system nor the situation was ideal, but after trial and error by both blacks and whites, economic relations did become stabilized, often at the expense of black autonomy. Out of the fluid agricultural conditions following the war, blacks attained a certain amount of independence by gaining some leverage through sharecropping. Within the limitations set by the government and society, the Texas assistant commissioners did what they felt was feasible. Undoubtedly, freedpeople suffered a great deal, but not because the Bureau failed to assist them. Generally, it made significant efforts in attempting to keep whites from completely dominating the black community. The Bureau also endeavored to promote a degree of black independence.

The four major Texas Bureau commissioners (Gregory, Kiddoo, Griffin, and Reynolds) all reiterated that civil law was a farce in postwar Texas. It was essentially a fruitless task, however. Reynolds was as despairing of the situation at the end of the Bureau's tenure as Gregory was when he assumed Bureau command. The condition of affairs in the state generally, he told Howard, was not comprehended by white Texans. Black civil rights were ignored and their complaints were simply dismissed, Reynolds believed, and his perceptions echoed those of every other assistant commissioner. For outrages "to be fully appreciated [they] must be experienced. The universal failure to execute criminal law is appalling."[90]

The most difficult problem facing the Texas Bureau was the rising tide of violence directed against the former slaves—a situation that would confront the assistant commissioners until the Bureau was discontinued. The constant abuse of blacks, in whatever form, simply could not be controlled or stopped by the Bureau. Most subdistricts encompassed two to five counties, and the agents faced a hostile white population with a minimum of assistance. The state was so large, and mounted troops so scarce, that protection could be afforded only to those blacks in the immediate vicinity of Bureau offices where troops were stationed. Many times the lives of the agents themselves were endangered, and threats were common.

By late 1868, Reynolds reported that six agents had been killed. Between 1865 and 1868, 761 murders had been perpetrated in the state, of which 464 victims were black. In addition, another 1,000 murders may have occurred between 1868 and 1870 after the Bureau was removed from the Lone Star State. The Bureau compiled a list of 2,225 cases of killings, assault and battery, whippings, hangings, shootings, and other assorted uses of force against both blacks and whites. How many violent acts went unreported will never be known. A perceptive Texas historian assessed the situation accurately when he wrote that the state "was the scene of a race war in which Negroes and their protectors suffered great loss of life."[91]

Neither a complete success nor a failure in Texas, the Bureau was not as detrimental to Texas society as many Texas historians have claimed. The controversy surrounding Edgar M. Gregory and his removal most certainly did not help the agency at its inception. Despite that, the assistant commissioners all encountered the same problems and maintained fairly consistent policies. Generally they tried to keep the Bureau away from politics and were surprisingly successful. Loyal or Union Leagues were established, but these were based more on the attitudes of the local agents than on any specific directive from headquarters. Bureau agents were involved in politics to the extent that they served as overseers of registration boards.[92]

When viewed from an administrative perspective, agents do not appear so much the Machiavellian figures when dressed in Bureau clothes as when in full military garb. It is interesting to note that the tone of military and Bureau letters are quite different. These men were attempting to please a divergent command—from Philip Sheridan to Oliver Howard—and to place the freedpeople within the mainstream of Texas society. Mistakes in performing their duties and responsibilities were made by all the Texas assistant commissioners, but a fair evaluation must credit them with positive marks in their attempt to elevate the status of former slaves and to provide services that would not otherwise have been available. They acquitted themselves well.

Whatever the merits or demerits of the assistant commissioners, it was on the regional and local level where contact with the Texas black community was most pervasive. The Texas Bureau chiefs could make all the administrative decisions they desired, and pass them along to the agents in the various subdistricts throughout Texas, but how they were accepted and enforced is a question that begs for investigation. After all, it was the Bureau agents who had to bear the brunt of the responsibility in assisting, advising, and promoting black welfare, civil rights, and economic viability. They had to contend with the hostility and violence of the white community. How they proceeded is the subject of the next three chapters.

3. The Texas Bureau in Microcosm: The Thirtieth Subdistrict During Reconstruction

FROM THE BEGINNING of the Texas Bureau, a subassistant commissioner, or agent, directed and supervised a specific section of the state known as a subdistrict, which was ill defined under the first two assistant commissioners. In any case, the vast distances within Texas, poor communication, shortage of funds, and lack of personnel made it difficult for the Bureau to expand its operations immediately beyond the coastal regions. Once the agency and the army merged under one commander, the state was divided into subdistricts, new agents were added, and affairs became better organized. Supervised by one man, a subdistrict generally encompassed from two to five counties and varied in size, racial composition, and economic factors.

Viewing such a subdistrict in microcosm makes a study of the Bureau at the local level a fascinating endeavor. An analysis of Bureau activities provides an insight into events in small communities across the South during Congressional Reconstruction when Congress controlled Southern affairs, strengthened the Bureau, legalized black rights, and enfranchised former slaves. For Reconstruction to succeed, change had to begin at the community level. The Bureau's task was to implement these laws, protect blacks in their newly won freedom, attempt to maintain peaceable relations between the two races, and provide economic direction. The agents of the Thirtieth Subdistrict responded in different ways to these responsibilities.

Under Assistant Commissioners Edgar M. Gregory and Joseph B. Kiddoo, agents presided over huge sections of the state. Preoccupied with making freedom a reality, stressing economics, and emphasizing education, these two men expanded the Bureau's geographical coverage very slowly. Before 1867 the subassistant commissioner, headquartered in Marshall, had jurisdiction over Smith County and adjacent areas. The Marshall agent had to take cognizance of all disputes between whites and blacks, promote education, and assist in negotiating contractual arrangements to make sure freedpeople received fair treatment by their employers. Numerous reports indicated that employers cheated them out of the proceeds of their labor.[1]

These conditions continued for two years after the end of the Civil War. Then the situation changed dramatically on both national and state scenes. Congress assumed control of reconstructing the South, passed a civil rights bill and a second Freedmen's Bureau law, and provided the agency with separate funding. In Texas, Governor James W. Throckmorton was removed as an "impediment to Reconstruction," and somewhat earlier, a new man became head of the Texas Bureau. Consequently, the organization of the Texas Freedmen's Bureau and the implementation of its various policies did not fully come to fruition until the assumption of the assistant commissionership by Charles Griffin.[2]

In mid-1867 Griffin divided Texas into subdistricts headed by subassistant commissioners. They were directly accountable to him, but because of geography and continuing communication difficulties, they would necessarily have to make some decisions on their own and later request approval from headquarters. During this reorganization, Griffin created the Thirtieth Subdistrict, which comprised Smith, Henderson, Wood, Van Zandt, and Cherokee counties, north of Rusk County inclusive. Tyler, a focal point of the region, became the agent's headquarters. The subdistrict covered approximately four thousand square miles, with a total population, according to the 1870 census, of 42,246 people, roughly 12,400 blacks and 29,900 whites.[3]

In the almost two years that the Thirtieth Subdistrict existed, its boundaries never changed, but its personnel did. Four subassistant commissioners and one assistant subassistant commissioner served at varying times during this period. The four agents included Captain David L. Montgomery, Major Levi C. Bootes, First Lieutenant Gregory Barrett, Jr., and Captain Horace Jewett, all of the United States Twenty-ninth Infantry; the assistant was DeWitt C. Brown. Their backgrounds and attitudes toward their job and the freedpeople varied considerably. Their successes and failures in the subdistrict mirrored the experience of other local agents across the Lone Star State and indeed the South. Agents encountered similar problems no matter where located.

Of the four subassistant commissioners who served in the Thirtieth Subdistrict, Montgomery was born in Pennsylvania in 1836; Barrett in Maryland in the same year; Bootes in Washington, D.C., in 1809 (the oldest of the agents); and Jewett in Maine in 1834. All four men had fought extensively for the Union army in the Civil War. The two most important agents, Montgomery and Barrett, both served in the area for six months. Bootes headed the subdistrict off and on for seven months, interspersed with Montgomery's tenure. Jewett directed the subdistrict for only ninety days, and the assistant subassistant commissioner, DeWitt C. Brown, a civilian agent from Ohio, stayed in Tyler but three months. The latter two had little influence on Bureau policy.[4]

About the same time that Congress gained control of Reconstruction, the first subassistant commissioner for the Thirtieth Subdistrict, David L. Montgomery, assumed his post at Tyler in March 1867. Enroute from Austin to Tyler, he had been approached by many former slaves who asked for protection of their person and property. After Montgomery's arrival in Tyler, many area blacks called upon him reiterating the same theme: abusive treatment. But before proceeding with any business, Montgomery had to establish an office. Eventually he found a place to serve as a local headquarters for fifteen dollars a month.[5] With this completed, the Pennsylvanian now assumed the arduous task of trying to bring the Thirtieth Subdistrict under Bureau control.

A month after establishing his office in Tyler, Montgomery made his first official report. Although he had heard several rumors that freedpeople were being terrorized, no satisfactory evidence had appeared that any violent acts had occurred since December 1866. (The general situation in Texas made this highly improbable.) Violence did exist, mainly in the form of assault and battery. The blacks did, however, commonly complain that they had not been paid for their labor. Montgomery referred these cases to civil authorities. Initially, he found local officials cooperative, and their actions met with his "full approbation." The forthcoming elections would noticeably increase the tensions between the two groups.[6]

As military rule had been reestablished, the scheduling of new elections became a priority. This necessitated registration of all eligible black and white male voters in the subdistrict. A supervisor (who directed registration in six to eleven counties) had to be appointed, and directly under his control was a board of registrars, usually three for each county. To expedite registration, the county was divided into precincts. In April, Montgomery searched for suitable men to serve as registrars in his five-county subdistrict. They had to be so situated that all those eligible to register would be able to do so with a minimum of difficulty and a maximum of efficiency. Montgomery managed these procedures effectively.[7]

Registration swung into operation in the Thirtieth Subdistrict in July 1867. Montgomery reported to Austin that the process progressed quietly and that the supervisor had begun a tour of his section. The election districts, divided differently than the Bureau's subdistricts, complicated registration, however. At the end of the first week, Smith County had enrolled 140 whites and 264 blacks. Registration proceeded apace in Van Zandt, and a supervisor had gone to Cherokee to ascertain the situation there. Continuing into 1868, agents had to contend with revised registration lists, general confusion, and numerous headaches. They had to make certain registration was completed and to assist in compiling the final voter lists.[8]

As suggested earlier, a reevaluation of the actual political influence that agents wielded in their local district is necessary. Clearly, they had to be involved in the registration and election processes as part of their required duties. Because agents symbolized the repository of governmental power, they, by necessity, had to deal with the political arena. It does not naturally follow, however, that they gravitated toward politics. Certainly they made political decisions when they selected registrars, made recommendations to headquarters about an individual's suitability for office, and attempted to enforce Congressional Reconstruction throughout their subdistrict. All this was required as part of their Bureau responsibilities.

Agents like Montgomery did become involved in politics as part of their responsibility. When they recommended individuals be appointed to registration boards or to serve as registrars, obviously they were making a political statement. They searched for persons who were sympathetic to Congressional Reconstruction, but headquarters had to approve their selections, and Montgomery's met the requirements. They had to work with the local power structure, and the job was demanding enough without worrying about clashes and conflicts with community officials. Some agents became more politicized than others, but most, particularly those in the Thirtieth Subdistrict kept their actual political participation to a minimum.

Race and Labor Relations

A supreme challenge to any subassistant commissioner's ability involved his effort to stabilize race relations in his subdistrict, an elusive goal and one that would have strained anyone's mental and physical capacities in any decade of the nineteenth century. An agent was especially vulnerable whenever politics became intertwined with the social and economic aspects of Reconstruction, and it became impossible for an agent, no matter how dedicated, to maintain harmony between the two races. White behavior and feeling toward blacks, Montgomery wrote, was "as various as the character of the people." Before the announcement of state elections, Montgomery had discovered no "unusually bad disposition" openly displayed by whites against the freedpeople.[9]

On the surface all seemed to be placid, but Montgomery, unquestionably overly optimistic, discovered his assessment of white attitudes to be misplaced. Area blacks, beginning to voice their concerns and disturbed by the increasing opposition of their white counterparts, became restive. Underneath, tensions, aggravated because of political and economic turmoil, increased because of the lack of black educational progress and the unresponsive reaction of civil authorities to black grievances. These factors quickly destroyed Montgomery's earlier confidence in the response the majority would make to black freedom and the assertiveness of the former slaves. Future actions proved the Pennsylvanian's first appraisal to be deeply flawed.

Except in occasional cases, Montgomery still assessed race relations favorably in mid-1867 and asserted that the outlook of whites toward blacks was "fair." But the agent now had additional support. Four companies of soldiers, comprising 179 men, now resided in Tyler to assist him. Montgomery unequivocally believed their presence to be "absolutely necessary for the protection of the freedpeople." Even with soldiers immediately available, race relations began to deteriorate under Montgomery's supervision. His earlier optimism had started to fade as the enormity of his task became clear. That troops were a necessity is not surprising, for a small social and political revolution seemed to be in the making.[10]

When Levi C. Bootes assumed direction of the Thirtieth Subdistrict for a temporary period in the late summer of 1867, a nadir in relations between the two races had been reached. White disposition toward blacks, characterized as bad except in rare cases, did not bode well for the future. Bootes also thought troops were indispensable. As long as a military detachment remained, it kept whites "in line" and ensured justice for blacks. During the succeeding months, the number of soldiers, constantly reduced, made it more difficult for agents to maintain any semblance of order or to force civil authorities to respect black rights. Whites and blacks treated each other warily until 1868, when Gregory Barrett, Jr., became the agent.[11]

Barrett encountered more trouble in performing his Bureau duties than either Montgomery or Bootes. He first reported white attitudes toward blacks around Tyler as "fair," but a "bad" feeling existed within the subdistrict generally. Troops had been withdrawn from Tyler, and as soon as the "Yankees" left, many whites threatened to "clean the blacks out." Violence against the freedpeople increased, and Barrett observed that the freedmen did not feel nearly so secure now that the troops were gone. Later he characterized white disposition as "very bad," and only the protection of the government (the little available) prevented whites from reducing the freedpeople "to a worse condition than slavery." [12]

Racial feelings became worse as outright hostility replaced underlying rage. In mid-1868 Barrett sadly concluded that relations were as "bad as can be." The only positive influence was the arrival of twenty soldiers (he needed one hundred). Troops were indispensable for the security of local blacks, and Barrett again stressed their necessity. Before Barrett left Tyler, he contended that white sentiment toward blacks had continued to spiral downward and that no sign indicated that relations between the two races would improve. In some portions of the subdistrict, a virtual "reign of terror" had commenced. Shortly afterward Barrett was relieved, and within three months the Bureau office in the Thirtieth Subdistrict had been discontinued. [13]

Attempting to implement the concept of free labor may have been the most important task of a Bureau agent. Planters experimented with various methods in keeping blacks tied closely to the land. What eventually evolved from a series of economic compromises that included yearly contracts and share wages was a modified form of black control over the land known as sharecropping. This semi-independence gave blacks some voice in determining crops and acreage. The Bureau assisted in this evolutionary scheme by promoting black economic and contractual rights. "Again and again the Bureau critics repeated this theme," Foner writes, "that by treating blacks with a semblance of equality, the Bureau 'demoralized' plantation labor." [14]

Across the South, most Bureau agents served in the area that had long been known as the Black Belt. Extending from South Carolina to Texas, slavery became the bastion of the labor system in this region. The principal crops of the Thirtieth Subdistrict included cotton and corn. Late in the harvest season or at the beginning of the year, black laborers contracted for a portion of the crop, usually one-third to one-half, depending upon what the planter furnished. If the planter supplied everything, blacks received one-third, if the freedmen furnished items for themselves then their share increased to one-half. Most worked for one-third, and a few labored for weekly or monthly wages. The agent checked the agreement to determine its equitableness.

Freedpeople had already contracted for 1867 when the Thirtieth Subdistrict became a reality. New orders from headquarters for the 1868 contracts confused Montgomery, for he believed the recent regulations would be detrimental to the former slaves. The controversy centered around blacks providing security (generally a clause in the contract) to ensure payment for provisions the planter supplied. If the planters did not willingly furnish provisions without ample security, the freedpeople would be treated unfairly, and the planters would gain an additional economic edge against the already impoverished blacks. Blacks should have the same privilege in entering into contracts that necessitated liens "as any other class of citizens." [15]

Besides the technical matters involving contracts, the agents of the Thirtieth Subdistrict discovered much of their time occupied with labor complaints. The agency probably handled more cases of this nature than any other. When Montgomery arrived in Tyler, his first encounter involved freedpeople who complained that they "experience[d] considerable difficulty in getting paid for their labor." In June 1868, Barrett tried nineteen cases under the category of "services rendered." Troops proved to be essential in assisting the agent in collecting the blacks' share. Without the army detachment, there would be small chance, if any, of black workers receiving their pay from dishonest whites. This problem existed until the Bureau left Texas. [16]

Not being paid for their labor became only one of many difficulties that blacks encountered while working in the agricultural sector. Violence, as it so often did in the Reconstruction years, infused and surrounded the working life of black laborers. Blacks constantly appeared at the subassistant commissioner's office to complain that they had been threatened, assaulted, shot at, and driven off the land they farmed. For example, Manuel Hamby, a freedman, filed a complaint with Barrett. Thomas Lloyd of Rusk County, Hamby's employer, had attacked Hamby with intent to kill. Later, he drove Hamby off the farm, retained his property, and threatened to kill him if he attempted to retrieve it. Similar cases occurred on several plantations. [17]

In one instance, a Henderson County planter named Stevenson threatened to hunt William Govan with dogs and then beat him if the black man left the plantation. Montgomery, appalled by these threats, believed such "amusements were a relic of barbarous days." The agent informed Govan that he had to abide strictly by the contract and told Stevenson that no violence against his laborers would be tolerated. [18] Beyond a veiled threat of punishment and an admonishment of strict adherence to the guidelines of the contract, there was little Montgomery could do. This may or may not have satisfied Govan (and probably enraged Stevenson), but the agent attempted to aid the former slave to the fullest extent of his limited capabilities, minimal without army support.

Until the end of the Bureau's existence, blacks who were driven from their crops after the harvest and forced to seek the Bureau agent hoped to negotiate an equitable distribution of what they had raised during the year. Black labor rhythms (see chapter 5) put them at odds with the planter's philosophy and produced critical reactions from the owners. Some freedpeople, undoubtedly irresponsible, lacked the strength of character to cultivate a crop industriously, which whites characterized as laziness. The majority, however, found themselves pushed into an economic condition in which the distribution of power favored the landowner, middlemen who kept the books, and generally subjected blacks to the pressures of the white community.

Remarkably, or so it seemed, blacks performed better, and the harvest was more abundant than observers expected. The agents looked after black economic interests as much as possible, but too many complaints, too much territory to cover, and too little assistance from military or civil authorities made their task almost insurmountable. An agent's effectiveness, limited to the immediate area surrounding the local headquarters, did not extend into the far reaches of the subdistrict. Blacks on the fringes of an agent's area of supervision often suffered for lack of contact. Agents had to refer cases to other subassistant commissioners because they were closer to the black complainant. A similar situation pervaded all other Texas subdistricts.

To complicate the labor situation, politics and violence became intertwined in the economic sphere. In late 1868 many whites refused to employ blacks for 1869 if the latter expressed a political difference. (Surely it is safe to say that most blacks supported the Republicans, and most planters the Democrats.) Employers also began to grumble, complaining they could not find "reliable" workers. The Ku Klux Klan made its appearance and drove blacks off the land, confiscating their arms and what little money they possessed. These actions further disrupted the labor scene. Strict planter demands and Klan violence became handy tools of coercion to maintain a stable black labor force. In many cases the strategy backfired.[19]

Freedpeople long desired to own the land they farmed. In the Thirtieth Subdistrict, no abandoned lands existed for cultivation, thus the government had nothing to lease to former slaves. Only a small minority of the black population had the means even to consider purchasing land. And if they did have the necessary funds, as a general rule, blacks found whites very reluctant to sell property to them. Owning land would make blacks more self-reliant, and whites would lose additional power over them. This they would not and could not allow. As long as blacks remained dependent upon whites for many necessities of life, they could be manipulated socially, economically, and politically.

Civil, Judicial, and Bureau Business

While serving these various constituencies and performing the many functions of an agent, a subassistant commissioner had to keep abreast of official Bureau business, which included ordering stationery, keeping copies of letters and financial accounts, approving and retaining copies of signed contracts, accounting for abandoned property, ordering wood for the office, and an endless array of numerous small details. Levi C. Bootes found it impossible "at my time of life" to perform everything expected of him without an "intelligent assistant." Headquarters sent DeWitt C. Brown, but he served only three months. With Bureau offices understaffed and with too much field work required of them, agents found little time for paperwork, which always seemed in arrears.[20]

Regulations required that many minor details critical to the operation of the Bureau be performed by the agent, a rule that exacerbated a generally tense situation and led to unnecessary petty squabbles. For example, Montgomery had trouble purchasing stationery, an item essential for conducting business. Since it was absolutely necessary for the office and none could be obtained through the normal channels, Montgomery had taken the initiative upon himself to obtain some writing materials without specific authorization from headquarters. The disbursing officer declined to reimburse Montgomery for the paper he had purchased because he had not received authorization from headquarters. Montgomery saw necessity as the key.

Montgomery argued that he could wait no longer for permission from the state office without "materially delaying the business of the office." Because of problems beyond his control, he assumed that in this instance special authority would be granted and the disbursement approved. Montgomery and the disbursing officer carried on a running feud for a number of months. Much of the difficulty centered around the "irregularity of the mails" as requisition forms and required reports never arrived at headquarters or were invariably late. Occasionally, correspondence took over two months to reach Tyler from Galveston. At one point Montgomery had to travel forty miles to Palestine to retrieve his mail.[21]

Bureau agents found themselves in constant contact with the civil and judicial officials of their subdistrict. An agent's working relationship with these individuals often depended upon their political persuasion, which frequently meant strained encounters. Montgomery informed the commander of the District of Texas that he had traveled over a large portion of the central and northern part of Texas and that he was fully satisfied that more disaffection existed toward the government in this section "than any other point he had visited or heard from" in the state. The agent believed that the Bureau and the military should work closely together and should adopt severe measures that would lead to the "abatement of this political nuisance."[22]

Montgomery had been urged by the Unionist-leaning citizens of Tyler to join in a petition to headquarters to remove several civil officers. These individuals, the Unionists informed the subassistant commissioner, had been enthusiastic supporters of the Confederacy. Montgomery adopted a cautious approach and declined to cooperate until he could investigate the charges himself. If he became convinced, Montgomery informed the petitioners, that sufficient cause existed for such removals then he would take up the matter with headquarters. Montgomery did recommend, without explanation, the removal of F. A. Godley, a member of the Tyler town council, and the appointment of Jesse Rasberry in his stead.[23]

Confirmation of the "Unionist-leaning" citizens' attitude and belief about the members of the Tyler town government soon occurred. Montgomery clashed with the elected officials. He had been at his post scarcely three months when the mayor, three town council members, and the city marshal resigned. They not only removed themselves from office but simultaneously accepted their own resignations. The officials then informed Montgomery that Tyler had no municipal government. With no civil or legal officials, it became imperative that replacements be quickly agreed upon. Montgomery, disgusted by the action of the five town officials, wrote that they performed in such a manner which "prove[d] their disaffection to the General Government."[24]

Finding suitable officials for Tyler continued to engage the Bureau agent's attention. Over a year after Montgomery's difficulties, Barrett enclosed a petition, once again from the "loyal citizens" of the town, for presentation to the Texas assistant commissioner, requesting the appointment of various corporation officers and two justices of the peace. Tyler needed new officials immediately, Barrett asserted, because he believed that much lawlessness that took place could be checked through the power of active civil authorities. Barrett supported the petition and recommended its acceptance so that he could relinquish many cases of disloyalty on his docket to the new city officers.[25]

Many white Southerners openly expressed a deep resentment toward the Freedmen's Bureau. Texans were no exception. The idea of an agency designed to provide a brief period of guardianship for blacks galled inhabitants of the Lone Star State. Montgomery had to contend with this prejudice, as did most Bureau agents, which hindered them in the performance of their duties. The citizens and their leaders defiantly expressed their hostility, Montgomery complained. Various judicial officers encouraged and abetted this resentment. He had heard a Texas Supreme Court judge and D. W. Crow, a justice of the peace, while on the bench with court in session, "express sentiments strongly derogatory to the Bureau and calculated to destroy its efficiency."[26]

Jurisdictional disputes commonly arose during the Bureau's operation in the Thirtieth Subdistrict. The delicate question of whether the civil authorities should, would, or could aid Bureau agents also appeared. In Texas the subassistant commissioners assumed the duties of justices of the peace. They attempted to monitor trials in cases in which they did not have jurisdiction to make certain the freedpeople received justice and their civil rights were upheld. Generally at a disadvantage, the subassistant commissioner had received no training in the law but often had to serve as counsel, judge, and jury. Not an ideal system, nevertheless it provided area blacks with some protection of their civil liberties that they otherwise might not have received.[27]

A subassistant commissioner did not adjudicate all trials that came before him. He immediately referred some to the civil authorities, but often these officials procrastinated and found various excuses for delaying cases where blacks desired jury trials. When Montgomery first attempted this course of action, no trials took place because local officials stated that no jury could be obtained due to governmental restrictions requiring the loyalty oath. Montgomery had little confidence in the judiciary, particularly when a district judge in Quitman (Wood County) failed to obtain a jury. The subassistant commissioner contended that two hundred or three hundred men in that county could take the necessary oath to serve on a jury.[28]

During the existence of the Bureau in the Thirtieth Subdistrict, the agents compiled a list of 452 complaints, an average of about twenty-eight complaints a month, or one a day. This provided ample opportunity for conflicts to arise with civil officials. In cases where the agents presided, usually for sums amounting to $100 or less, they generally disposed of them in the following manner. When they received a complaint, both parties were summoned to appear on a specified day. On that date (if the contesting parties appeared), the agent heard the evidence, any witnesses testified, and the subassistant commissioner decided the case. An agent spent much time presiding over these Bureau court cases with mixed results.[29]

When an agent issued a summons not everyone honored it. Blacks did, but whites often ignored it. If the individual failed to appear, the agent sent cavalrymen, if he had them, to deliver the person to his office. Too often, however, the agent had no military support for this purpose. All the agents claimed that they had found no method, short of physical force, to compel attendance. Moreover, no authority had been given by the Texas Bureau chief for agents to incur expenses for the purpose of being issued horses. Previously they had used government mules (unsatisfactory) but had been deprived of that privilege. If an agent had no troops available, then he requested that the sheriff secure custody of the offending party.[30]

Montgomery's customary routine followed a pattern of hearing and determining without reference to the civil authorities two classes of complaints. First, in cases where the complainants, especially blacks, would "suffer for the necessaries of life" because of trial delays by the civil authorities, the agent would take immediate action. Second, where the local officials failed to act in criminal cases, he would try to initiate the proper proceedings as quickly as possible. Discontent was caused in the black community because many criminal acts had been legally ignored by local officials. Later, Winfield Scott Hancock, commander of the Fifth Military District, eliminated the Bureau's judicial power and ordered the agents to refer all cases to civil officials.[31]

Barrett became embroiled in numerous legal controversies with officials in the Thirtieth Subdistrict. Although most of the civil and judicial authorities pretended to be loyal to the government, they effectively hid their disloyalty from the public and refused to provide blacks legal equality. Even if an appearance of justice could be maintained, juries demonstrated little sympathy for blacks or white Unionists. Believing this lack of justice, Barrett, like Montgomery, tried all cases himself if the parties could be brought before him. Not many cases could be disposed of in this manner, however, as individuals refused to obey the summons. When this occurred, Barrett placed the summons in the sheriff's hand. Often ignored, the agent found the pursuit of justice a fruitless endeavor.[32]

One example involved a case in which officials refused to arrest or serve papers upon a white man who had been accused of assaulting a black man. Previously, Montgomery had referred the case to the civil authorities, and the sheriff had been ordered to arrest the accused party, but no action was taken. Barrett, "credibly informed" that the accused person still lived in the area close to where the crime occurred, believed he should be taken into custody and notified the sheriff of this fact, but he still refused to arrest the man. Had he had soldiers, Barrett claimed, he would not hesitate to guarantee full justice to blacks throughout the subdistrict. Troops, "indispensable to the safety and protection of the freedmen," would render the assistance of the sheriff unnecessary.[33]

Barrett complained that Julius A. Robinson, the Smith County sheriff, and James Sprinks, a Rusk County justice of the peace, ignored their responsibilities. J. M. Hoge, another Rusk County justice of the peace, refused to arrest a person when required to do so by the agent. Barrett encountered trouble with other local officials besides those in Smith and Rusk counties. A black man declared that Squire Shurford, justice of the peace in Wood County, had levied a false judgment against him and had issued an attachment on his cow and corn. Barrett, after investigation, believed Shurford's decision discriminatory and ordered him to withdraw the attachment, allowing the freedman to retain his animal and the necessary feed.[34]

In a controversial Tyler case, Barrett further angered civil authorities and alienated public opinion. On April 4, 1868, T. J. Warren, a white man, shot and killed James W. Bates, described as a "white ruffian." Warren was arrested on the same day of the shooting along with Wiley Adams, a black man, charged with complicity in the killing. Adams, the agent contended, had proved himself a "respectable, hard working man." His only crime, the agent believed, was that he took too much interest in the late election and provided the agent information concerning white outrages perpetrated upon blacks. Barrett observed that the local whites had used Adams' alleged participation in the killing as an excuse to arrest and confine him.[35]

Barrett interviewed Adams. After their conversation, the agent became more convinced than ever that Adams had nothing to do with the murder. The subassistant commissioner took legal steps to secure Adams' release. The case came before a "rebel magistrate," S. S. Johnson, who jailed the freedman in lieu of twenty-thousand-dollar bond. Barrett thought the bail excessive and that the testimony did not support requiring such an exorbitant sum. Furthermore, he believed that at the grand jury's next session Adams would be indicted on the charge of complicity to murder in order to detain him in jail for six to twelve months. Barrett requested that he be granted the authority to forbid the sheriff or his deputy from serving any warrant on Adams.[36]

Although he concentrated his assistance upon Adams, Barrett refused to see two innocent men "railroaded" for exercising their legal rights. "Knowing the hatred of the rebels" in the subdistrict "for all blacks and their determination to get rid of any freedman who will make himself prominent in the cause of reconstruction," Barrett challenged the previous ruling through legal channels. On a writ of habeas corpus, he had Adams brought before the Texas Supreme Court, then in session at Tyler. In a unanimous decision, the judges vindicated Barrett's faith in Adams' character and innocence. Discharged after a full hearing, both men went free: Warren on a self-defense plea and Adams because the charges of complicity were patently false.[37]

In an attempt to bolster his authority, Barrett sent a letter to the sheriffs of Van Zandt, Henderson, Wood, and Rusk counties. He also enclosed an order from the District of Texas headquarters that directed them to obey and execute all writs issued by Bureau agents. He also requested the officials to notify the people of their respective counties that any refusal to obey a summons issued by a Bureau officer would subject them to arrest by the sheriff or his deputies. All persons arrested had to be brought to the agent's office. Barrett believed a majority of these individuals to be disloyal, people who would not hesitate to inform whites who had committed outrages against blacks, so they could escape. He understood the order would have a minimal impact.[38]

Barrett thought it strange that every county officer to whom he had addressed a communication about arresting accused people, especially whites, had taken pains to lecture the agent on the limits of his jurisdiction. His orders required that his mode of proceeding "is to conform" to that of a justice of the peace. Nothing in the order prevented a person accused of murder from being arrested and held until proper testimony could be taken. Governor Elisha M. Pease had asserted that the laws of the state should govern all criminal and civil actions. This legal interpretation Barrett followed, with one significant exception. The reimposition of military government meant that civilian authority be subordinate to the Bureau.[39]

Pease and all other state civil officers, creatures of the military government and "allowed only by it," Gregory wrote to Cherokee County sheriff Thomas Clairbourne, were "subject to change by it when deemed necessary." Congressional enactments governed Texas, he continued, while in "its present rebellious condition, and all other laws are subservient thereto." If state laws conflicted with those of Congress, then Barrett's authority superseded that of local officials. The only duty required of Clairbourne: to obey the writs he issued. If the agent's course should be determined to be erroneous, then others would make that decision, not Sheriff Clairbourne. Barrett's only desire was to uphold the law and to see criminals arrested.[40]

Because the sheriffs and their deputies showed a disloyal attitude and would not hesitate to give information to people who had committed crimes against blacks, troops became a necessity. Although Barrett could not directly sustain this assertion, his prior knowledge of the situation and the fact that *"no criminal"* who committed an outrage upon the freedpeople had yet been arrested would bear out his assessment. The conflict between the law officers and the Bureau had reached a stalemate. Barrett requested that John H. Morrison, the Palestine agent, try a case involving a black who had been assaulted with pistols and then stripped and beaten because any reference to the civil authorities in his subdistrict "would be a farce."[41]

Barrett no longer had any faith in the civil officials, but he continued to make efforts at cooperation and sent them letters requesting the arrest and confinement of individuals who had committed crimes. "If a disloyal person be injured," he wrote, the "guilty ones will be arrested, but the murderers of freedpeople never." Relations became so bad in June 1868 that Barrett received private threats that he would be run out of town. His greatest crime, he believed, was that he would not allow the citizens to run over the freedpeople. Barrett also actively participated in defending the former slaves in court when he believed them innocent, and he observed court proceedings and jury trials whenever blacks were parties to a suit.[42]

Barrett, at some risk to his life, maintained his endeavors in behalf of legal equality and justice for the local black population. When a freedwoman reported that she had been seriously assaulted, he ordered the Henderson County sheriff to arrest the alleged criminal. If the woman subsequently died, no bail would be allowed the prisoner. Moreover, if a Henderson County judicial official or a jury discharged the white man of the crime, then the sheriff would be required to bring the man to Tyler. In one letter he proceeded to give Thomas Clairbourne another long lecture about his duties, the responsibilities of the Bureau, and the intent of the laws in relation to former slaves.[43]

Sheriffs continued to refuse to arrest alleged criminals. They now changed their tactic and returned the writs endorsed "not found." Barrett accused Julius A. Robinson, the Smith County sheriff, of being especially derelict in his duty. The agent desired his removal.

Robinson would not execute the writs the agent requested from him. In a case where a white man had been accused of stabbing a freedman, a warrant given Robinson to arrest the alleged criminal still languished. The man who was accused of the assault remained at home and had not been taken into custody. Barrett stopped directing warrants to Robinson because they would simply be ignored. Of all the counties in the subdistrict, Smith County ranked last in protecting black rights.[44]

The Ann Doomis case confirmed Barrett's contention. This controversy combined black testimony, blacks serving on juries, and the agent's role on the local level. Doomis, a black woman, testified that she witnessed John Crumb's rape of a freedwoman. Although the defense witnesses made "a miserable attempt at an alibi," Crumb's lawyer played on community fears. He "implored" the jury "not to take the testimony of a negro, one of a race proverbial for dishonesty and lies." After Crumb's acquittal, Barrett took charge of the case and required that Crumb post bond so he would appear before the agent. For this action the community roundly condemned the sub-assistant commissioner for daring to scrutinize the action of a white jury.

Barrett, in response, observed that juries rarely failed to convict a black or to acquit a white. He had more than once attempted to have a jury empaneled that would be composed in whole or in part by blacks, but the clerk of the Eighth Judicial District, J. U. Wright, swore publicly that before he would take a "nigger as a juror he would leave the court." Barrett recommended Wright's removal as "disloyal" and as "an obstacle to reconstruction." Ann Doomis, who cooked for Wright, claimed she heard Wright "angrily" state that Barrett would get his head shot off for "meddling with the Court too much" and because "he had turned the niggers to be damned fools." And, she claimed, if the meddling persisted, the agent and local blacks would be killed.[45]

In a long letter to headquarters, Barrett summarized the particular failings of the judicial system. The civil officials failed to put into the jury pool the names of freedmen but included only whites, of which a great majority could be considered disloyal to the Union. From their failure to be allowed to sit on juries, blacks obviously did not receive justice before the civil courts. As they had meager resources, most could not afford to hire proper legal counsel. Barrett's assistance was solicited by some blacks who were charged with killing a stray steer and who had no money for a lawyer. They believed they needed counsel because the jurors were thought to be prejudiced against the defendants.[46]

Barrett thought that Section I of the 1866 Civil Rights Bill had been overlooked in the "stray steer" case. This provision declared that freedpeople were guaranteed the full and equal benefit of all the laws and proceedings for the security of person and property as enjoyed by whites. Barrett's objections were overruled by Judge Samuel L. Earle, who claimed he had no control over who the citizens selected as jurors and thus could not interfere. Barrett, who knew something about law, proceeded to cite various precedents, but to no avail. He firmly believed that the Civil Rights Bill legally gave blacks the same right to sit on juries as whites. In his eyes any other interpretation violated the intention of this major congressional enactment.[47]

Barrett strongly supported the power of the law to change attitudes. If blacks did not have the protection that the law gave them, he wrote, "they had far better be returned to slavery, subject as they are to conviction on the oath of people little given to respect oath, and to trial before rebel juries." Whites who served on juries did not believe in the legality of the Reconstruction laws, thus the laws did not have to be obeyed, he wrote. Not only would whites resort to any scheme to defraud blacks of their wages and rights but, if this ruse did not succeed, he reported, they trumped up charges to be used in court. Any freedperson could be readily convicted because every witness believed that blacks had no "rights which a white man is bound to respect."[48]

The Black Community

Bureau agents of the Thirtieth Subdistrict had frequent contact with black individuals and their communities. Many unique problems confronted black Texans in the early years of Reconstruction, and they quickly turned to the Bureau for resolution. Four familial concerns engaged the attention of blacks in the Thirtieth Subdistrict. These interrelated family matters included the reunification of families, the new marriage regulations applicable to blacks, the status of black children and the apprenticing law, and an attempt to find assistance for indigent members of the black community. In trying to resolve these matters, agents once again found themselves at odds with local civil and judicial officials.

After emancipation, one of the foremost priorities of blacks was the reunification of their families. Under slavery, black family life had a precarious existence, but once slaves attained freedom, the circumstances surrounding the family drastically changed. Now free to move, search, and seek Bureau travel assistance to locate relatives from whom they had long been separated, blacks appealed to the Bureau, which aided wherever it could. Agents spent considerable time trying to locate missing family members. The Bureau and the black community also posted printed circulars and made announcements at social and religious gatherings in their quest for an individual. They employed every conceivable method possible in trying to reconstruct black families.[49]

The Bureau and its agents also took steps to legitimize black marriages in the aftermath of war. The flexible state of matrimony in the antebellum years, and its lack of legal sanctions, led to numerous disruptions among man and wife once they were allowed freely to choose a mate. Divorce, wife and child abuse, desertion and abandonment, and child custody complaints, all quite naturally surfaced in the black community. Although it certainly cannot be fully attributed to the presence of the Bureau, the 1870 manuscript census returns for Smith County suggest a more cohesive character among black families and many characteristics similar to the white family structure.[50]

A serious problem encountered by black parents and the Bureau involved the apprenticing or "binding out" of children without the parents' knowledge or consent. The state apprentice law, part of the 1866 Black Codes, gave the Bureau numerous problems because it appeared to treat the children of the two races equally. Inevitably, a clash between agents and county officers occurred when the latter attempted "legally" to apprentice black children under this law. The situation was remedied by the local Bureau through the insistence of the black community and the intervention of state Bureau headquarters, which ordered agents to disregard the apprentice law. In some cases previously bound black children were returned.[51]

Under the Texas apprentice law, publication of intent to bind out a child had to be made in a newspaper. Despite the fact that a majority of the parents or friends of black children being bound out could not read or write, they did not receive advice as to the intention of the law or its legal ramifications. Local courts apprenticed children without their knowledge or consent. With the establishment of the Thirtieth Subdistrict, black parents appeared at the Tyler office complaining of these practices, extremely anxious to obtain possession of their children. When Edom Smith complained to Montgomery that Matthew and Samuel Rogers held his two sons without consent, Montgomery ordered them returned to their father.[52]

The same pattern of complaints and results followed other apprenticeship or slavery cases which blacks called to Montgomery's attention. In some cases, Montgomery made decisions that removed children from a black environment. Where black children seemed to be properly cared for and legally bound to a white family, or the agent satisfied himself that the letter of the law had been complied with, he took no action. Headquarters, however, did not agree with Montgomery's decisions, repudiated them, and returned the children to their parents or relatives. With the exception of Montgomery, Thirtieth Subdistrict agents actively returned black children to their natural parents whenever possible. Indeed, they succeeded in a surprising number of cases.[53]

Indigency, although not a significant problem among black communities in the Thirtieth Subdistrict, did present a creative challenge for Bureau agents. Invariably, the individuals who evinced this kind of suffering were older blacks who could not work, had been turned off a plantation by uncaring planters, or could not be supported by the black community. In short, they needed relief. The Bureau did provide some rations in Texas, but the state agency, through its national connections, did not have the financial wherewithal to continue any type of permanent subsistence. Those deemed truly indigent became the responsibility of the particular county in which they resided and would be cared for by local officials.[54]

Hostile planters, uncooperative county officials, and some black laborers also contributed to the problem of indigency. Barrett reported that a number of blacks in a state of "idleness" had congregated at Tyler. Some had been driven off their land by lawless persons, "but a great portion are simply lazy." Barrett wanted to enforce the old state vagrant law to remove them from the town. Thinking that such a course would be productive, the assistant commissioner directed Barrett to call on the civil authorities to enforce the provisions of the vagrancy law. These officials undoubtedly required them to return to work. Idleness never became a significant problem, and the Bureau did not issue any rations in the Thirtieth Subdistrict.[55]

Black Education

A major accomplishment of the Bureau's existence in Texas concerned its involvement in assisting those schools that blacks had already established. Additionally, the Bureau through its organizational network, along with black insistence, began to promote black schools across the eastern portion of the state. Many Texas agents saw promotion of black education as one of the key functions of their job. Montgomery, immediately after his arrival in Tyler, surveyed the area for educational purposes. He wanted to ascertain the necessary requirements to undertake the formation of more black schools in the Thirtieth Subdistrict. Supervising a five-county region and performing necessary duties, in addition to responsibility for black education, became no mean task.

The freedpeople had begun a school and conducted it at their own expense before the Bureau came to the Thirtieth Subdistrict. Montgomery subsequently found blacks maintaining schools at Selma, at J. W. Brooke's plantation in Cherokee County, and at Colonel Hubbard's farm in Smith County. He applauded these demonstrations of self-help but believed it exceedingly important that schools be organized throughout the remainder of the area. Montgomery toured the area and proposed that schools be located at twenty-one sites in the Thirtieth Subdistrict. Although he requested special authority to commence his plan, it never became a reality. Later he reported that only the private schools still functioned.[56]

The freedpeople had exhausted their educational funds, Montgomery believed, overreaching "on every hand, before the arrival of the troops." Whites generally made no objection to blacks receiving an education. Though they put no obstacles in the freedpeople's way, only in rare instances did they offer aid. But neither Montgomery nor the freedpeople could locate teachers to staff the schools. Montgomery complained that his heavy work load prevented him from traveling the area to look after the educational aspect of an agent's duties. Later, Montgomery's assistant DeWitt C. Brown, toured the district to try to hire buildings suitable for schools and to take the necessary steps to establish them at the locations Montgomery had earlier suggested.[57]

Montgomery continued his limited assistance to black education in the subdistrict. One attempt to secure a teacher from New Orleans failed. When Jesse Chancellor proposed opening a school, the agent inquired whether the Bureau would be authorized to rent another room, besides his office, for the purpose of beginning another school. Chancellor also had to be paid. Montgomery wondered whether the Bureau would provide a stipend of forty dollars a month if Chancellor did not obtain a sufficient number of scholars to support his school on a self-sustaining basis. The plan failed.[58] Throughout the history of the Thirtieth Subdistrict, agents had difficulties in finding teachers and in increasing the number of schools in operation.

Progress always remained slow on the education front no matter how hard the agents worked. The constant interruption of schools—so that children could labor in the fields because black families had to muster all the help they could to subsist financially—made instruction difficult. Consequently, the children's learning suffered. By late 1867 Montgomery reported but one school in Tyler. The Bureau paid seven dollars a month rent for the building, and the government eventually raised the subsidy to fifteen dollars. Taught by Mary Stripling, the school had an initial attendance of fifty-five pupils. She was the only teacher Montgomery employed on a full-time basis, although he frequently made known throughout the Thirtieth Subdistrict the necessity for more instructors.[59]

Another school that had a brief existence had to be discontinued because of teacher incompetency and the revoking of the Bureau rent contract. Early in 1868 George Richardson, a black man, began yet another school, with an attendance of seventeen students: five in the day session and twelve at night. The contract had to be annulled because of finances. Even in their straightened economic condition, blacks maintained schools on their own. Although not supported by the Bureau, by April 1868, Mary Stripling still taught thirty-two pupils in day school and forty in a Sunday school. These figures fluctuated from month to month. In May, Barrett reported that she had increased her day attendance to fifty-six, while her Sunday class had lost four.[60]

Under Barrett's stewardship, whites gave no assistance, but they generally did not harass blacks who desired an education. Instead, he complained that local blacks did not make much of an effort to promote and establish schools for themselves. Economics provided the answer. Because of a bad cotton crop, local blacks could not afford to pay tuition to support a school. Barrett attempted a solution. He suggested that if the Bureau paid a teacher's salary, then it would allow those blacks not able to pay tuition to attend free of charge. Unfortunately, headquarters vetoed this idea and only permitted Barrett to continue to rent the school at the same monthly rate as previously had been allowed Montgomery.[61]

For all the educational setbacks because of the Bureau's and freedpeople's financial difficulties, Barrett remained optimistic. The continuation of the rent contract brightened his outlook. He contended that any cessation of the school would be fatal to black educational efforts and that the teacher would be forced to look elsewhere for employment. Since March 1868 the school had grown rapidly, and the pupils had progressed at a steady rate. In Tyler, blacks did relatively well, but in other parts of the subdistrict the former slaves, for want of protection, seemed to be at a standstill in relation to their educational needs. Barrett believed that it would be dangerous to establish schools in locations from which no government office could be reached easily.[62]

Originally, Barrett had reported mixed feelings among the white population about blacks being educated: some were in favor; some were opposed. In June 1868 white hostility toward black education openly manifested itself. Black children who attended the Tyler school were attacked by whites, beaten with clubs, and stoned. The assault alarmed the black community, frightened the children, who refused to attend school, and forced its temporary suspension. Mary Stripling, the white teacher, along with various members of the black community, informed the agent that area whites planned to burn the schoolhouse. Understandably, a tense racial situation ensued, and attention focused upon identifying the attackers of the black children.

Barrett gathered information about the incident from freedpeople who were employed by whites throughout Tyler and also spoke with certain members of the white community to assess their attitudes. Complicating matters, the people who committed the violence remained unidentified. Prosecution was therefore impossible. The sheriff could do nothing without a warrant, which could not be issued, since no one could identify the attackers. Barrett believed that if the sheriff had attempted immediately to arrest the individuals responsible, and if their identity had been known, it would inevitably have led to resistance. Whites, agitated over the incident, expressed ugly feelings, and tensions between the two races increased.[63]

A spokesman for the white community now emerged. Lawyer and former Tyler mayor, F. D. Crow, intimated that local whites had attacked the black children because of offenses by their elders. Any attempt by the Bureau to arrest those responsible for the incident, he declared, would result in the "killing of all the 'Yankees' and 'Niggers' in the place." If necessary, he would tear "the damned 'Nigger' school out" himself or would be an "active participant" with any group intending to clean the "damned 'Niggers' out." The insult alluded to by Crow involved social deference. Blacks broke a long-established pattern by "not walking out in the road when ordered to do so by the whites."[64]

To gain a measure of revenge for these insults, unknown whites cowardly retaliated by attacking black children. Barrett informed Crow that he would be held accountable for any further trouble and that if more occurred Crow would be arrested. Crow detested the Bureau's presence, challenged Barrett's authority, and claimed that the agent did not have the necessary troops to take him into custody. Although Barrett reiterated his stand, he admitted privately to headquarters that any attempt to take Crow into custody would probably lead to bloodshed. There is some evidence, although it is not substantial, that those whites who committed the outrages upon the black children came from outside the community.[65]

Whoever attacked the black children did not repeat the violence, and the crisis passed. The school resumed full operation, gaining enrollment. Stripling now had sixty-two pupils in her day school and seventy-five in her Sunday class. Another school had been established at Garden Valley (Smith County) by Guilford Murphy, a black man, with twenty day pupils. Henry Black, another black teacher, started a school about ten miles southeast of Tyler with twenty-five day students. These schools operated continuously until crops had to be harvested. When harvest season arrived, the enrollment of Stripling's day school dropped, but she later gained eight, although she lost ten in her Sunday class. The Murphy and Black schools continued with a steady enrollment.[66]

By mid-1868 Stripling still had not received her pay from the Bureau for teaching in October, November, and December 1867. Although Barrett had forwarded the requisite pay vouchers, headquarters had never received them. The school, now on a self-sustaining basis, continually struggled and did not generate much income. Stripling had not totaled one hundred dollars in tuition payments for nine months' service. She had to pay for the wood the school used during the winter and six dollars a month for house rent. Also, she reported that she now had an opportunity to migrate to western Texas with a younger brother. But she had given her word to stay, and she would never leave without Barrett's full approval. Stripling stated she would rather rely on the agent for protection than her brother.[67]

In concluding his Bureau service, Barrett pessimistically wrote that area whites still opposed the education of the freedpeople. Optimistically, however, two more schools had been established in Smith County since the arrival of troops, and the Tyler school would do better after the gathering of the crops. Barrett definitely wanted the expansion to continue, requesting authority for A. C. Prince, a freedman, to found a school near Douglassville with full Bureau and military protection. Although blacks remained financially distressed and the Bureau only rendered limited financial assistance in the Thirtieth Subdistrict, they never ceased their efforts to expand the number of schools so that more black children could receive an education.[68]

The schools continued in operation until the end of 1868, when the Bureau agents withdrew. Stripling was forced to vacate her position somewhat earlier because black parents could not pay the amounts due for their children's tuition. Some were five months in arrears. As Stripling also depended upon this money for her subsistence, she could no longer continue to teach. The Bureau decided not to renew the property lease after October 31 unless new arrangements could be negotiated. The building in which the school held classes, not worth more than five dollars a month, needed repairs. With the withdrawal of the Bureau and its limited finances, interest in promoting schooling among the black community seemed to wane.[69]

W. H. Hartz, a temporary agent who closed Bureau operations in the Thirtieth Subdistrict, complained that a "proper interest does not appear to be maintained by the Colored people in keeping up their schools." He was unaware of how blacks maintained their schools in other parts of the subdistrict because, he said, numerous duties prevented him from making a personal inspection. He considered the agency's educational effort in behalf of the black populace more important than any other Bureau responsibility. Education alone required the oversight of one individual. This same theme had been reiterated at one time or another by every Bureau agent who had served in the Thirtieth Subdistrict. Manpower and money shortages retarded school efforts in the region.[70]

Although all other phases of its work ceased in 1868, the Freedmen's Bureau continued its educational operations through state authorities and a state superintendent until 1872. During the year and a half that agents promoted black schooling in the Thirtieth Subdistrict, they achieved some small successes but were never able to assist the black community in a substantial and permanent manner. If Montgomery's original education plan had been put into operation, then more black schools would have been established in the subdistrict, and the efforts already begun by the black community would have been enhanced. Nevertheless, black educational efforts in the Thirtieth Subdistrict and across the state did create a solid foundation for future progress.

The Bureau, through its various educational policies and its philosophy, constantly promoted the idea of black self-help and independence. Freedpeople, with little money and very few individuals who could read or write, organized schools and found literate people from the community to serve as instructors. Schools also sprang up on plantations in the region. When local resources became inadequate, they turned to the Bureau. With agent assistance, and a dedicated woman, they maintained schools intermittently in Tyler and other locations. Blacks' zealous desire to acquire some type of schooling compensated, in some respects, for the lack of funds, especially to pay teachers. The Bureau assisted whenever and wherever possible.

Violence

The most unfortunate and dismaying aspect of an agent's work for the Texas Freedmen's Bureau involved the unsuccessful attempt to protect the black population against numerous forms of violence. In the Thirtieth Subdistrict, the subassistant commissioners enjoyed only limited success in preventing outrages against the former slaves. Soon after Montgomery's arrival in Tyler, local blacks began to appear at his office to recount physical violence to which they had been subjected and their vulnerability to violent attacks. Often attacked for no easily discernible reason, blacks found themselves in a constant state of wariness due to unprovoked assaults. Freedmen's bodies were found in all areas of the subdistrict.[71]

Violence surrounded all aspects of a former slave's life, from work to school, from politics to social relations. In the labor arena, violence continually surfaced from the signing of the contract through the division of the crop. Whether attending religious meetings, harassed and broken up by disgruntled whites, or school, where white assailants attacked the children, blacks found mundane activities dangerous. Transgression of established white mores led to physical conflict, and political participation by blacks intensified white racial attitudes, engendering more violence. An unsavory element also inhabited the Thirtieth Subdistrict. Blacks never reported many of the outrages committed upon them because they feared the "murderous ruffians who infest Smith County."[72]

In June 1868, after the failure of President Andrew Johnson's removal by the United States Senate, Barrett perceived the disappointment and resentment reflected in the demeanor of the white citizens. The people "exhibited a spirit as bitter and hostile to the government as was shown by them during the rebellion." No day or night passed without some type of violence, and white outrages committed upon blacks became "alarmingly numerous." Concealing their identities, these desperadoes rode at night, and during the day many of the attackers seemed to be strangers and unknown in the area. At least, no one came forward to identify them. In addition, the Ku Klux Klan had finally made its appearance in the Thirtieth Subdistrict.[73]

Under Barrett, he reported, the intensity of violence directed at district blacks increased. He proposed two methods to alleviate the widespread lawlessness. First, he requested authority from headquarters (which was rejected) to raise a local militia force, whose responsibility would be to rid the area of undesirable elements, the members to be paid by the county. The "rebels" might be quelled, but unquestionably "strife" would ensue and perhaps even a "race war." Second, a temporary mounted force of twenty-five men could be detached to him. Either way, the agent needed assistance and pleaded for soldiers. Without them, Barrett exclaimed, he would "be at the mercy of the rebel mob." Although sympathetic, headquarters did little to assist him.[74]

Finding himself in a desperate situation (he had been shot at three times), Barrett reported that he would refuse to allow whites to do as they pleased with blacks. If capitulating to the "rebels" was the only way to effect change, he desired no part of it. In no uncertain terms, Barrett screamed for some type of protection, preferably cavalry. His earlier proposal to form a militia contradicted his description of there being "few loyal whites" in the area. Moreover, they could not be depended upon to assist him, he told headquarters, because they had been broken down by past misfortunes and by the "rebels" who controlled the region. But if soldiers could not be promised by headquarters, then some type of protection had to be organized.[75]

A good example of the type of pressure under which an agent labored involved Barrett's living arrangements. He needed to know how much longer, or even if, he would be retained as subassistant commissioner. If the main office extended his tenure, Barrett would have to find another place to room and board, as he would be unable to stay at the hotel. Because of the agent's presence, all the other occupants had gone, and the proprietor would be forced to close if Barrett did not make other living arrangements. This would entail renting a house himself, if he could find one, as he would not be allowed to stay in a private home. Even sympathetic individuals would not board him, as the chances for a violent confrontation would be increased.[76]

Violence touched the agent personally in an altercation with a man named George Kennedy. Described by Barrett as a "notorious ruffian," Kennedy had a reputation for harassing the freedpeople. A freedwoman appeared at Barrett's office and complained that she had been assaulted by Kennedy. On the day Barrett scheduled the case to be heard and knowing Kennedy to be a "reckless man" with many friends in the area, he stationed two soldiers and his clerk in the office. Found guilty, ordered to pay a fifty-dollar fine and to give bond to keep the peace, Kennedy made a break for the door, drawing his revolver. In the ensuing shoot-out (involving thirty of Kennedy's cohorts), two soldiers and the Bureau clerk received wounds. Barrett shot, but did not kill Kennedy.[77]

Local sentiment bitterly turned against Barrett, and a full-scale riot seemed in the offing. "I have a thorough knowledge of these people," he wrote, "know what they say in the recesses of their dwellings and know that their hatred of the government is as deep and damning as perdition itself." Pleading for more troops, Barrett believed that these "people have such a hatred of myself that whenever their black hearts can be sufficiently fired they will attempt to get rid of me." The agent could say "these things with no prejudice, for I have used every means to get along smoothly, but say sorrowfully that the easier they are treated the worse they become, and the only remedy is sharp, quick punishment."[78]

The difficulties of geography and the availability of soldiers to assist an agent in his duties could never be overcome in the Thirtieth Subdistrict. When troops were detached to the area, although never entirely peaceful, less violence did occur. The withdrawal of troops in March 1868 meant that it became virtually impossible to provide any kind of protection, except of a very minimal nature, for area blacks and Unionist whites. The agent could only despair at their fate. Too much area to cover, too many people to oversee, and too little assistance made the plight of a Bureau agent a precarious one indeed. Violence could erupt at any time, and the agent had few weapons with which to combat it.

Conclusion

Considering the vast area to be supervised, the host of responsibilities that an agent had to shoulder, and the general community resentment at their presence, it seems little short of astonishing that subassistant commissioners performed as well as they did. Enough difficulties surfaced in Smith County alone to keep an agent fully occupied without having to be concerned about three and one-half other counties. Fortunately, agents from other subdistricts assisted one another, so the outlying residents of an agent's area might be aided through a closer Bureau office. Contending with almost insurmountable obstacles, the Thirtieth Subdistrict agents attempted to make the Bureau's presence a positive force for change.

Montgomery, who seems to have been one of the abler agents in the Texas Bureau organization, expressed his feelings about the Bureau and perhaps summarized the attitude of many of the agents who saw service in the Thirtieth Subdistrict. Writing in early 1868 to Congressman Thomas D. Eliot, chairman of the Committee on Freedmen's Affairs, Montgomery contended that "in good hands the Bureau is capable of accomplishing a great deal of good and vice versa." After serving as an agent for eleven months, he believed the

"Bureau should be continued." In the future, however, "great care should be taken in the selection of Officers and Agents to place in charge of the Offices," so the agency would be respected by blacks and be above suspicion.[79]

During Congressional Reconstruction, life for Bureau agents in the Thirtieth Subdistrict must have been like riding an emotional roller coaster. Depending upon the political and economic situation, the degree of white hostility, and the assertiveness of blacks, sub-assistant commissioners had to respond in a variety of ways, trying always to avoid exacerbating the feelings of either race. Serving in numerous capacities, they came into contact with the leaders and power structure of both the black and white communities. The position was terrifically demanding, and the agents evinced varying degrees of enthusiasm for their job. In the Thirtieth Subdistrict, they seemed to have done as much as they could to assist, encourage, and protect the black population.

What life would have been like for the freedpeople in the aftermath of war without the presence of the Freedmen's Bureau is difficult to ascertain. Some of its accomplishments were unquestionably minimal, yet the Bureau served as an organization that aided blacks in their transition from slavery to freedom in various economic, social, political, and judicial circumstances. The Bureau provided a partial buffer between hostile whites and the black community. Blacks could legally challenge whites with the hope of obtaining justice in the Bureau courts. Freedom for Southern blacks during the early years of Reconstruction had an elusive quality. The Bureau assisted in enhancing the realities and nuances of that freedom.

This overview of the Thirtieth Subdistrict and those agents who supervised the area demonstrates that the local subassistant commissioners faced a herculean job. Largely isolated, with little community support, and looked upon with some suspicion by the black populace, the agent needed a strong resolve to survive in performing his duties. To understand what a local agent endured after this detailed examination of one subdistrict, it is necessary to investigate the performance of a single agent, in one region, over a period of time. In adopting this even more microcosmic approach to a study of the workings of the Texas Freedmen's Bureau, we begin to comprehend what an enormous responsibility confronted the agency and the agent.

4. To Die in Boston (Texas, That Is)

BUREAU AGENTS BECAME the embodiment of all war-related frustrations for white society. Blamed for the evils that beset the postwar South, these individuals often served in isolated places, where a hostile populace resided, with no troops for protection. Depending upon the agents' demeanor and relations with blacks and whites, they often became targets of abuse, ostracism, and violence. Thus, their personal safety could never be guaranteed, and security often bordered on the precarious. "The agents which the Bureau could command," W. E. B. Du Bois wrote, "varied all the way from unselfish philanthropists to narrow-minded busybodies and thieves," but more often than not the "average was far better than the worst."[1]

A local agent's duties and responsibilities can be described only as "daunting." Activities "included introducing a workable system of free labor in the South, establishing schools for freedmen, providing aid to the destitute, aged, ill, and insane, adjudicating disputes among blacks and between the races, and attempting to secure for blacks and white Unionists equal justice from the state and local governments." Serving as "diplomat, marriage counselor, educator, supervisor of labor contracts, sheriff, judge, and jury," they had to "win the confidence of blacks and whites alike in a situation where race and labor relations had been poisoned by mutual distrust and conflicting interests," writes Eric Foner.[2]

The career of one specific Texas Bureau agent is illustrative of the vicissitudes that such an individual faced in the course of his duties. Whether this man can be described as typical (atypical because he was murdered) of Texas Bureau agents is uncertain, as there are so few studies of these field personnel. Nevertheless, a detailed analysis of his tenure as a Bureau agent provides an in-depth portrayal of what the life of an agent entailed and the accompanying responsibilities. It also suggests the complex nature of governing a conquered region and the role agents played in implementing Reconstruction policies under a recalcitrant president, a partially supportive Congress, and an outraged citizenry.

All the questions originally raised during the Civil War, and the Congressional legislation applied to the emancipated slaves, arose in Southern communities during the postwar era. Here the Bureau attempted to solve questions and apply the law. How a Bureau agent went about performing his job, how the black and white communities reacted to him, what efforts he made in behalf of the former slaves, and the pressure under which he labored, are important clues in understanding the Bureau, the South, and the Reconstruction process. The conclusions that can be drawn from the experience of one Texas Bureau agent among all the larger questions posed by the results of the Civil War suggest how the Bureau functioned at the most basic level, the community.

The Killing

It had been raining hard two weeks previous to the assassination. On an early fall morning, October 7, 1868, at 2:00 A.M., the agent prepared to leave Boston (Texas, that is) to travel to Bureau headquarters in Austin. Hearing a noise outside his office (actually someone calling him to come out), he proceeded to investigate. The shots came from the shadows, around the corner of the building from his office. Seventeen rounds were fired, only one by the agent. Dead before he hit the ground, he had buckshot and ball in the breast, shoulder, and side, and a revolver bullet through the ear. When the gunfire echoes ceased, someone hollered, "All is well."

The clerk of the county court, Nathan B. Anderson, who lived nearby and with whom the dead man boarded (the murdered man had been responsible for Anderson's appointment as court clerk), told a black man to see who had been shot. Four men in a boarding house and two citizens of the town heard the shots but refused to take any action, and none went near the body. The alarmed townspeople, afraid of "personal assault," refused to take any action. Although Boston (Bowie County) may not have been a typical Southern town where a Bureau agent would be located (which says something about the size of Texas and its vast distances), the danger an agent confronted is exemplified in the death of this particular man.

Approximately forty-five minutes after the killing, two men examined the body, the dead man's gun still clenched in his hand. They spotted the black man who waited to identify the man who had been shot down. The two men bluntly gave him a choice: either shoot or leave. The black man ran into the house but not before he determined who had been killed. He then informed Anderson. Into the early morning hours, the body lay where it had fallen, everyone afraid to investigate further. When the corpse was examined later, the pockets of his trousers had been turned out, the revolver gone; missing also were three twenty-dollar gold pieces, a small roll of bills, a watch and chain, and the dead man's horse.[3]

After the inquest, held the next day, Anderson, William A. Payne (a merchant with whom the dead man had all his financial dealings), a Mr. Morrow, and others made the funeral and burial arrangements. (The government later reimbursed them.) The agent, originally buried in Old Peters graveyard in Boston, had an escort of a few soldiers, and a "large number" of local citizens attended the service. Although not respected by everyone, the dead man was described by one observer as "esteemed by all good citizens who knew him as a man of most unswerving integrity, earnest, fearless, and faithful in the discharge of every duty," an appropriate epitaph for any Bureau agent.[4]

The official appointed by the Texas Freedmen's Bureau to investigate the killing of the Boston Bureau agent belonged to the agency himself, a man named George Shorkley, whose headquarters were in Clarksville (Red River County). Although not on an enviable mission, Shorkley had originally intended to visit Boston on October 10, three days after the murder. Advised by a local judge and other community members to delay his inquiry, he wisely did so. Local citizens were "disturbed" over the killing of the government official, and all manner of rumors floated about the town, creating further confusion. As yet, no steps had been taken by the local law enforcement officials to apprehend the killers.

Shorkley's impressions are worth noting, for they reveal numerous insights into the milieu in which the dead man labored. When he finally made the journey to Boston on October 13, he hired a light two-horse wagon, with a black driver, and "traveled as a citizen on business." There were compelling reasons for assuming this disguise. Shorkley first visited Anderson, the county clerk, who indicated a reluctance to discuss the incident. But after Shorkley identified himself and stated the purpose of his visit, Anderson urged him to continue to conceal his background while in the area. It was not safe for any government officer to enter the town, Anderson informed Shorkley, without a "sufficient force of men for protection."[5]

Shorkley's evaluation of the Boston region suggested an area that remained bitter because of the war and unreconstructed. The Clarksville agent quickly perceived that the Bowie County civil courts were "unwilling or unable" to administer civil or criminal law to blacks or Unionists. Injustices abounded. State laws afforded no protection for person or property in the county. No additional steps had been taken to arrest the individuals involved in killing the Bureau agent, the "officers and citizens admit[ting]" to Shorkley that "they dare not move in the matter." The cause of this state of affairs: a "notorious desperado" named Cullen Montgomery Baker (whose activities will later be described in detail).

Local individuals would not even use Baker's name, simply referring to him as "that man" or "he." Many of Boston's inhabitants believed that Baker had associates living in town and spies lurking about. All of Bowie County, in fact, the surrounding region, Shorkley observed, whether black or white, stood in "awe" of Baker and his gang. The residents expressed an abiding fear for their safety, especially if they supplied information that could be traced back to them. Baker's escapades not only had frightened the town but had forced movement among the freedpeople. Some of the area freedmen, who farmed for themselves, left their places, either going back "for safety" to their "old masters" or moving from the county.[6]

The next morning after the Boston Bureau agent had been murdered, Baker, with four men, "called" at the dead man's office. What they came for had "already been accomplished," according to Shorkley. After making a few purchases, the five men rode out of town, their visit described as "uneventful." R. H. Watlington, a schoolteacher and farmer who settled in Boston in 1866, met Baker on October 9 at a friend's house. Baker credited himself with killing the Bureau agent and stated that his men were camped a short distance away. They planned to return to Boston and "clean up" the entire garrison. An hour later, Baker, at the head of a "dozen or more of his clan, all heavily armed" and many "drunk or nearly so," rode off.[7]

Shorkley believed, but not very enthusiastically, that the citizens of Boston might be able to do something about the chaotic nature of local affairs but were afraid to take action, fearing that they or their families would be murdered. Only the presence of soldiers would make a difference. He recommended a one-company garrison be stationed at Boston, the county courts be revived, then compelled "vigorously [to] enforce their own laws" until better ones could be enacted. This course should be pursued as long as necessary, or until its desired effects were achieved. The result would be that many good citizens who dared not speak out "in favor of law and order" would be encouraged to do so.

The former slaves needed special protection, but it would be unwise to send any assistance in the way of a garrison unless a company could be stationed *"permanently."* In that way black and white law-abiding citizens would be influenced to take active measures in support of "law and order without the fear of future consequences." Shorkley hoped the government would be "untiring in its efforts to visit upon" the Boston agent's murderers the "swift vengeance of an outraged law." He informed William A. Payne that he wished the merchant would continue his activities to improve conditions in the county. The Clarksville agent, "most anxious to relieve the people in some manner acceptable to them," offered any assistance in his power.[8]

With this background, it might be asked, what chain of events led to these unsettled conditions in Boston and the surrounding area and the killing of a Bureau agent? The murdered man's name is not found in history books, but his story and job are important because as events unfold it becomes clear that the motive for killing was not robbery, although some may have wished it to appear that way. What follows is the story of a dedicated Freedmen's Bureau agent. When an agent demonstrated sympathy and concern for the local black population, then events outside his control often engulfed him. This is an account of one of those forgotten agents in a forgotten Texas town. Here is the legacy of William G. Kirkman.

Kirkman and His Subdistrict

Born in Jacksonville (Morgan County), Illinois, in 1843, Kirkman was completing last minute business, preparing to leave his post when killed.[9] When the Civil War began, Kirkman enlisted in Company K of the Thirty-ninth Illinois Infantry on August 19, 1861. He served as telegraph operator in the United States Telegraph Company, Department of the South, in South Carolina, in 1863 and 1864, being mustered out in the latter year. Kirkman was five feet four and three-quarter inches in height, with dark complexion, dark eyes, and black hair. Precisely how he got to Texas and became a Freedmen's Bureau agent is unknown. More than likely he was encouraged to do so by his brother, Joel T. Kirkman, a member of the Texas Bureau headquarters staff.[10]

Kirkman's decision to leave his post came from a combination of factors. By late 1868 the Texas Freedmen's Bureau faced dismantlement. Bureau Assistant Commissioner Joseph J. Reynolds had officially relieved the agent of his position in September 1868, two weeks before Kirkman's assassination. Reynolds, "unwilling that" Kirkman's "life should be imperiled further," ordered him to leave Boston. Kirkman had reiterated the same theme for several months:

serving as an agent in northeastern Texas constituted a dangerous occupation. Kirkman had also been indicted by a grand jury for murder. Headquarters authorized him to disregard the summons, for the laws passed by Congress creating the Bureau exempted him from arrest.[11]

Kirkman, a capable, honest, and persevering individual, supervised as subassistant commissioner the Fifty-eighth Subdistrict of Texas, which included Bowie and later Cass (renamed Davis between 1861 and 1871) counties. This section, in far northeastern Texas, is adjacent to Arkansas and, during that time, the "Indian Nation," now Oklahoma. The area comprised 1,838 square miles, with 13,558 people, divided between 7,930 whites and 5,628 blacks. Whites composed 58 percent and blacks 42 percent of the two counties' population. Davis ranked twenty-eighth and Bowie forty-fourth among Texas counties in terms of black residents. Kirkman's headquarters, the rather small and isolated village of Boston, had a population of about three or four hundred people.[12]

Special Order no. 67, dated June 22, 1867, of the Texas Freedmen's Bureau, officially made Kirkman an agent, his pay being one hundred dollars a month. He arrived in Boston on Friday, July 5, 1867, accomplishing his three-hundred-mile journey from coastal Galveston to Boston "without unnecessary delay." Traversing eastern Texas from bottom to top may have inadvertently saved Kirkman's life for the assassin's bullets. That summer of 1867 saw the Texas coast and parts of the interior ravaged by a yellow fever epidemic. Located in Galveston at that time, Bureau headquarters lost many personnel to the disease. Kirkman may have been somewhat infected, for shortly after settling in Boston he fell ill and had to consult a physician.

While his sickness continued (Kirkman never thereafter complained of any illness), he also had to locate and rent an office and perform other official duties. For fifteen dollars a month, he rented a small building in one corner of the Anderson property on the south side of the courthouse. (Remember, he also roomed and boarded with the Anderson family, the father serving as county clerk.) The new agent arranged to have a table with a drawer and three stools constructed for the grand total of one dollar. (When Kirkman later sought reimbursement for these items, the government paperwork frustrated him, and many of his efforts were returned by headquarters as improperly filled out.) He also purchased a broom for fifty cents.[13]

Beginning his official duties on July 8, 1867, Kirkman needed to familiarize himself with the area. After touring and inspecting the vicinity, Kirkman relayed his observations and assessments to head-quarters. From what he could judge through personal scrutiny and inquiries, Bowie County blacks appeared to be "working well." He thought in a "majority of cases" that planters willingly gave freed-people "their just rights and a faithful settlement of contracts." Un-fortunately that year, all but a few of the Red River plantations had been subjected to "bad" overflows that would cause "great loss" among the planters and create, he wrote, a "great amount of destitu-tion among the freedpeople."

Although Kirkman had interviewed various people, he did not find much feeling one way or another in relation to establishing schools to educate local blacks. He had heard of a few efforts being taken to promote black education, but good intentions did not trans-late into positive action. Three Davis County white women dis-cussed and promoted the founding of schools for black children, but due to threats and intimidation they abandoned the idea. Through this kind of pressure, blacks and those who desired to assist them in their fight against illiteracy could be persuaded to disregard any no-tions of educating the freedpeople. Throughout Kirkman's subassis-tant commissionership, establishing schools for blacks continued to be a major problem.

Violence was not yet a problem at this stage of Kirkman's tenure. Bowie County seemed relatively quiet, and only a few instances of "outrages and mistreatment" of black citizens had been reported. The disposition of the white community, according to the agent, en-couraged the fair administration of justice "both to themselves and to the freedpeople," but in fact, Kirkman contradicted himself on this point. Later, he contended that blacks did not "have the bene-fit" of equality before the law. To maintain the "publick peace" and to ensure the "execution of severely rendered justice," Kirkman had nine soldiers assigned to him. Without troops, he believed it would be impossible to secure anything approaching equal justice for the black populace.

Violence saturated neighboring Davis County. "Bad and reckless men" had murdered several blacks and whites. Freedmen could not walk on a public road "without suffering personal violence and dan-ger of life." One black man, described as "peaceful, quiet and indus-trious," had been shot five times (four in the heart) by Baker because he worked a small farm "on his own account." (As yet, Kirkman had not encountered the famous Baker but described him as having a "bad reputation." The rumor circulated that a person could hire him "to shoot a freedman for a few dollars.") Reportedly, two "hard and reckless men," operating out of Linden (the Davis County seat), had murdered blacks, stolen horses, and escaped to New Orleans or Memphis.

The most violent section of the area, six miles east of Douglassville and ten miles south of the Sulphur River, safe for neither blacks nor "peaceful white citizens," became a haven for desperadoes. A majority of the people, anxious for some kind of law to be imposed, were "tired of the lawless state their county is in." He recommended that an agent, supported by troops, be stationed at Douglassville or Linden. An individual named Robert Perryman applied to be an agent. A man of family and property, Perryman thought he could take the amnesty oath, as he had not engaged in the rebellion. The Boston agent had little doubt that Perryman could and would faithfully execute the duties of a Bureau agent. Headquarters, however, ignored Kirkman's recommendation.[14]

Kirkman's initial impressions of Boston, Texas, and its environs, did not bode well for the future. He actively entered upon his many Bureau responsibilities and attempted to make cautious observations about the people he would be dealing with in the course of his official duties. Except for his comments about the violent nature of Davis County, Kirkman's surveillance of the area exhibited a rather positive note, which he later realized to be quite erroneous. How Kirkman went about managing the new race and labor relations, civil and judicial officials, Bureau business, violence and crime, Cullen Montgomery Baker, and how he assisted the Boston area black community to fulfill its aspirations becomes the focus of his Bureau career.

Race and Labor Relations

In the aftermath of war and the destruction of slavery, harmonious race relations did not characterize Bowie and Davis counties. Numerous reports suggested an unstable situation. With a minimal military presence, little protection could be afforded the black inhabitants. The Fort Smith, Arkansas, agent reported in May 1866 that "Freedmen are coming almost daily from Texas in a destitute condition and report that anarchy and despotism reign supreme." Whites selected "the most intelligent Freedmen" to be "driven from their homes and families, many have been shot and hung for expressing a desire to enjoy their rights as Freedmen, while others are intimidated by vile threats, and cruel treatment, rendering their condition most deplorable."[15]

By mid-1866 the violence against blacks so alarmed the Arkansas assistant commissioner that he felt compelled to write Commis-

sioner Oliver Otis Howard that "numerous reports from reliable
sources reach me to the effect that crime and lawlessness go almost
unchecked in that part of Texas near the southwest border of Arkansas." Freedpeople were still held and treated as slaves, and if black
Texans attempted "to leave they are shot down, and white persons
from Arkansas who wish to employ them, dare not go into that part
of Texas to seek laborers." The "injurious effects" of the lawlessness
now extended into southwest Arkansas. Local citizens, in a state of
panic and afraid to challenge this reign of terror, sought help from
the Bureau.[16]

Throughout 1867 and early 1868, the attitude of whites toward
blacks changed little. Kirkman believed that overall race relations
appeared "more liberal" and "more quiet." Blacks and whites attempted to "get along as quietly and as peacefully as possible."
These feelings, Kirkman admitted, did not extend much below the
surface. By mid-1868 the Boston agent depicted white feelings as
"undescribable." The two races had but "little sympathy for each
other." Kirkman contended that the situation had to change "for the
better" if the two peoples remained "as situated as they were now,
and if they were to have any quiet and peace." Blacks also had "very
many opinions [about whites] that [were] erroneous, and unjust."[17]

Kirkman, with few soldiers at his disposal, could not prevent violence directed against blacks or their white sympathizers. When the
contingent withdrew, as occurred in areas adjacent to Kirkman's
geographical domain, then depredations, including murder, against
blacks and whites increased proportionately. Keenly aware of the in-
flammable situation in his subdistrict, Kirkman did not want to be-
tray black trust. But he simply could not predict the result if area
blacks were deprived of the little military protection they did receive and had to fend for themselves. Kirkman could only wonder
whether events would follow the same pattern that had taken place
in other sections when the government withdrew.[18]

The organization of the labor system dominated much of Kirkman's time during his tenure as subassistant commissioner in the
Fifty-eighth Subdistrict. He ordered that labor contracts be approved
by a specific date and be ratified by one of the following: a justice of
the peace, a county judge, a county clerk, a notary public, or two
"disinterested witnesses." An original and two certified copies had
to be submitted for the approval of the Bureau agent. Kirkman required planters to "strictly abide by the contract and . . . not discharge workers unless by mutual consent." Anxious to "promote
prosperity through the medium of free labor," Kirkman attempted
to "convey impartial justice" in accepting agreements.[19]

Forms of payment for the labor of black workers varied. The least popular method was paying wages. Women, as usual, received lower pay than their male counterparts, being paid five to seven dollars a month; men, eight to ten dollars a month. Kirkman had approved wages at twenty dollars for a male fieldhand, but this figure could certainly not be considered "average." Contract labor, the type of agreement most preferred by black farmers, promised blacks one-half the crop if they furnished their own food and clothing, one-fourth if the planter provided the provisions. Before the Boston agent accepted a contract as valid, he struck out the section that related to the 1866 Texas labor law.[20]

Kirkman made every attempt to protect blacks from being defrauded and to force planters to deal fairly with them. For those planters who had not used written contracts for 1867 (remember Kirkman did not arrive until July), he required them to file a written statement, certified by a proper official, which listed the names of the freedpeople who had worked for them, what the agreement stipulated, and the date the contract expired. In addition, the portion of the crop the freedpeople received had to be listed, along with the number of days they missed due to lost time or neglect of their labor. The planters had to agree to the latter section, according to Kirkman, "*the same* [as] *being under oath.*"[21]

The year 1867 did not turn out to be a productive agricultural one in Bowie County. When the freedpeople sold all they had produced, it would not "pay for the clothing and groceries purchased." Planters, seeking repayment for advances, "in almost every division of the crop" took more "than what the laborers crop would sell for to pay" for the provisions that had been charged on credit. Some freedpeople had been "injudicious and had done wrong in running themselves in debt so heavily." It might be a lesson, surmised Kirkman, that when "contracting debts they are not only contracting them but would have to pay too." To protect the industrious black laborers, Kirkman assessed fines against planters when their accounts charged the "freedmen above the market value."[22]

By 1868 the labor system of the Fifty-eighth Subdistrict varied, but contracts predominated. These included blacks who worked for one-third of the crop, and the employer furnished rations and other items necessary to cultivate the crop. Blacks who received one-half fed themselves, and the planter supplied all else. Freedpeople "were almost universally inclined" to work for a share (nonrenters) of the crop, but a small minority rented land with one-quarter of the crop pledged for payment. In 1868 the contract system had evolved so that the agreements appeared "more liberal, systematic, and just" than previous ones. Kirkman charged a fee to approve contracts, which he used to promote Bureau educational efforts. A few blacks succeeded in buying land.[23]

Natural difficulties intervened once again in 1868. Although the river had overflowed (not as disastrously as in 1867), the rains had come earlier and "at a more seasonable time." Heavy rains continued, making the river "bank full" but "at a stand still." Grasshoppers then appeared. Initially, the damage appeared minimal, as they fed on grass and burrs, but they had to be killed before becoming full grown or the crops would be destroyed. Nature dealt an additional blow in May, when the area was hit by a violent storm that brought destructive rain, hail, and winds, "washing and cutting" corn and cotton "up by the roots, completely destroying the crops." Replanting efforts partially succeeded.[24]

Sometimes conflict occurred on the plantation that ended in dissolving the labor agreement. The planter, if desiring to dismiss a laborer, had to prove the other party "has utterly failed in their obligation or done something to deserve being discharged." For his part the laborer "must show something" about the planter. When Granville Betts appeared before Kirkman, the black man desired that he be discharged from E. R. Fort's employ as the latter had not "done anything toward making a crop." Although it was "not customary to move hands off the plantation when labor had been agreed upon," Kirkman wrote, if Fort would settle his account with Betts, then he could be discharged and his name eliminated from the contract.[25]

In March 1868 a planter accused Eli Ball of violating his contract through the use of abusive language and running away. Kirkman ordered Ball's arrest, and the freedman appeared the next day, confronting his white female employer, Mrs. M. A. Paxton. Until another "place could be found" for him, Ball had to return to Mrs. Paxton's employ and pay court costs. The freedman "promised" to return but ran away again. Rearrested by Kirkman, the agent "compelled [Ball] to carry a large block of wood on his back for 6 hours" and be "confined in the county jail for two days." The evidence suggests that Ball absolutely refused to return to the employ of Paxton. Hired out to a Mr. Ottoway, Ball worked for him "at stated wages."[26]

One of the individuals whom Kirkman confronted over contractual problems, Hardin R. Runnels (governor of Texas, 1857–59), first appeared before the Boston agent in late 1867, attempting to collect some accounts due him from freedmen in Arkansas. Runnels had leased a plantation to two men named Fowler and Campbell, but still retained some control over the laboring force. Runnels proceeded to discharge one of the black workers for voting. He also in-

formed Kirkman that he held a lien on the entire crop until his rent
had been paid, including the freedmen's one-third, which Fowler had
promised the laborers. Kirkman informed Runnels that his claims
"could be founded on no principles of right or justice."

To approve Fowler's contract, and the agent so advised the hands,
on the back of each agreement Runnels had to agree not to interfere
with the workers' interest. Initially, the former governor refused.
Kirkman also wanted a bond guaranteeing that one-third of the crop
be turned over to the laborers or its equivalent value be paid to them.
Fowler and Campbell gave bond for five thousand dollars, with two
securities, that they would "truly and faithfully" comply with the
contract. The agreement stated that if Runnels failed to settle one-
third on the workers, the lessees, freed from any rent liens, would
pay the laborers one-third of the harvest. Fowler and Campbell accepted the contract, Runnels' opposition notwithstanding.[27]

When time for settlement of accounts occurred, Kirkman became
distressed. A few planters willingly gave the freedpeople "their
rights, but in many cases they certainly do not hold their contracts,
and the fear of the almighty before their eyes as they should, by
which means the freedpeople many times are brought out in their
debt. When the truth is arrived at they found that they were indebted to the colored man."[28] Planters failed to appear for numerous
reasons. When Kirkman fined the individuals for nonappearance,
they sent appeals to headquarters. He also legally attached crops to
force employers to settle with their employees. Even blacks dis-
agreed among themselves and brought their disputes before the
Boston agent for resolution.[29]

One lengthy case serves as a prime example of the conflicts between white employers and black laborers. A. R. Moores, a white
man, had employed several black laborers to work his plantation for
the 1867 harvest year. At settlement, blacks lodged several complaints against Moores. A few stated that they had never been compensated for 1866. After examining the accounts, Kirkman found
them indebted to Moores in the sums of twenty-five to forty dollars.
In addition, they accused Moores of assault and battery upon a black
woman. Kirkman referred this complaint to the civil authorities,
and Martha Tyler, in civil court, won her case as Moores confessed
that he had beat her with a "quilting frame." Moores paid a five-
dollar fine and court costs.[30]

Moreover, Flood Tyler, described by Kirkman as a "freedboy"
around nineteen years of age, charged Moores with "shooting at"
and "whipping" him. This case Kirkman took before a justice of the
peace, who evinced little interest in the complaint, but did preside

over the trial. He demonstrated a lack of enthusiasm for the case when he "decided the case on very little testimony and without inquiring into the particulars," Moores receiving a fine of one dollar and costs. Kirkman ordered Moores and Tyler to appear at his office. When a soldier attempted to serve a summons on Moores, he drew his revolver. Moores wrote on the back of the summons that he would not be tried twice for the same indictment.

Kirkman took Tyler before a local judge and asked him to investigate the case, the agent promising no interference. Moores sent word to Kirkman that he would not appear for trial, but the agent could send someone to arrest him. Kirkman proceeded with the case; Tyler appeared but Moores did not. Kirkman fined Moores twenty-five dollars and sent word through Moores' friends that he had three days to pay. "I fined him no more than I probably should have done," Kirkman informed headquarters, "had he obeyed the order." Moores did appear to pay the fine "without protesting" verbally. (Kirkman wrote that he "should not have received it under protest.") In all dealings, Kirkman claimed that he "treated [Moores] as a gentleman."

Moores did request that Kirkman remit part of the fine as he had "voluntarily" paid. Kirkman, who described Moores as "disloyal" and a planter who still used "corporal punishment and threatening language toward his laborers," offered to remit five dollars. Moores appealed the case to Bureau headquarters, arguing that the money should be returned because the commander of the Fifth Military District, Winfield Scott Hancock, had disallowed fines imposed by agents. Although the assistant commissioner did not fully approve of Kirkman's approach (he did not deem it "advisable or strictly legal to rearrest a person after they had once been tried and convicted"), he did sustain the agent's action. The "fine could not be remitted."[31]

Kirkman used various tactics to gain financial settlements for the local freedpeople. At times, he resorted to legalities, informing one planter that once a settlement had been made according to the law, the note the freedman held contained prima facie evidence that the planter owed that amount of money or its worth in property. Kirkman informed J. E. Rosser that "it would not be just" to charge a freedman for use of all the teams, only his portion, which amounted to about ten dollars currency. Rosser could deduct the sum from the final settlement figure and pay the balance of the note, though Kirkman believed "it was probably an accommodation" to the planter to have the freedman "take the stock."[32]

Although at a considerable disadvantage, blacks did not always end the year financially impoverished. Kirkman assisted freedpeople

in gaining their fair share. For example, Alf Richie, a freedman, sued
T. E. Rosser for his 1867 wages, claiming Rosser owed him $290.50.
After deducting $155.39 for accounts against him, the DeKalb black
man should have received $135.11, but Richie agreed to accept nine
cows and nine calves instead of cash. After settling his contract with
A. Stevens, W. Dorsey, a Boston area freedman, received 182 bushels
of corn. Peter Vaughn came away with 727 pounds of cotton, about
100 bushels of corn, and five dollars. Ben Tickle received three
months wages at thirteen dollars a month, minus fifteen dollars for a
cow and a calf he had purchased, leaving him with twenty-four
dollars.[33]

Laborers found it time-consuming when they attempted to collect
the proceeds of their labor when a planter died. One freedman won
a judgment of seventy-two dollars for his son from the estate of
W. Smith and William Lee. In another instance, Kirkman spent five
days negotiating a settlement with the ninety workers hired to W. C.
James, who had died. A freedman later made a claim against the
James estate but had "to wait for reimbursement until the plantation was sold." Black laborers sued the L. S. Johnson estate, the
settlement being negotiated by two people: one picked by Kirkman
with the consent of the workers and the other by the administrator.
The hands won, and the crop was held until they received the final
balance due them.[34]

Violence also surrounded the everyday lives of black laborers,
leading to demands for contract dissolution and compensation. Preston W. Roberts claimed inhumane treatment by V. M. Lassiter and
desired that their agreement be terminated as "no probability"
existed of the "two getting along peacefully." Roberts argued that he
should be paid one-half the amount agreed upon in the contract for
the work so far completed. When Susan Sherrell, a Boston freedwoman, produced evidence of an assault, her contract with Anderson Sherrell was annulled, and she received compensation for the
time labored. Other cases involved abuse, mistreatment, and the use
of violence to negate any obligation, such as planters refusing to pay
for the previous year's work.[35]

Abusive language became a source of contention between whites
and blacks in the workplace. Whites still expected the former slaves
to defer to them in matters of social etiquette. Blacks saw freedom
as altering past customs and refused to accept being demeaned. In
one case a black woman, Mary Ann Jeanes, and a white man,
W. Johnson, both received fines for verbal abuse: the latter five dollars and the former two dollars and fifty cents. Simon Terry, a black
man, paid a fine of one dollar and fifty cents, plus loss of time for a

day's absence from work, for "disrespectful" comments to his employer's family and noncompliance with his contract. Terry pleaded
guilty to all charges.[36]

It is worth comparing Kirkman's record relating to labor settlements with a broader Bureau perspective. "Far from an absolute
rule," writes George R. Bentley, the decisions "were often as arbitrary and prejudiced as they were painted" by white Southerners.[37]
This is not confirmed by evidence from the Fifty-eighth Subdistrict.
Even with Kirkman dispensing mostly evenhanded justice, blacks
did not emerge in very stable financial condition. Persistent in their
claims, once Kirkman established himself, individuals came to him
seeking compensation for their labor. Not as many black women as
men protested labor injustices, but women did actively pursue their
economic rights. Freedpeople even instituted legal action against
each other.[38]

The Black Community

Bureau agents became entangled in many other concerns besides labor and race relations that impinged upon Texas black communities
in the years following the Civil War. There has been much controversy about how blacks actually viewed the Freedmen's Bureau and
to what extent they received a fair hearing for their complaints and
grievances. How black Texans perceived the Bureau, responded to its
agents, and used the agency's limited power are important issues in
understanding the Reconstruction black community, whether in
Boston or in other Southern towns. Their unceasing effort to learn to
read and write is one of the most significant achievements of their
postwar experience.

Black education in the Fifty-eighth Subdistrict did not extend
much beyond the environs of Boston during the period that Kirkman
served as Bureau agent. What efforts local blacks made to begin the
educational process before Kirkman arrived is not known. The little
available evidence indicates it had become an important community
priority but that it did not progress very rapidly. Kirkman wasted little time in exploring the possibilities for establishing black schools.
He met with a temporary committee of the "Colored School" and
encouraged them to continue their work in organizing a school. In
mid-July he predicted that with the cooperation of the community,
both black and white, one or more schools could be organized by October 1 and ready for teachers.

In an August meeting in Myrtle Springs, a large group of freedpeople agreed to organize a school and unanimously elected for their

three trustees, Forrest Hooks, Major Halloway, and Henry Fort. For this school, which Kirkman thought would average about one hundred pupils daily, they preferred a male teacher because the school was located some distance from any plantation where an instructor could board. Therefore, the isolation and possible white opposition dictated that a male would be a much more practical choice. Although Kirkman stated that he would render any assistance in his power if they hired a woman teacher, he made it clear that because of the remoteness of the area a woman might find the situation difficult.[39]

Blacks organized Sunday (Sabbath) schools. Myrtle Springs had four classes with a total of forty students. They also constructed a building, fourteen miles from Boston and three and one-half from Myrtle Springs, and installed desks. As they still owed considerable money, Kirkman suggested the government might assist them with $300 to $350. In addition, Kirkman had attended two meetings to raise money to pay for the school and maintain the Sabbath school. (These latter schools should not be lightly dismissed as the Bureau agent believed black children made "considerable progress in learning.") Attempts to interrupt other meetings for school support by two white men with shotguns did not dampen the enthusiasm of local blacks.[40]

White response to black education varied both individually and communally. Kirkman believed that the majority of white citizens felt blacks should educate themselves, so they made no effort to promote schooling for the former slaves. This same attitude prevailed into 1868. The agent thought that it a "rather exceptional case" that whites, who employed black children as house servants, did not try "to learn them 'their book.'" Not all whites disapproved of educating blacks, Kirkman observed, and "some men of considerable influence" favored it. One local doctor offered to donate an acre of land to erect a church and a school. Kirkman originally rejected the offer because the freedpeople "had so little means."[41]

By the end of the first quarter of 1868, however, blacks had organized their efforts and believed they could secure the money, materials, and labor to build a wood-framed box house. As the doctor still demonstrated a willingness to deed the land, Kirkman remarked that "if the freedpeople could succeed towards making a good advance toward the building" he would "accept the property." Kirkman also assisted in providing reading material, even if religious in nature, by requesting that the state superintendent of education send Bibles and other "religious papers." Not only would traditional

Christian values be inculcated into the children but they would have material to aid them in their quest for learning how to read.[42]

Much of Kirkman's educational concentration centered on a black preacher from Myrtle Springs named Forrest Hooks. The Boston agent sought a teacher's commission for Hooks. His qualifications, according to Kirkman, were that he "writes a good common hand, could figure, and read." (Kirkman, in fact, sent two specimens of the preacher's writings to headquarters.) Hooks, also a "very good carpenter," agreed to repair and expand the church and school at Myrtle Springs. The conveyance deed rested with the three black trustees, which included Hooks. The contract between Hooks and the Bureau set a sum of $250 for the building, with Hooks assuming a debt of $148. He paid this off from the proceeds of his 1867 crop.[43]

When Hooks received his authorization from the Bureau's superintendent of education to teach school, Kirkman carefully instructed him. The school "must not" exceed fifty pupils, must be conducted like an "ordinary common school," and must be in session six hours a day five days a week. Hooks would open the schoolday with a hymn or prayer and then call the roll. He could "correct the pupils and demand obedience to the rules." If unruly behavior continued by a student, the trustees had the authority to remove the offender. As a subscription school, the monthly tuition charge would be one dollar a month, except where two students from the same household attended, then it dropped to seventy-five cents each.

If a household contained more than two children, the family paid a standard fee of two dollars. Because the school operated on a self-sustaining basis, Hooks' salary would be determined by the black trustees. Once the Bureau's financial position improved, the agency assumed Hooks' monthly compensation, paying him ten dollars a month. Hooks also had to report once a month in person to Kirkman. The black teacher made steady headway until the fall of 1868. His students progressed satisfactorily and learned to spell, read, and make figures. Hooks' day school averaged around thirty pupils and his Sunday school approximately fifty. By that time, however, his life had been threatened by whites opposed to black education, and the school was in danger from their outrages.[44]

Even when blacks made an initial effort to provide their children with an education, they found their efforts stymied, or even stalled, until they could raise a crop or some benevolent society or the government came to their assistance. With little money, they maintained what they had rather than expanding educational opportunities. Admitting that they had limited resources, Kirkman nevertheless complained that the Myrtle Springs blacks did not use "any efforts to promote" schooling "further than supporting the school" already established. He visited black schools whenever he sensed they might be having financial difficulties and gave constant encouragement. Among the freedpeople, there existed "quite an anxiety for the privilege" of education.[45]

Besides education, family difficulties and problems of destitution came to Kirkman's attention. Blacks complained of desertion; a freedman desired the return of his son; and the Boston agent had to be cognizant of indigent and vagrant freedpeople and their treatment. The records do not indicate overwhelming numbers of indigent and vagrant Bowie County blacks, but a few cases did arise that Kirkman turned over to the chief justice of the county. Contrary to what some historians have written, an agent did not have the means or funds to do more than refer cases to the proper county officials. Kirkman, in an odd statement, found no "pilfering vagrants," although he did hire out one individual.[46]

Another issue that arose concerned black ministers who performed marriage ceremonies but did not have ordination papers. To officiate at a legally sanctioned marriage, the preacher had to be ordained in a recognized church. This requirement, expressly spelled out in state law, meant that Kirkman had to apprise these "earnest and sound" individuals of that fact. As the freedpeople "disliked very much" being married by a white minister, Kirkman, although he had not had an opportunity to initiate any action, had encouraged those ministers capable of being ordained to do so. The real problem, however, was that the state had not legalized black marriage and would not do so until 1869. Their legal family status would remain in limbo until that time.[47]

Kirkman also had to make certain that Texas laws, such as the Black Codes passed by the Eleventh Legislature, would not be implemented. The codes dealt specifically with labor, vagrancy, and apprenticing, and Kirkman, like other Texas agents, had received instructions to disallow them. Previous practices died hard, however. Apprenticing of black children by white justices and courts became a particular concern of the black community. Kirkman believed that in many of the instances "an utter disregard to the feelings and wishes of the wards relatives" had been a conscious policy. "Is not a law unconstitutional," he queried headquarters, "that deprives them of their civil rights?"

In one case Kirkman returned a black girl named Julia (who had been legally apprenticed to E. S. Runnels, the former governor's brother) to her grandfather because he believed the law morally wrong. He also ordered the return of other black children. Kirkman did allow the courts to prosecute blacks, both men and women, for enticing an apprentice away from the legal guardian. Although the Boston agent felt that "too much feeling on the part of jurors to look at a man's color instead of the law" may have influenced the case, he did not interfere in the decision. Apprenticing became a significant issue during Kirkman's early months in Boston, but through his perseverance he nullified many of its unfortunate aspects.[48]

Although much has been said about Bureau participation in Republican politics, Kirkman's ties with the political process may be more typical. In July 1867, when the Boston agent assumed his post, Congressional Reconstruction had just begun. Both black and white voters had to be registered. "The colored people," the agent wrote, "are just beginning to learn of the registering." Kirkman observed that those formerly entitled to vote and still qualified "were not intending to register." Whites might appear to allow blacks to vote according to the dictates of their "conscience," wrote Kirkman, but "appearances showed that one way or another their votes may be partly controlled otherwise" than according to blacks' "own wishes."[49]

Kirkman, invited to hear opposition speeches, politely declined. No evidence exists that he attended black political gatherings either. His political philosophy suggested that a black "should vote for the candidate whom he thinks will befriend his rights—vote for a convention—and for one whom will try and promote education among them." Once blacks took the initiative and cast ballots, then white attitudes dramatically shifted. Local citizens, like A. R. Moores, openly began to threaten black voters. By 1868 the "prevalent feeling from the [white] public" indicated that the freedpeople had "no right in being allowed a voice in deciding the difficulties of the nation at the present stage" of Reconstruction.[50]

Kirkman believed that "one characteristic instinct of the freedpeople" was that when in doubt they "ask advice of those in whom they have confidence." From the records Kirkman left, there can be little doubt that the freedpeople who came into contact with him generally respected his judgment. They also found that the Boston agent made considerable efforts in their behalf, even though, surely, they had gone away disappointed at times. Considering the nature of the task that had to be accomplished and the circumstances, inevitably Kirkman would sometimes fail the black inhabitants of the Fifty-eighth Subdistrict. Kirkman fought for black equality under the law, an action which engendered constant battles with local civil and judicial officials.[51]

Civil, Judicial, and Bureau Business

Kirkman's Reconstruction philosophy, embedded in his relations with civil and judicial authorities and the local population, had as its underpinning the concept of legal equality. The Boston agent initially believed that civil officers appeared "fully disposed" to give blacks the "full protection of the law." Dissidents did appear among the local population. Hardin R. Runnels, one of the most prominent of these, and approximately a half dozen other individuals, "who yet seemed to be disloyal" and disinclined to provide Bowie County blacks with the "full benefit of the *reconstruction acts*."[52] The Bowie County sheriff was included among the troublesome people. These officials made Kirkman's job quite difficult.

Kirkman complained to headquarters about local officials who neglected or improperly performed their responsibilities. One name often mentioned was that of W. E. Duke, sheriff of Bowie County. The Boston agent lodged several charges against Duke, including "total incompetency," "no moral character," a "continual visitor of whiskey saloons," neglect of duty, and other "grave charges." Duke's behavior toward prisoners did not accord "with the customs of a progressive age." Moreover, when transacting business with blacks, his treatment of them "could be proven to be unlawful," demonstrating a "want of proper spirit of integrity" for an officer of that rank.[53] A local black man brought charges against the sheriff for his offensive actions.

Dennis Burns, a freedman, charged Duke with unlawfully keeping $10 for three months and with failure to make any progress on an account placed in his hands for collection. Indicted for failing to disperse the rioters during the Orton Circus incident (more on this later), a jury found him negligent and assessed a $12.50 fine. Kirkman also summoned Duke to appear to show cause why a fine assessed against him should not be collected. For a change, the agent received support from the civilian sector when the county commissioners' court supported the punishment. The sheriff's performance became so problematic that the commissioners' court directed him to furnish additional security on his official bond. The sheriff failed to do so.[54]

Kirkman, zealous in attempting to rid the area of disruptive individuals, received a caution from headquarters over his procedure in arresting criminals. "It was not deemed advisable," they warned the agent, "to arrest men supposed to be criminals, or guilty of assisting criminals to escape, unless charges could be proven against them." The Boston agent did realize, however, that the law provided that a peace officer or "any other person" could, without a warrant, "arrest an offender when an offense was committed in his presence or within his view." Then the warrants would be made out and executed later by the sheriff. Although not always successful, Kirkman understood the necessity of working closely with local officials.[55]

It seemed an unending task to try to find competent individuals who sympathized with Reconstruction principles to serve in local positions, although Kirkman did not make this latter idea a hard and fast rule. One man appointed county clerk resigned because the duties did not match his assumption of what they would be like. Kirkman recommended Nathaniel B. Anderson, the man he boarded with, be immediately appointed. When the county assessor announced his intention to resign, Kirkman suggested that the man's deputy assume the office. The deputy seemed a "reliable" individual, and the Boston agent did not know "anyone that was better qualified for the position." However, the deputy could not take the loyalty oath.

Because he had to work with them and frequently required their assistance, indeed protection, Kirkman often advised headquarters about whom should be selected or recommended for local and town offices. "If the civil officers were of a grade that were conscientious, in executing their duties," he wrote in late 1867, "there would be no doubt but justice would be rendered without the presence of the military." To ensure that conscientious individuals would be chosen by the assistant commissioner, Kirkman suggested that "an inspection" at "frequent intervals" of these officials "would be of considerable service and use to the Bureau in promoting the interests of all classes of people throughout the state."[56]

So that he could determine the jurisdiction of Texas justices of the peace and county courts, Kirkman requested a copy of *Sayles Treatise* to learn about all "required forms of process." He received a copy of the Oldham and White law digest, "considered equally good." After reading the general order that outlined an agent's jurisdiction, he believed that if "strictly construed," it limited an agent's power to that of a precinct overseen by a justice of the peace. His perception of the "spirit" embodied in the order suggested to Kirkman that the "restriction" should be employed throughout his district. Headquarters informed him his jurisdiction, like all other agents, "extended to the whole of his sub-district."[57]

Kirkman made two penetrating observations about the judicial process and the reason for lack of black participation. Local blacks lodged their complaints with the agent, Kirkman wrote, because they "have not yet the confidence in the Southern white people that

would prompt them to apply to them, for redress, for grievances."
He had never known of an instance in his district where a "colored
man had been drawn to serve as a juror." If a black person appeared
before the court "in any cause," the individual should be "tried by
an impartial jury and it would be but right and justice if he or they so
elect that they have the right to have his, or their cause, decided before a jury composed in numbers, one-half his own color and similar
in their feelings."[58]

Kirkman always desired that he be "permanently" detailed "good
and reliable" soldiers. But continuous problems arose about personnel and equipment. The cavalrymen needed revolvers in one instance, and in another, men were being returned to their companies
whom Kirkman needed as witnesses. At times, headquarters assigned infantry when he required cavalry. Accommodations also had
to be provided, or the men would be forced to "encamp in tents."
Command problems surfaced as there was "general dissatisfaction"
with the "non-commissioned officers in command of the men."
Kirkman was not a commissioned officer, but he thought the problems could be remedied by "more explicit instructions or orders
being issued to them."[59]

Kirkman complained that some of the soldiers were "overbear-
ing," "getting drunk," and creating image problems in the community. The commander who assigned soldiers could not ensure their
good conduct. Although their "habits at times made" them "unfit
for duty," it was incumbent upon the agent to "work with the material the Gov[ernmen]t furnishes us," he wrote, "and do the best we
can with it." The difficulty was that Kirkman's area of supervision
was an exceedingly violent one, and any soldiers detailed to him
were at risk of being killed. Soldiers deserted, were murdered, shot
at, and harassed. It was a dangerous area, and even with unfit personnel, Kirkman rued the day all assistance was removed.

Kirkman attempted an arrangement with the Mount Pleasant
commander to maintain the small force available, pleading that if
the cavalry detachment were "precipitously removed," it would
render him liable to "insult[s] and other violence." His life would be
in danger because of the unsettled condition of the country, and he
knew that he would have "trouble with" Baker's "sympathizers,"
not to mention the outlaw himself. Even troops that caused him
difficulties were preferable to none at all. When the soldiers finally
departed, Kirkman stated that he would remain "as long as he
thought he could do so in safety," or until Baker and his gang made it
impossible for him to stay in Boston.[60]

Bureau formality tended to overwhelm Kirkman. Even though he had conflicts with headquarters over procedural matters, he always believed that this was a secondary aspect of his field position. Officials in the central Bureau office became exasperated at the Boston agent's lack of propriety when it came to Bureau forms, but he did keep quite detailed records about all facets of his work, which is the reason we know so much about his relations with local civil and judicial officials and how he responded to the assistant commissioner's office. Kirkman found himself in a difficult position as he attempted to placate the civil authorities, ensure justice for all citizens, and maintain peace and the dignity of his office.

Violence and Crime

Violence and crime, an ever-present reality during Kirkman's stay in Boston and the Fifty-eighth Subdistrict, engaged much of his time, which is not surprising considering the background and isolation of the town. C. Vann Woodward applied the proper perspective when he wrote that "in the South of the supposedly vanquished and helpless white" the unmistaken attitude was "'advance'—aggressive, determined, and ruthless advance of racial oppression and white supremacy." The South, he lamented, "seems to have been one of the most violent communities of comparable size in all Christendom." Others agreed, viewing the defeat of Reconstruction as being "accomplished only through the use of violence on a massive scale."[61]

Disorder within the town of Boston became a frequent occurrence. A few months after Kirkman assumed his Bureau post, he wrote to the assistant commissioner describing "with regret[,] another disturbance in this place." A circus precipitated this violence. During late 1867 it had been advertised that the Orton Circus would appear in Boston. The troupe finally arrived on November 21 from Rondoe, Arkansas. Circus workers erected the tents and opened the show that evening. Kirkman had long believed that when the circus arrived "it would be the forerunning of a disturbance or riot." However, no one informed Kirkman "until they had been here some time that they were composed in great part by men from different parts of the North."

While circus activity took place, a "considerable number of people had accumulated in town," among them a "number of young men who were drinking very freely," preparing to "disrupt" the performance. "Under the influence of liquor," they harassed the individuals involved in the show, calling them "yankies" [sic], swearing they would kill somebody. John Tiller pulled out a revolver and "made a good many dangerous motions with it" until someone disarmed him. Tiller also offended the circus women. When the circus closed for dinner, a dozen men "occupied their time" by riding around town and on the galleries, running their horses, disturbing the peace, and drawing their six-shooters when they believed they had been insulted.

Kirkman, who had no desire to interfere, wished only that the sheriff would do his duty. But the agent made up his mind that he would make an effort to arrest them if they did not leave town. He spoke to the sheriff about it and informed him that he would personally assist "in their arrest." The sheriff demurred, wishing to delay a confrontation, hoping the young men would return home. They were told, however, that if they did not disburse by a specific time they would be arrested. A "number left town but some of the most desperate remained." Kirkman observed that trouble was "brewing" but thought that "after what had [previously] happened there would be no serious difficulty in the evening."

He was mistaken. The proprietor of the circus, Mr. Orton, "an honest and quiet gentleman," told Kirkman that during the evening show it had become "customary" to permit soldiers to attend and inquired whether the agent would allow any men on duty in Boston who wished to see the circus to do so. Kirkman complied. The men viewed the performance a few at a time, and the Bureau agent decided to enjoy himself for an evening. Kirkman accompanied Orton inside the tent and immediately observed that the men who had created the morning excitement were grouped together, with one individual, John Richardson (whom Kirkman subsequently wounded in the arm), pacing around the horse ring with a double-barreled shotgun on his shoulder.

Kirkman sat down to watch the performance but noticed that their "motions and signs" indicated that some plan was in progress. (The agent thought they might try to take the horses from the soldiers' quarters.) As the men left their seats, Thomas Duke, an overseer on a local plantation, rode into the ring, holding a revolver by his side. At that point Kirkman knew trouble was in the offing and made his way secretly outside the tent to procure a gun from his room and to alert the army detachment, which supported him, that a serious confrontation was about to ensue. The soldiers made their way to the circus and took their places as two men rode around the ring. Richardson continued his shotgun vigil.

Trouble ensued. One of the rioters deliberately shotgunned and severely wounded a little boy belonging to a performer, who had entered the ring to retrieve an object. When the rioters attempted to flee, the soldiers opened fire. Duke, another man riding inside the ring, and his horse were immediately cut down. One man who challenged Kirkman (the agent wielded a double-barrel shotgun) tried to escape and was arrested after not finding an exit. It turned out to be Richardson, the man who had patrolled the circus ring. Richardson, relieved of a pistol, of which "all of the barrels having been recently discharged and having the old caps on," had been wounded in the right arm, had a slight bruise on his side, and a hole in his pants from a stray bullet.

During the original confrontation inside the tent, Jeff Dillingham, a black man, received a serious hip wound. The bullet completely shattered the bone, so his leg had to be amputated. Ironically, although none of the soldiers suffered injuries in the fracas, Kirkman admitted that Dillingham had been shot by accident, he thought by "one of our guns." Kirkman had to assume responsibility for payment before the physician would treat Dillingham. The Bureau agent believed that the "instigators" should be made to pay the bill. Acting upon this belief, Kirkman systematically began to impound the horses of those men responsible, so the animals might be sold later to pay the doctor's bill.

In addition, he had arrested Richardson, Tiller, and a "German named Johnson." The latter supplied the young men with a bucket of whiskey; the young men, in turn, promised to "tear down" the circus tents and "clean out the Yankees in the show." Kirkman refused to release Richardson, Tiller, and Johnson on bond. Johnson remained confined only because his bondsman refused to sign the bond that required Johnson to keep the peace and not to leave the county or state without permission. Finally released on a fifteen-hundred-dollar bond, Johnson agreed to report every Monday, abide by his trial, keep the peace, and not leave the county. T. A. Shipp, also one of the perpetrators, gave bond. Shipp had led one of the horses into the ring.[62]

The Orton Circus saga did not end in Boston, however. The performers, on their way to Mexico would pass through Austin, now Bureau headquarters, and Kirkman suggested that evidence from the circus people could be gathered at that time by staff officials. More important, on the local scene, District Judge A. G. Haskins and Runnels, the former governor, approached Kirkman with a proposition that amounted to a compromise. If the remaining "young men" would voluntarily surrender, Kirkman would allow them to be tried by civil authorities. The agent accepted the terms but retained the right to try one individual, whose name he did not mention to Haskins or Runnels.[63]

During the night the situation changed. A man who Tiller

claimed had refused to identify himself, smuggled two guns into the jail. On December 18, shortly before the attempted escape, Kirkman visited the jail. John Richardson (the "chief instigator" in the "riot") and John Tiller forced a corporal to free them and fled with drawn pistols. They exchanged gunfire with the soldiers and a corporal killed Richardson. Tiller surrendered, and was placed in irons and returned to the guardhouse. Kirkman believed that Tiller "was to blame" but that Richardson had "put it in his head." The two men had anticipated being turned over to the civil courts. Instead, Richardson was dead, and Tiller was remanded to the military post at Mount Pleasant.[64]

The Tiller dilemma continued. His friends suggested that Kirkman grant him bail, and if allowed, the sum to be set at two thousand dollars. Tiller agreed to obey the laws of Texas and the United States and report to Kirkman twice a month and once a month to the Mount Pleasant post. He would also have to appear before whatever commission the assistant commissioner directed. Tiller was granted bail. After the grand jury found a bill of indictment against him, Kirkman thought a change of venue would be expedient, but this violated state law. Meanwhile, Tiller did not comply with the stipulations of his bond. He failed to keep the peace in Boston and never reported to Kirkman as agreed upon. Kirkman apprised the district court judge of these facts.[65]

Although blacks continually reported incidents to the subassistant commissioner and to the civil authorities and swore to depositions, without military assistance the Boston agent could do very little. Local blacks, who banded together at times, attempted to protect their own and also to relay information of impending violence. This unquestionably saved some black lives but Boston's isolation, forty-two miles from the nearest military post, meant protection often arrived too little and too late. Local violence, often sporadic, occurred because of a particular incident or emotional outburst. The violence committed by men like Cullen Montgomery Baker, who occupied much of Kirkman's time, came in the form of guerrilla activities.[66]

Cullen Montgomery Baker

Within three weeks of Kirkman's arrival, he encountered his major nemesis and the man directly responsible for his death, the notorious Texas desperado, Cullen Montgomery Baker. On the morning of July 24, 1867, Kirkman, DeWitt C. Brown, and three cavalrymen from the Mount Pleasant post traveled nineteen miles into Davis

County to arrest Baker, his "first lieutenant," a man named L. R. Rollins, and other members of the gang. Unable to locate him, Kirkman and his group began the return trip to Boston. After crossing the Sulphur River at Pettit's Ferry, the soldiers confronted Baker and his men. Baker's band "fired a good many shots" at the federal officials. The agent and the soldiers retreated into Boston.[67]

Later the same morning, upon hearing that Baker had followed them into town, Kirkman and the soldiers attacked the building in which Baker was hiding. Baker fired "16 or more shots" from the window, striking Private A. P. Titus of the Twentieth U.S. Infantry with "15 large buckshot," killing him instantly. Baker received a wound in the right arm before he made a successful escape, but the Boston agent expected him to return. Kirkman described the condition of the area that Baker inhabited in the western part of Davis County as "bad." Baker terrorized both blacks and Unionist whites in that county, and Kirkman requested additional troops from three different places. The necessity for soldiers to "preserve the lives of innocent men from being murdered" should be clear to everyone, he declared.[68]

Baker, who later killed an Arkansas Bureau agent named Hiram F. Willis, became an absolute "terror" (Kirkman's word) to blacks, Unionist whites, and the Union army in Davis and Bowie counties and in neighboring Arkansas. In effect, in northeastern Texas, western Arkansas, and northwestern Louisiana, he and numerous other desperadoes began what has often been labeled the "New Rebellion." An Arkansas Bureau agent described him as "a notorious Texas desperado who has killed several soldiers in the adjoining county to this in Texas and boasts that he has killed an hundred negroes." His hatred seemed to know no bounds, and his life, according to Kirkman, appeared "to be of no value to himself."[69]

Cullen Montgomery Baker, dubbed the Swamp Fox of the Sulphur, brought terror and death to northeastern Texas. Too often in Texas history, he has been written about in tones of adulation. Although fictionally immortalized by Louis L'Amour in *The First Fast Draw*, Baker exhibited the traits of a psychopath. He was born in Tennessee in 1835, and his family settled in 1842 in Cass County, where Baker killed his first man when he was nineteen. When the Civil War came, he joined the Confederacy. In his absence, the legend continues, blacks began robbing his family, and so to assist his beleaguered kin he deserted. Baker expected to return to the service, but it took so long to "clean up" the blacks who stole from "his people" that he overstayed his leave and never returned.[70]

Baker recruited a group of outcasts, including "ex-Confederate

Soldiers, bush whackers and renegades, all, or many, already with a price on their heads." According to one description, they were "as rough, daring, lawless cutthroats as ever swore fealty to a murderous, out-lawed chief." R. H. Watlington, who met Baker twice, had no fond remembrance of a man who murdered blacks "for the mere sport of killing" and terrorized local citizens so that the "bare mention of 'Baker and his clan,' brought foreboding of direful portent." Watlington described him as a "sallow, thin, hatchet-face, taciturn man of yore." He saw Baker as "bold, out-spoken, [and] red face[d]," with "every feature deeply stamped with marks of dissipation."[71]

One Arkansas Bureau agent captured the nexus of Baker's appeal when he wrote that "such a character" is as "essential to the ends and aims of the citizens of this part of the country as hounds are to a hunter. Through such instrumentalities the chivalry govern the lower grades of society even more effectually than they could by legal enactments by narrating their deeds of valor to the ignorant freedmen who recount them by their evening firesides with horror and consternation." He wondered why, if the government could spend thousands to protect United States citizens in foreign countries, "can she not protect her soldiers in her own territory." But then, the government, national, state, or local could not stop Baker's depredations either.[72]

Kirkman sent Baker's description to various military commanders in the area. He believed that Baker could be located and "brought to justice" if the government offered a large reward for his arrest. One Arkansas agent exclaimed that the "Government should offer a reward for his head and levy a tax on the citizens of his county to meet it for allowing a highwayman and murderer to 'run the road' with impunity, and harbor him from justice because he confines his depredations to soldiers, union citizens and negroes." (Baker occasionally worked a farm in Davis County and had sisters in the area who "harbored him" when necessary; he never strayed too far from home.) Kirkman even enlisted Governor E. M. Pease in his reward scheme.[73]

Kirkman coordinated his efforts to capture Baker with Hiram F. Willis, a Bureau agent serving in Rocky Comfort, Arkansas. Willis, familiar with Baker and knowing his "desperate character," enthusiastically assisted in the effort to capture him. Willis now had twelve soldiers assigned to his station. In the meantime Baker struck again. On October 6, 1867, he and Ben Griffith ambushed a "team" bringing rations to Kirkman. They killed the teamster. The Boston agent requested that a detachment from the Mount Pleasant post be ordered to Davis County, as Baker still remained at large after killing another soldier. His band reportedly numbered from fifteen to thirty, so a large force would be necessary.[74]

Along with Cullen Baker, other desperadoes such as Ben Griffith and his "band of ruffians," created problems for Kirkman and local blacks. A coconspirator of Baker's, Griffith harassed and disarmed the freedpeople whenever possible. He tended to operate more in Arkansas than in Texas but still menaced the order and stability of the Bowie County area. A freedman, King Battle, stated that Griffith had killed his son, Jacob, who worked for Griffith at the time. Griffith had also murdered local whites. Griffith stole army supplies, killed at least two soldiers, and wounded a Bureau agent. At various times Kirkman attempted to apprehend Griffith but failed. A Bureau agent later killed Griffith in Clarksville.[75]

Less than three weeks after Baker killed Kirkman, he murdered Willis, the Arkansas agent, and J. P. Andrews, an assistant United States assessor.[76] Baker's exploits became the material for a local legend (there is an annual county fair in his honor). His nickname, Swamp Fox, reputedly came from the time he swam, while "severely wounded," the "flood-swollen Black Bayou in 1887" (he was long dead) under fire from some two hundred pursuers and went to his "grave vowing to overthrow the Yankee forces that occupied the South after the Civil War." By "terrorizing carpetbaggers," Baker "won the loyalty of countless law-abiding citizens." When Civil War widows encountered trouble, they knew Baker would "help out around their farms."[77]

Baker, credited with riding with such guerrillas as William Quantrill and outlaws such as John Wesley Hardin and "Wild Bill" Longley, probably did not perform half the deeds attributed to him. His teenage bride, Martha, once reportedly rode two hundred miles because she feared Baker was going to be hanged. When she later died, Baker made an effigy of her and talked to it for days, vowing vengeance on the Yankees. The final portion of this fanciful folklore recounts that when officials displayed Baker's bullet-riddled body in the Jefferson town square, it was actually someone else, giving Baker time to escape to Cuba, where he assisted the Cubans in gaining independence from Spain. Baker, however, had been killed by his brother-in-law and others on January 6, 1869.[78]

Conclusion

When Kirkman first entered upon his duties, he sensed a "cold shoulder" being presented to him by many of the townspeople of

Boston, Texas. His ideas on how to deal with those townspeople are
worth considering. He thought that a "lasting" peace had to "begin
at the heart of those who are now so biased, and warped in their
views." The Bureau should be "conducted in a spirit of *kindness,
justice* and firmness and upon the principle *to forgive* some of their
errors when penitent, or when they are strongly prejudiced, that
they do not know right from wrong." Regardless of "what their *war*
principles may have been," they should be encouraged to participate
in the reconstruction of the Union and to compromise. Around this
nucleus of individuals could be assembled a larger group who would
support Reconstruction.[79]

By mid-May 1868 Kirkman decided to resign his Bureau position
after having been employed by the Bureau for nearly one year. His
aim had been to "do his duty" and to "pursue a mild and just course"
in all affairs. He thought that the people of the area would now be
"more subject to the law" because of his influence. The Boston
agent allowed himself and state headquarters two months to complete the closing operations, so his resignation was to take effect
July 16. He thanked the officers at Austin for their assistance, the
kindness of one particular individual in Boston (probably Anderson),
and the soldiers who had been stationed with him. Without them,
he said, his job would have been twice as difficult.[80]

Kirkman rather innocently stated in one letter: "There are some
very bad characters in this county, as in all other communities." The
Boston agent attempted to do "exactly his duties," perform his responsibilities, and "make the Bureau as little *odious* as possible."
Despite his cautious attitude, "there were still unprincipled men
which only force controlled." Kirkman contended that when the Bureau and the military had been removed, "some lawless men and
persons of the female sex will again give vent to unbridled passion in
the abuse of not only freedmen but of those that love Union, freedom and peace." Kirkman's violent death did nothing to alleviate
the already tense feelings that characterized the area.[81]

Kirkman's encounters with lawless men never ceased. Not long
before his scheduled departure from the Fifty-eighth Subdistrict,
"armed bodies of men," numbering four or five, dressed as citizens,
passed through his area robbing the freedpeople. A spirit of rest-
lessness pervaded the district. Baker had been visiting the county
"for no good purpose," which further excited the populace. The
Boston agent had been briefly absent from Boston during this time
because he was detained south of the Sulphur River by high water
and by a thigh wound received in "breaking up an assembly of freed-

people in Davis County." With the mustering out of military units at this time, support from the army could not be arranged.[82]

Less than a month before Kirkman's assassination, a Bowie County grand jury indicted him for murder. Richardson (from the Orton Circus incident), in the custody of the soldiers assigned to Kirkman, escaped from jail. The soldiers subsequently shot and killed him. Kirkman believed that Richardson, running away in an escape attempt, "tumbled forward several steps after being shot," which created an impression that "he was stumbling." If Richardson had been standing still, "his motions," in Kirkman's estimation, would "have been different." The "force of the motion" accounted for his action. Kirkman was charged with shooting Richardson after he surrendered, although he had not fired at the slain victim but merely had observed the shooting.[83]

The indictment deeply disturbed Kirkman, and Anderson, the county clerk, became concerned about the state of the agent's mental health. Banks, the district judge, requested that Anderson, with whom the Boston agent roomed, inform him of what had occurred. Anderson complied with the request but did not know what course Kirkman would pursue. Clearly, Anderson was concerned and desired to help. He was "fearful" that Kirkman would fail to give bond, although he had not yet been arrested. He did not know whether Kirkman would even try to post the required sum. "He is in my opinion," Anderson wrote Assistant Commissioner Joseph J. Reynolds, "partially deranged, and not capable of realizing what course to persue [sic]."[84]

Anderson had no illusions about his personal status. He had been appointed under the direction of Winfield Scott Hancock, and the "same hatred that is against Kirkman is against me." In other words, "the same party that hate him hate me," and something "ought to be done" for the agent. Anderson did not feel safe, particularly if called upon to post Kirkman's bond. He thought that Kirkman and the soldiers were only performing their duty in attempting to recapture the escaped prisoner and had killed him in self-defense. The grand jury witnesses testified that Kirkman ordered the man shot, "but I don't think that Kirkman did so, nor does any one else but ultra men, and for this reason I think it a malitious [sic] thing." He hoped the situation would be "promptly attend[ed] to."[85]

The Boston agent regrouped his damaged psyche and began to query headquarters about his course of action. Kirkman's interpretation of the original Bureau act of 1865 suggested to him that it protected military officers while discharging their duties. Kirkman traveled to Clarksville to consult with Judge Banks of the Eighth Judicial District on what course of action should be taken. The Boston agent also employed the services of B. W. Gray, a Clarksville attorney who represented him before the court. A week later Kirkman's case was tried on a writ of habeas corpus before Banks, who rendered a decision "in compliance with the Reconstruction Acts" absolving the agent of all charges.[86]

Kirkman, undoubtedly relieved at his exoneration, knew he could leave with a clear conscience. No evidence exists that he conspired to murder Richardson. The agent's murder, on the other hand, had a ripple effect throughout the Boston community. The life of anyone who befriended Kirkman could not be considered safe, and ramifications of Kirkman's assassination were felt by Boston citizens, like Anderson, who knew the agent well. The man who supported Kirkman decided to leave the area after Baker killed the agent. Anderson, in contact with Kirkman's brothers, decided to move to Sherman, "fearing personal violence if he remained longer in Boston." Baker's influence and reputation deeply affected Anderson's decision to migrate.[87]

Historians have concluded that the "efforts of Bureau agents to protect and enforce freedmen's rights were insufficient and ineffective." Agents, according to Robert J. Kaczorowski, "exercised sufficient civil legal authority to secure the civil rights and personal safety of the freedmen of the South." And an agent's "ineffectiveness" cannot be attributed to the "insufficiency" of Bureau legislation or "national civil rights law": their "inadequacy was due primarily to the virtually insurmountable practical obstacles to civil rights enforcement that confronted" them. "Bureau failure," Kaczorowski concludes, was "due to an insufficiency of political power and failure of will, not to an insufficiency of civil legal authority."[88]

This situation is exemplified in the career of William G. Kirkman. He may not have been a typical Bureau agent for Texas or for other parts of the South. But Kirkman was probably closer to the norm of the type of individual who became a Freedmen's Bureau agent than has previously been realized. Officially listed as a civilian agent, he had prior military experience. This Northerner from Illinois really suggests what Reconstruction was all about. Serving in an isolated area infested with desperadoes and undermanned by the military, he attempted to use common sense and fairness in treating both blacks and whites. Kirkman's murder may indicate that he was too successful.

Anti-Northern sentiment and resentment of the Freedmen's Bureau prevailed throughout the subdistrict. Kirkman may not have been headquarters' ideal agent when it came to following proper Bureau procedure, but in the field he was precisely the kind of individual who produced results. The black population in every Southern state would have benefited from similar individuals. In all activities touched by his subassistant commissionership, Kirkman made concerted efforts to see that the freedpeople were treated as fairly as his limits would allow. Active, conscientious, and sympathetic to black aspirations, Kirkman believed in the ideals of Reconstruction and lost his life in attempting to implement them.

Few Freedmen's Bureau agents had to contend with the likes of Baker and his cohorts. But they always had to be cognizant of the relations between blacks and whites in their subdistricts. The freedpeople, at the heart of the social, economic, and political reconstruction of the South, needed the Bureau's assistance. Their status depended upon their numbers in any particular area and the degree of social and political organization. As Reconstruction progressed, black community leaders emerged and challenged white dominance. Race relations changed and took new shape as blacks registered to vote, joined the Union League, and strove for economic independence. Violence thus became a major factor in crushing black aspirations.

5. Reconstructing Brazos County: Race Relations and the Freedmen's Bureau, 1865–1868

WRITING FROM Bryan (Brazos County), Texas in early August 1868, the plantation manager for an absentee owner expressed disgust at the direction of Reconstruction events in Texas. Distressed by the freeing of the slaves, S. L. Love viewed blacks' involvement in politics and their propensity for violence as an ominous sign for the future. Attempting to turn a profit for Mrs. S. V. Young, a North Carolina resident, he complained that "politics is [a] business now and no one can tell what may turn up before the beginning of the next year." Suggesting that whites be held blameless for the recent upheavals between the two races, Love asserted that "Negro riots are of frequent occurrence here."[1]

Two significant disturbances had "occurred near" Bryan within the last month, and the result, Love laconically wrote, was the death of several blacks. Especially noteworthy also was the "riot" at Millican that erupted between blacks and whites in mid-July. He believed that the local black community had been "incited to violence by unprincipled" Northern whites. These actions by "outsiders" could not be allowed "with impunity" by native Texas whites. After the tragic conclusion to the altercation, according to Love, the white community "gave a barbecue" to "assure the colored population that they would be protected from violence provided they would conduct themselves in proper manners."[2]

Exploring the background of why racial tensions reached such an impasse in Brazos County, resulting in a racial confrontation at Millican in 1868, is important for social, political, and economic reasons. This background provides a basis for delineating and analyzing the course of local Reconstruction events and the fluctuating state of relations between whites and blacks, and the Freedmen's Bureau in a confined area (a county and a town) during the early years of Reconstruction. During this period black participation in the political structure of the county became a reality, if only a fleeting one, and whites became so angered that they willingly resorted to violence to dissuade blacks from continuing their political and military activities.

From war's end until the advent of Congressional Reconstruction, race relations in Millican and the surrounding county exhibited an unstable character. As a focal point for the frustrations of the white community, and the hopes and dashed illusions of the black, Millican illustrated the complexity of life in the post–Civil War South. The initial confrontation, leading to the death of several freedmen, occurred when the Ku Klux Klan rode into the Millican black settlement, intending to break up a meeting of the Union (Loyal) League. Long before this event, a series of nagging social, economic, and political problems fed a smoldering hostility that existed mostly in the eyes of the white community.

Brazos County racial violence did not reach the magnitude of the 1866 New Orleans and Memphis riots. Compared to other racial disturbances that erupted throughout the postwar South, the Millican imbroglio does not rank high on the scale of numbers killed.[3] Nevertheless, a study that includes blacks, whites, the Freedmen's Bureau, county background, the participants involved, and the origins and consequences of racial violence portrays a fairly complete picture of everyday life in small locales across the South during the postwar era. Millican can be viewed as Reconstruction in microcosm because the pattern of events there undoubtedly was similar to that in other rural communities throughout the South.

An examination of race relations where the black and white communities had an almost evenly balanced population and experienced nagging labor difficulties, even with the Bureau's presence, provides an intensive look at how Reconstruction progressed at the community level. Although more is known about the background of the white than the black community, enough can be pieced together from the material discussing the latter to see the emergence of a communal spirit. A brief survey of what has been written about the Millican affair points to numerous misconceptions of the entire event. Historians view this period according to their own backgrounds and make their moral judgments in conformance. Some place the blame for Reconstruction problems on the blacks; some, on the whites.

Charles W. Ramsdell blamed Brazos County blacks, as did Love, for the confrontation that developed at Millican. "Despite the fact that Texas was now under the unhampered control of General [Joseph J.] Reynolds," wrote Ramsdell, the "late summer and fall of 1868 saw no apparent abatement of the general disorder and lawlessness." The freedpeople "were beginning to show the effects of the teachings of reckless carpet-baggers [Love's "unprincipled" Northern whites] and 'scalawags.'" Violence occurred, Ramsdell contended, "because a mob of negroes, who were attempting to lynch another negro, refused to disperse at the order of a deputy sheriff." A white posse formed, a "fight ensued, and a number of negroes were killed."[4]

Two decades later, a historian of Brazos County, Elmer G. Marshall, followed much the same interpretation. A "rumor" circulated that a black man had been "lynched" on the Holiday farm, his body left hanging to a limb. Assembled under the leadership of an "itinerant Negro minister," local blacks organized to search for the lynchers. On the way they encountered the sheriff and his posse. The sheriff supposedly had gone forward to speak with the minister when a black man, "some distance behind the others, accidentally discharged his gun." The whites, thinking they were attacked, began firing. When the shooting stopped, according to this account, twenty blacks lay dead, eighty had been wounded, and the whites had lost four men.[5]

The same evening, July 15, Mayor G. A. Wheat issued a call to all able-bodied white men in the county who could bear arms. In Bryan, five hundred responded, commandeered a train, and started for Millican. After the mob arrived, several blacks, later killed, allegedly entered the town and began firing at the white people. The riot "continued several days" with whites shooting and hanging a "number" of freedpeople in the area. During this time, no federal soldiers were stationed in the county, but the government sent officers to Millican "with orders to punish the citizens of the county." Robert C. Meyers, a "strong Union man, used his influence to prevent further friction" and to avert any punishment.[6]

Marshall, more than any previous or later chronicler of the Millican riot, focused considerable attention upon the activities of the Freedmen's Bureau. Essentially a "them against us" interpretation, with the Southern elements portrayed as virtuous and the Bureau and the Loyal League (the "Northern element") seen as disruptive and evil. "Perhaps no organization in the county was more active in fomenting trouble between the whites and negroes" than the Bureau, wrote Marshall. "All the business activities of the Negro had to be done through" the agency, and every aspect of "economic relations between the two races came within their perview [sic] . . . [and the] amount of land rented to a Negro, the crops he planted, and the goods sold to him."[7]

In 1970 Michael Wallace wrote his brief account of the Millican riot in a much different racial and social environment. Surveying the violence committed by whites upon blacks after the Civil War, he observed that Millican "blacks, hearing that a comrade had been lynched, marched on the town in armed formation, led by a black preacher, and attempted to hang the guilty white." Additional "whites came to his rescue and, in the ensuing shoot-out, twenty blacks and four whites died and at least seventy-five were wounded." In Wallace's perception (the exact opposite of Ramsdell's and Marshall's) local blacks attempted to avenge the killing of one of their own; whites resented their extralegal practices; and a racial conflict resulted.[8]

The events leading to the armed shoot-out between whites and blacks and the resulting consequences do not support the earlier thesis blaming the blacks—and by extension, carpetbaggers and scalawags—for initiating the violence. Wallace, on the other hand, emphasizes black action. Although his brief narrative is partially correct, he exaggerates the number of dead and wounded, as did Marshall, who based his estimates on oral testimony. Ramsdell did not specify the number of blacks killed. All three historians reflect the historiographical climate surrounding Reconstruction in the age in which they wrote. None attempted to evaluate the immediate or long-range effects of the incident on Millican or the Brazos County black community.

Many factors and reasons led to the bloody episode that erupted in Brazos County. The riot demonstrated the growing political awareness of a local black population and how, fearing white intentions, they made efforts to protect themselves and their community. Black assertiveness contradicted white expectations. It frightened them, and they used violence to control disruptive elements. The killings left a black community virtually leaderless, exacerbated race relations, and maintained emotions at a fever pitch for several months after the riot. The background of the town, the people, and the arrival of Bureau agents are a necessary prelude to what became the first important racial confrontation of Radical Reconstruction in the summer of 1868.[9]

The County and the Town

Located in the east central part of the Lone Star State, Brazos County is approximately one hundred miles north of the Gulf of Mexico. Forty-one miles in length and twenty-four miles wide, the county is bounded on two sides by the Brazos and the Navasota rivers. It covers a geographical area of 578 square miles, or 369,920 acres. Even with quite fertile soil, Brazos County never became a large slave-holding area in comparison to other counties in the region. By 1864 the county contained 2,013 slaves, almost doubling the size of the chattel population from the 1860 figures. At the war's conclusion, the county had two major towns, Bryan and Millican. In the latter place, much of the trouble between the two races originated.[10]

Millican, located eighty miles northwest of Houston, was established in 1860 as a terminus for the Houston and Texas Central Railroad. Situated three miles east of the Brazos River and twenty miles east of Bryan (which became the county seat in 1866), it had only two hundred inhabitants. Blacks made up 41 percent of its population. (Millican was one of the South's rare examples of a town that had a population almost evenly balanced between the two races.) A major shipping center for agricultural products of the counties contiguous to it and northward for "hundreds of miles," extending as far as Dallas and Fort Worth, Millican was the most extreme point that could be reached by railroad in the interior of eastern Texas.[11]

Fluidity and mobility characterized the black and white citizens of the town and surrounding county. Because of their instability and lack of roots, white transients compounded the difficulties already present in relations between the two races. A Bureau agent complained in 1867 that because it was a railhead Millican became a haven for "many strangers," which included "gamblers and blacklegs." These disreputable characters stayed for "days and weeks," and violence accompanied their appearance. One white man was killed, and numerous lesser aggravations occurred. In an atmosphere already strained, the presence of these individuals added to the animosity that began to develop between the two races.[12]

The U.S. army arrived in the summer of 1865. According to Marshall, the occupying forces removed the civil officers and replaced them with "unscrupulous carpetbaggers." With county government already in a "turbulent condition," federal officials needed military assistance. Blacks, allegedly chosen for this task and clothed in "uniforms of the northern army," patrolled the streets. Encouraged by the army, local blacks "soon lost all fear of their former masters." Informed that "they were as good as the whites," freedpeople walked the streets singing that Jefferson Davis was a "fool." County whites refused to have their "spirit crushed." They would "gallop into town on horseback," fire their guns, scare the black troublemakers, and disappear.[13]

The Bureau

The Texas Bureau assigned an agent to supervise Millican and the surrounding area beginning in late 1865. In July 1866 a vacancy occurred. Millican could be considered "one of the most if not the most important point so far as the Bureau is concerned" in the eastern part of the state, wrote one Bureau official. All complaints between blacks and their employers over crop division centered here. If no labor settlement had been arranged, then the Bureau immediately stopped the cotton shipments. Millican became such a critical spot that post Commander L. H. Sanger of the Seventeenth U.S. Infantry frantically telegraphed Texas Bureau Assistant Commissioner Joseph B. Kiddoo: "Please send an agent here it is insufferable."[14]

The Freedmen's Bureau did not fully complete its organization in Brazos County and the surrounding area until May 1867. Charles Griffin, the new assistant commissioner, reorganized the state and created the Twentieth Subdistrict. Three significant Bureau agents served varying lengths of time while the subdistrict remained in existence. They included Samuel C. Sloan, Edward Miller, and Nathan H. Randlett. Randlett served as the agent when the actual incident took place. As a background for what eventually occurred at Millican in July 1868, it is necessary to look at the many difficulties the agents had to cope with and, most important, how they handled race relations and responded to the needs of blacks and their new political status.[15]

The Bureau's Twentieth Subdistrict comprised more than just Brazos County and Millican; it encompassed approximately two and one-half counties: Brazos, Grimes, and that portion of Burleson County east of the railroad running north and south through Caldwell County. A substantial area, the subdistrict had an equitable population distribution. It covered 1,726 square miles with 13,192 blacks and 13,265 whites. According to the 1870 census, Grimes County ranked third in black population among the state's counties with 7,921; whites totaled 5,294. Burleson ranked thirty-fourth with 3,021, compared to 5,051 whites. And Brazos County ranked twenty-third in black population among Texas counties in 1870 with 3,759 blacks and 5,446 whites.[16]

All three agents had fought in the Civil War. Two, Miller and Randlett, had suffered wounds. Miller had been shot in the chest and had had his left arm amputated. Afflicted with chronic rheumatism, nephritis, and acute uremia, he was physically unable to perform the demanding responsibilities of a Bureau agent. During the war Randlett had received a bullet in the left thigh and had contracted malaria. Although not as impaired in the performance of his duties as Miller, Randlett certainly suffered. Sloan, the healthiest of the three, had no physical problems. Both Sloan and Randlett became agents in their late twenties, but Miller was almost forty. Of the three, Sloan served in the Twentieth Subdistrict seven months; Miller, ten; and Randlett, nine.[17]

An agent assigned to the Twentieth Subdistrict assumed a very large responsibility. It was a position that demanded perseverance and required the dedicated endeavors of an observant, stable, and bold individual. Headquarters, aware of the onerous nature of an agent's activities in this region, periodically required an inspection of the agent's performance. When William H. Sinclair, inspector for the Texas Bureau, visited Millican during Christmas 1866, he immediately observed that the duties of the local agent assigned to this particular station were "great and of the most vexatious character." The Bureau official in this area had "more work and the most important of any agent in the whole state" except Houston.[18]

Samuel C. Sloan arrived in Millican in August 1866, shortly after Sanger's urgent plea to Bureau headquarters for assistance. The agent perceived that he had entered an active business center and expressed distress over the denial of justice to the freedmen in their problematic labor relations with employers. The "entirely nerveless" civil authorities largely ignored criminal offenses against blacks. Texas whites, Sloan asserted, evidently "cannot realize the changed status of the freedman" and so "injustice will ever be done" to them when complaints are left to the discretion of civil officials. Juries would not convict whites for murdering or committing any type of outrage upon blacks, but for blacks, justice would come swift and vengeful, he thought.[19]

Sloan had been in Millican only a month when a freedman, without the slightest shred of evidence against him, was hanged for rape. He was helpless to counteract the violence perpetrated by whites upon blacks because no troops were available. Without support, Sloan could only alert the attention of civil authorities to such crimes. He continually followed this procedure but discovered it a largely fruitless gesture. Another Bureau official, who personally toured Brazos County, confirmed Sloan's assessment. After the conclusion of his trip, the individual wrote that in the county generally, and Millican specifically, "civil law is so much of a farce in Texas that [alerting civil officials] amounts to nothing."[20]

With a sympathetic state government in power in Austin, local whites understood that they could ignore the Bureau agent and any attempts he made at protecting black rights, for little progress had been made in race relations since the end of the war. The Millican black community, beginning to stir and to believe they should be protected in their legal rights, received an unsympathetic response. Although the confrontation between the two races would not occur for another year and a half, whites had begun to set limits on black freedom, and any black straying beyond these bounds would be dealt with quickly and harshly. These constant irritations and the harassment of blacks by whites would continue to fester until open conflict resulted.

Sloan attempted to steer a balanced course. Sinclair, a dedicated champion of black rights, believed that Sloan did his job "faithfully." When Sloan first arrived in Millican, he had no troops and was "comparatively helpless." The Bureau inspector observed that while Sloan did much better than anticipated he did need troops immediately, for although he was respected by the planters, he also insisted "on every cent due the freedpeople." Such an important shipping post as Brazos County needed careful Bureau attention, and any attempt to swindle blacks out of their share of the crop had to be discovered in Millican before the cotton was transported. Sloan did complain that in settling accounts he too often had to perform in a "sort of compromising manner."[21]

Edward Miller, the agent who replaced Sloan, brought to the subassistant commissionership a very different perspective. However, although Miller reported only two criminal offenses committed against the freedpeople in March 1867, his complaint about local officials echoed Sloan's. He reiterated the fact that they reluctantly arrested offenders who perpetrated crimes against the freedpeople and almost never brought them to trial. One of the two offenses reported, the murder of a black man, occurred within five miles of the Brazos County sheriff's residence. The sheriff permitted the alleged killer to remain at his home for two days before arresting him and then released the man on his own recognizance.[22]

Deeply troubled by the lack of civil action, the black community decided to demonstrate their displeasure. They arose en masse, confronted the sheriff, and demanded that the accused be taken into custody instead of being allowed to roam freely about the countryside. To them, the entire procedure was unacceptable. The blacks who participated in this protest may have been amazed when the sheriff arrested them on the charge of being "rioters." Miller believed that such action indicated gross misconduct and that officers such as the sheriff should be removed. To Miller, law, order, and justice would be upheld by Brazos County whites, but almost always at the expense of the black population.[23]

Whereas Sloan encountered trouble with, and had little faith in the civil authorities, Miller's position vacillated. Miller naively believed he could maintain peace without troops because the local officials "always" willingly assisted him. But some civil officials could not "assist" Miller because of their alcoholism or corruption, and so he recommended the removal of two men, a justice of the peace because of habitual drunkenness and a deputy sheriff for extortion from area blacks, as unfit to perform their jobs. A month later he requested a detachment of troops, necessary, he wrote headquarters, for the protection of Unionists and freedmen. During this time Miller had one sergeant and three privates to aid him in his duties.[24]

Miller, whether from physical exhaustion, sickness, or a lack of commitment to Reconstruction principles, finally capitulated to the white power structure of Brazos County. Although no soldiers had been dispatched, Miller once again had unbounded faith in local officials. "In nearly every instance," the agent informed headquarters, whites dispensed justice to the black inhabitants. The reason for their change in attitude, he wrote, was the "fear" of being "removed from office." Miller's confidence in local government continued to grow. Just before he left office, he requested Bureau headquarters to return the four soldiers assigned to him to their company. He deemed them no longer necessary, as community officials always cooperated.[25]

For an eight-month period in 1867 (April to November), Miller knew of no criminal offenses committed against the freedpeople. Compared with events both before and after his tenure, this lack of violence is rather astounding and unbelievable. Miller showed increasing hostility toward blacks and an affinity with the planters. To him, the disposition of Millican whites appeared "to be very friendly," or "friendly in all respects," or blacks and whites lived on the "best of terms." Miller based his judgments on the premise that all seemed to be fine because blacks made few complaints of bad treatment. Blacks clearly understood that if they brought grievances before the agent, he would do nothing, so they did not complain.[26]

Combined with Miller's newfound respect for local governing authorities, he evinced a disparaging and unsympathetic view of black life. Internal problems beset the Brazos County black community. These tensions centered around marriage and family life. Miller suggested that some order be instituted regulating the marriages of the freedmen, apparently unaware that state headquarters had already issued a circular defining the status of black marriages. Miller believed they practiced polygamy, claiming few black males lived with their lawful wives and "less who have but one wife." Talking with and advising the freedpeople had no effect, and he feared that prevailing customs would "materially injure the whole race."[27]

Miller also complained that a number of freedwomen caused him difficulties. Characterized by "utter depravity and wantonness," a "majority of the females" practiced "unlimited prostitution." Virtue, an unknown practice or known only to a few, did not pervade the black community. The most disgusting aspect of this situation: "white people take no interest to remedy this state of affairs, but take delight in pointing out such cases and bringing them before the public, thereby injuring the whole race."[28] That such cases needed to be magnified suggests that Miller exaggerated their prevalence. Unfaithfulness and prostitution existed in the black community, but not on the scale that Miller described.

Although Miller appeared to view the black community unsympathetically, he did believe they had a right to vote. Why he naively believed he could continue to court the goodwill of the whites, while becoming involved in black political organization, is uncertain. On July 22, 1867 (almost precisely a year before the riot), Miller reported that he had formed a Union League Council in Millican. (Miller is one of a handful of Texas Bureau agents who informed headquarters that they actually had participated in Union League activities.) The league included twenty blacks and three whites. "Most of its work," one report suggested, "was done among Negro women." Urged not to do work of a menial nature for white people," they turned to politics.[29]

Considering Miller's perceptions of black women and his less than enthusiastic support of black legal rights, he expressed optimism about his Union League connection. "I expect the best results from this movement," he penned headquarters. Miller hoped to be able to report at "least 50 members at the end" of August 1867.[30] It is impossible to ascertain just why Miller believed his league activities would not affect his standing among the white community. After all, whites generally opposed the Bureau and the Union League, and Miller's unenthusiastic support of black rights in whatever form meant that he would receive little encouragement from either race. Apparently, he never reflected a great deal upon his action, but a major consequence would be the exacerbation of race relations.

Miller, like Sloan, found himself evaluated by a Bureau inspector, but in Miller's case the evaluator proved to be black. George T. Ruby, one of the few Southern black agents, visited Miller in June 1867, when the agent suffered from an attack of "bilious fever." Ruby's inspection occurred about halfway through Miller's subassistant commissionership. Miller spoke to Ruby about the "multiplicity of his duties and of his wish to be transferred to some field where he would have less labor and care." Miller "impressed" Ruby, who subsequently "saw him transact business," as an "earnest officer" and one "who would do all he could but who rather lacks the 'savoir faire' in execution."[31]

Ruby canvassed the local black population to ascertain their feelings about Miller. The "freedmen have more or less complaints against him," he wrote. The more "thoughtful ones" alleged Miller's unenthusiastic "conduct," contending that with murder being "so rampant" he "dared not act as he should." He confirmed this when he wrote that the Twentieth Subdistrict "is an exceedingly rough one." He found conditions in Brazos County "nearly as bad" as those in Robertson County. "The people need a little rough handling," he asserted, "and this I do not believe Cap't M. can do as he is incapacitated for much activity from debility etc." The Bureau needed an *"energetic faithful* officer" who could "materially aid in the work of 'Reconstruction.'"[32]

Labor

The introduction of a new labor system, based upon Northern precepts, consumed much of a Bureau agent's attention. From this theorem (only free labor could be successful), blacks would become part of the American system by making decisions for themselves. Every other personal or legal right flowed from this axiom. Thus, an economic struggle now ensued between the planters and the freedpeople (now actually endowed with constitutional rights) over how the latter would allow their labor to be used and under what conditions. Planters could not visualize blacks as "economic entities" or "capable of self-direction." The laborers desired more independence and a hiatus from the cruelty of the past.

Even before the Bureau came to the South, change swept the region. The transformation of Southern society continued under the Bureau. Everything seemed to center upon economics. An agent's task was to stabilize blacks into an efficient working class, based upon the Republican concept of free labor ideology, and to make sure that planters dealt with them fairly. In constant demand and essential to the South's agrarian economy, black laborers found a small wedge to assert their independence. Bureau agents understood this and often referred to the black farmer as the "sinew and bone of the land." The employers still viewed them as semislaves. Blacks had some bargaining power, as the state experienced a drastic shortage of agricultural workers.

Sloan admitted that whites expressed little vocal bias against blacks. Nonetheless, he became convinced that most of the "apparent acts of kindness and humanity offered" by whites toward blacks were "done in a patronizing way and in a selfish interest." Whites evinced a different psychological response when dealing with blacks economically. A significant majority of the planters, "extremely exacting in their demands," found that blacks balked at these methods and had no desire to labor under antebellum restrictions. Until employers changed their requirements and ceased treating them badly, blacks preferred working by the job and refused year-long contracts.[33]

Sloan indicated that whites had adopted subtle tactics to mask their beliefs and had become adept at presenting the proper face to the Bureau agent. Miller quickly noticed the animosity that existed between planters and freedpeople. Blacks demonstrated a wariness in their encounters with whites and suspected deviousness on their part. They opposed allowing anyone but an agent to approve their contracts. Brazos County whites took notice when Congress assumed Reconstruction controls. A "complete change seems to have come over the people since the new military bill has become law," Miller wrote, "and they promise to do anything, if they only will be saved from confiscation."[34]

Whites also began to bicker among themselves. They found themselves accusing each other of dealing unfairly with the freedpeople at the end of the 1866 contracting season. "Good faithful laborers are petted," Miller wrote, and all their "reasonable wishes complied with." Whites began to understand that new methods of negotiation and treatment had to be adopted. The "importance of the freedman is daily acknowledged by the white man," stated the agent. The "welfare of the County depend[ed] upon the [black] laborer," so employers "trie[d] to get the good will and confidence of the freedman." There would be "no trouble whatsoever," Miller lamented, if only the blacks would be "industrious and cultivate the land."[35]

Planters sacrificed a small portion of their past dignity when they hired black laborers, but it did not extend to recognizing the federal government's authority. Whatever methods planters used to entice blacks to labor for them in the upcoming year, they conveniently neglected to file copies of their contracts with the agent. Contracts could also be approved before civil officers and then checked by the Bureau. The majority of agreements had been approved by persons Miller referred to as "*disinterested* witnesses." In the subdistrict about one-half of the blacks worked for wages, and one-half toiled under contractual agreements in which they labored for one-third of the crop with rations provided or one-half without.[36]

Once contracts had been approved and the growing season had commenced, planters began a litany of complaints about the idleness of the black workers. To prove their contention, planters declared that the agricultural books they kept demonstrated that many hands had only worked about half time. On a tour, Miller claimed he had seen only three plantations where the freedmen's idleness had "materially injured" the crop. Despite all the talk of a lack of intensive work habits, the freedmen indeed labored industriously. By mid-1867 the crops progressed satisfactorily, and the expected corn yield would be above average. Nature, more than black work rhythms, drastically changed Miller's optimistic appraisal.[37]

Army worms appeared and extensively damaged the cotton crop; no remedy could be applied to save the damaged plants. Nature struck again when yellow fever and cholera invaded Brazos County. Although many people fled from Millican, "there were scores who died," according to one historian. At one point during the epidemic, a man later testified that "only three able-bodied men" remained in the town to "look after the sick and dying."[38] Local blacks materially assisted in the effort to nurse the white population back to health, but the effects of the sickness lingered long after the disease had passed. Although the epidemic and natural factors played their role in the relative failure of the crop, work attitudes unquestionably remained important.

The charge of black farmer "idleness" by the planters led to increased tensions among whites and blacks. The two races had a fundamentally different perception and conception of laboring patterns. What a planter may have perceived as a black laborer's lack of initiative may have had more to do with the way the former slaves approached their work. Certain patterns accrued from agricultural labor, and blacks understood this better than almost anyone. With emancipation, a black work ethic began to become clearer to whites, even as the agents of a Northern economic philosophy attempted the introduction of a free labor ideology. The crucial difference between employers and employees involved the terms and definition of "time" and "task."

Southern whites maintained a distorted image of the Puritan work ethic, which called for the appearance of constant toil and bragging about one's laborious feats. It often failed to account for nature and the change of seasons. Concerned about appearance and industriousness, planters failed to understand the labor ethos of the freedpeople. It is important to "emphasize the essential conditioning in differing notations of time provided by different work-situations and their relation to 'natural' rhythms," writes E. P. Thompson. Blacks desired to labor according to "task-orientation." During slavery this labor feature became, in many areas, an integral part of the agricultural process, regardless of the laborer's status.[39]

Task orientation had three important aspects: first, in an agricultural setting, it is "more humanly comprehensive than time labour"; the laborer "appears to attend upon what is an observed necessity." Second, there is the least demarcation between "life" and "work." Last, this work ethos appears "wasteful and lacking in urgency" to those habituated to the clock and not the seasons.[40] If the planters knew all this, where is the conflict? Laborers worked at a task until they finished it; a crop had to be harvested when ready, which might mean working from dawn to dusk or dawn to noon. Working at various tasks, as weather dictated, made much more sense to those blacks who contracted or sharecropped than appearing to be at constant toil.

The planters, on the other hand, largely saw their employees in terms of the "time is money" principle. As long as a worker had signed a contract, a planter (as during slavery) felt entitled to all his time. Black laborers resented this attitude and demonstrated through their actions that they considered such thinking wrongheaded. They had a clear perception of what their labor was worth. Reflecting upon this situation, Miller largely misinterpreted what the freedmen did or what principle they were trying to establish. He wrote headquarters that the freedmen are "inclined to confound freedom with independence, and they leave plantations and stop work, to attend to their own business whenever they please."[41]

The idea of being able to move about without permission became an attractive lure for blacks. Freedom not only endowed them with mobility but also implied that they might be able to negotiate with an employer for improved working conditions. On a larger scale, it may not have meant much, but for those who had spent a lifetime in bondage, confined largely to a plantation, the possibilities seemed considerable. Laborers felt it necessary to make the planters aware of the new guidelines. Most important, some distinction had to be made between what amount of time belonged to the employer and what amount of time blacks would enjoy for their own pursuits or business. Blacks made sure that their employers knew and understood this division.

Few planter complaints about their laborers surfaced during harvesttime as older collective rhythms broke through planter obtuseness. For blacks, the "weight of folk-lore and of rural custom" appeared in their collective consciousness. Social distinctions "momentarily" disappeared, and the ritual functions embodied in the "harvest-home" asserted themselves and engendered a "psychic satisfaction." Blacks clearly understood that their portion of the crop determined profits. After the harvest, the old rhythms faded, and the new ones became dominant once again. Whites resented lack of structure in black work habits. The agricultural pattern, one of "intense labour and of idleness," might be the "'natural' human work rhythm."[42]

Whatever the role of black work rhythms, or the continued expectations of whites, every societal condition suggested upheaval. By the time Nathan H. Randlett (the final Bureau agent) arrived in Bryan City in February 1868, the situation seemed to be deteriorating. The people had been devastated by the yellow fever epidemic. Crops generally had failed, and the shortage left the freedpeople much worse off than at the end of the previous year. Though the 1867 crop yielded below one-half the normal amount, the freedpeople had better luck in making contracts for the next season at a slightly higher figure (than the one-third and food, or one-half and provide for themselves) that had previously held sway. But the economic outlook did not brighten.[43]

In the first six months of 1868, race relations reached a nadir, with politics having much to do with the decline in social accommodation. Conditions, further aggravated, Randlett thought, by the upcoming elections and the freedmen's "interest in the political situation, and their rights of suffrage." As elections approached, whites grew more "hostile and bitter" toward blacks, and in many instances "hostility to the Government" became "openly and fearlessly expressed." They directed these attitudes at those blacks who actively participated in the election, and the attitudes gained widespread acceptance among the white community. By April the excitement and some of the overt hostility had subsided, but the agent concluded that "it is bad enough yet."[44]

Randlett often queried headquarters about how he could protect the freedpeople and white Unionists with a limited contingent of troops. He had only five soldiers to assist him, and eventually one of these left. Civil authorities could not or would not safeguard black rights. Even when blacks testified, their statements made little difference to a jury in cases where whites had been charged with crimes against blacks. Like most agents, Randlett requested mounted troops, but headquarters could never spare them; even a small number would have been of assistance. Randlett attempted to bolster his case by citing the example of Grimes County, where crimes quadrupled when soldiers were removed from that area.[45]

In early June 1868, Randlett asserted that he had a greater need for additional troops than there had been immediately after the war. "My opinion," he wrote, "is that the presence of troops has a very beneficial effect upon the disposition of these people." Blacks complained of injustice, but the white citizens held the general belief that nothing could be executed but the civil law, which almost always favored the status quo. More important, whites expressed grave fear of social equality which, Randlett said, "[I] fear is near consummation by the rapid change in color now taking place."[46] Race relations rapidly deteriorated; black political participation increased; and whites openly began to voice long subdued fears.

The Riot

The threats of the Ku Klux Klan, which by 1868 had made its appearance in the Twentieth Subdistrict, contributed to the uneasiness of Millican blacks. Not only had the Klan made its presence known in the area, but whites manifested a "considerable ill feeling" toward freedmen. Politics intensified the racial tension. To solidify their social and political supremacy, the white community made the first move. On June 7, 1868, a group of about fifteen people dressed as Klansmen, marched through the freedpeople's village at the outskirts of Millican in "an attempt to frighten black members of the Loyal League, who were meeting in a member's house." (In another account blacks had congregated in their church for services.)

"To the Millican whites' genuine shock," writes Melinda Meek Hennessey, the most authoritative source on Reconstruction race riots, when the Klansmen "fired off their weapons," blacks "responded in kind." They commenced firing with muskets and pistols at their white-draped tormentors. The Klansmen "ingloriously fled," leaving the ground littered with masks, winding sheets, other wearing apparel, and two revolvers.[47] The retaliation by blacks undoubtedly caught the whites off guard as their hasty retreat demonstrated. The sense of indignation among the whites over the incident can hardly be imagined; they had been humiliated. The black community, to protect itself, began to arm its people and commenced drilling in formation.

Whites believed blacks intended to form a "military organization," and white civil authorities requested that Randlett forbid blacks to bear arms. Whites also accused blacks of initiating the practice of carrying guns everywhere. Randlett informed them that as soon as they stopped the depredations of the Klan he would forbid "any warlike preparations" among the freedpeople. After some delay and negotiation, Randlett accomplished this. In turn, he ordered that "no *armed* band, organization or secret society not authorized by law" would be permitted, according to general orders, District of Texas. "The drills, meetings, and enthusiasm of the Brazos blacks worried and angered local whites."[48]

Headquarters refused to allow Randlett to disarm the blacks. Although "no further trouble occurred," the disposition of the whites toward the blacks was characterized as "very bad, and seemingly growing worse." Many attempts, Randlett reported, "are made to control freedmen by threats of the Ku Klux of which they have a mortal horror." (Their earlier response suggested that whites exaggerated black fears about the Klan.) After the brief encounter of June 7, Randlett took it upon himself to travel around the vicinity, trying to undo the mischief of the Klan.[49] Nevertheless, race relations were extremely strained by now, and more trouble could be expected. Whites planned to "show" blacks that they would not back down from a demonstration of force.

On July 15, the rumor circulated that a freedman named Miles Brown had been hanged. Brown previously worked as a blacksmith on the plantation of William and Andrew Holiday (also spelled Holliday), about six miles outside of Millican, and a recent altercation had ensued with the Holidays over compensation due him. Appearing at the plantation intoxicated, Brown desired his money. The brothers were absent, but the mother and sister, home alone, became "badly frightened." The next day, when sober, Brown heard that the two women had described his behavior as "insulting." Brown decided a short trip might be wise. He neglected to tell anyone he planned to leave the area, and the story spread that he had been hanged by the Holidays.[50]

George E. Brooks, a preacher, schoolteacher, registrar, leader of the four-month-old chapter of the Union League, and head of the Millican black community, directed Harry Thomas, another community leader, to raise a sufficient force of men to hunt for Brown's body. Collecting approximately thirty men, the group marched through Millican in military order. Thomas proceeded to the Brazos River, and there an additional twenty men joined him. As they made their way to the site where they supposedly would find Brown, they met Andrew Holiday, who exchanged words with a freedman named Robert. Holiday sent word to Millican for assistance, stating the freedmen had surrounded his house and threatened to hang him.[51]

About 3 : 00 P.M., after receiving information from Holiday, thirty whites armed themselves, and under the leadership of Mayor G. A. Wheat and a deputy sheriff, they marched to the Holidays' rescue. Fearing trouble, the deputy sheriff summoned more men, who overtook the first group. Meanwhile, after failing to locate Brown's body, the black group began to disperse. As the white posse rounded a bend, it came face to face with the black group. While Mayor Wheat and the deputy sheriff talked to the freedmen, someone fired a musket (Wheat claimed that it was a young black man), whether accidentally or purposefully cannot definitely be ascertained. Whites commenced firing. Blacks fled, and the white party returned to the town.[52]

After the white posse returned to Millican and reconnoitered the town, the mayor, along with two or three other officials, went to the freedpeople's village to discuss the recent turn of events with Brooks, who had not accompanied the black band in the search for Brown. Brooks, very unpopular with the white community, suspected that his life might be in danger. Randlett contended that "there has been for some time past great antipathy against this freedman Brooks by the white population, and accusations of a grave character have been made against him." Although the agent did not specify the "grave" accusations, he dismissed them as "mere prejudice, which could not "be sustained by the facts."

During the course of the meeting with the white civil officers, Brooks claimed that his men had been killed. Initially, the black minister declined to negotiate any terms of peace. After his refusal became generally known among Millican whites, they became extremely agitated once again. Rumors circulated that blacks had organized, intent on taking revenge for their slain comrades. Negotiations between the leaders of the two respective communities continued, and a settlement was finally reached. The mayor and some of the leading citizens agreed with Brooks to lay down their arms. They also compromised about a neutral arbitrator and mutually decided to submit all difficulties to the proper authorities the following day.[53]

Working in his office at Bryan, twenty miles from Millican, Randlett, informed that a serious riot was in progress and a sheriff's posse had been summoned, proceeded to the depot. He found an estimated 200 citizens, fully armed, and much agitated over the reports from Millican. Chaos reigned as the impromptu posse prepared to depart for Millican on the 9 : 00 P.M. passenger train of the Houston and Texas Central Railroad. This excitement, coupled with the influence of liquor, caused Randlett to "fear the result." About 150 men boarded the train, including Randlett and Sheriff J. Neil, and arrived in Millican around 11:00 P.M. By the time they had reached their destination, the cease fire agreement between black and white leaders had been finalized.[54]

Whites stationed guards around Millican and cordoned off the village. About dark, when two freedmen attempted to enter town, whites fired upon them, killing one. About 6:00 A.M. the next morning—July 16—several blacks came to Randlett to seek protection. He had no troops but suggested they could remain with him, and he would make every effort to protect them. Two hours later, Randlett met with Mayor Wheat and Sheriff Neil, who had a later meeting scheduled with Brooks. Randlett accompanied the two men, but the black leader never appeared. Touring the freedpeople's town, the agent and mayor found it peaceful. Nearly all the inhabitants had left their homes, apparently hiding in the countryside.[55]

While the agent and the sheriff absented themselves from Millican, numerous rumors circulated that hundreds of blacks had congregated with the intention of attacking and burning the town. Randlett was met by a group of citizens who requested that he allow the train to return to Bryan for additional reinforcements. The agent opposed this plan, suggesting instead that the train should proceed to Navasota, the nearest telegraph station, and forward a telegram to Brenham for soldiers. Calmer emotions prevailed, and the offer was accepted. Randlett requested that the sheriff forbid any men to leave town, having no "confidence" that he "would restrain" the men under his command "if they met any freedmen in the vicinity."[56]

All remained quiet until 11:00 A.M. when another tale circulated that nearly one thousand armed blacks had massed near the Brazos River. In a state of panic, whites demanded reinforcements. Once again, they requested that Randlett authorize the return of the train to Bryan for two hundred men. This time he felt that he would be overruled, so he acquiesced. The sheriff was to send for as many men as necessary, "but to accept no men that he could not control." Seizing the train, the sheriff requested fifty men. The train returned at 2:00 P.M. that afternoon, bringing men "highly excited" and "full of rumors." Luckily they found no freedmen with arms. Randlett surveyed the scene and claimed that less damage had been done than he anticipated.[57]

At 8:00 P.M. the same night, a cavalry detachment of twenty soldiers arrived, and so Randlett directed Sheriff Neil to have his men return to Bryan. Anxieties abated somewhat, and among whites a temporary level of sanity returned. The blacks, on the other hand, feared another confrontation, but when members of the white posse returned to Bryan, the freedpeople became calmer, and "quiet quickly replaced the excitement." Although rumors "persisted for several more days," the riot had "ended by nightfall."[58] The open confrontation between Millican whites and blacks may have ceased with the coming of darkness, but the nagging problem of Brooks' whereabouts disturbed the Millican black community. They could ill afford the loss of another leader.

The next day, July 17, another hysterical report spread through the white community that Brooks and approximately one hundred blacks had fortified themselves in a ravine three miles outside Millican. Randlett and Sheriff Neil at once investigated and found this rumor as unfounded as those of the previous day. But this was the area in which Brooks had apparently taken refuge. The black leader, afraid of being killed, wanted protection and needed to see Randlett. The agent told a freedman to find Brooks and inform him that he would be escorted to a safe place, as his life would be in danger if he remained at large. Brooks could designate any place for a meeting with Randlett alone, or with troops present, whatever he wished.[59]

Randlett never heard again from the freedman who had originally contacted him nor from Brooks. The black leader, the agent believed, could not be found because he feared for his life if he ventured into Millican. On the following day, July 18, a black man informed Randlett that Brooks had been hanged but could produce no evidence of that fact. However, on July 25, a black man discovered Brooks' body while searching for stray livestock. Identification was almost impossible because of the corpse's state of decomposition. Certain articles of clothing, a pencil, a knife, and that a finger was missing on the right hand confirmed that it was Brooks. Randlett labeled it a "deliberate murder" of a "most outrageous character."[60]

Brooks had been dead for several days; in fact, the probable reason Randlett never saw Brooks is because he had been killed long before. Brooks obviously knew that he needed protection. When or where he was killed—or even by whom—will probably never be known. At the time Randlett made his official report, he had not located enough evidence to convict anyone. One freedman told the agent that he had seen Brooks in the hands of a certain man (race not specified), but Randlett could not corroborate the black man's statement.[61]

The total number of persons killed and wounded in the violence that occurred at Millican during and after the initial confrontation included only members of the black community. Harry Thomas, who led the freedmen in search of Brown's body, died in the shooting on July 15, as did Moses Hardy, also black. King Holiday suffered a fatal wound in the same clash and died on July 17. Dan was shot on

July 16, apparently one of those who tried to enter the town after the whites had established guards. A Mr. Moore received a slight wound in the right shoulder. Robert, also black, was wounded and missing. In addition to Brooks, Dan Idle also died. In sum, six blacks had been killed and two wounded.[62]

Reports of the so-called riot quickly filtered back to Washington. On July 20, Oliver Otis Howard, commissioner of the Freedmen's Bureau, telegraphed the Texas assistant commissioner, Joseph J. Reynolds: "Are the Negroes in insurrection at Miliken [sic] as reported?" Reynolds immediately wired back that there had been a disturbance on July 15 and 16 and that a detachment of troops had been sent from Brenham, the nearest post. Although all the facts had not as yet been ascertained, he had been reliably informed that by the evening of July 16 all was quiet. The most reliable report estimated that five to fifteen blacks had been slain. Reynolds had received no other information and, as yet, no detailed information or analysis.[63]

Two weeks after the violence, race relations remained "bitter" in Millican and throughout the Twentieth Subdistrict. Randlett complained that people "ignore any action that is taken" and that civil authorities refused to make any attempt to protect local blacks. Enforcing peace, good order, and claims against a "people who consider it no crime to deceive, cheat, or murder a freedman" became impossible. A month later the situation had calmed considerably because everyone was too busy gathering the crops to cause more problems. The corn crop resulted in a satisfactory yield, but cotton produced only about one-half the normal amount. Worms and rain had done most of the damage. And considerable uneasiness still prevailed.[64]

Conclusion

Randlett originally believed that a white man had fired the first shot, basing his theory upon the evidence of a black man who had been wounded during the July events in Millican. Whites, however, indicated that the shot had come from the black group. Describing the Millican affair in a supplementary letter, Randlett wrote that he had since become convinced that blacks fired the first shot. Millican's mayor, G. A. Wheat, and Brazos County Deputy Sheriff Patillo both claimed they saw a freedman fire a gun and signed affidavits to that effect. Two other white witnesses confirmed their statements. No evidence exists that anyone consulted the blacks about who fired the opening salvo.[65]

Who fired the opening shot is impossible to determine. Freedmen's declarations did not seem to carry the same weight as those of the white civic leaders. Blacks may have been dismayed that Randlett allowed white affidavits to become such an important part of his investigation. Even the white community expressed unhappiness with his conclusions. Since the report had become public, the agent had been "assaulted, insulted," and his "life threatened." No Bureau business could be transacted due to the townspeople's excited state. Randlett requested that his letter not be published, as it would render his stay "very unpleasant if not dangerous." He needed troops in the district for the protection of those "suspected of loyalty to the Government."[66]

An interesting aspect of the Millican affair is a comparison of Bureau records with contemporary newspaper accounts of the clash. In rough outline, newspaper stories substantially agreed. The dead and wounded figures for the two opposing forces, especially for blacks, were wildly exaggerated. For whatever reason (possibly to stress what would happen if blacks challenged white authority) newspapers reported that between fifteen and sixty freedmen were killed, and the blame was invariably attributed to their own actions. Not one newspaper, no matter how friendly, mentioned anything about the Ku Klux Klan and its marching into the blacks' village, interrupting a community meeting.[67]

Two major Texas newspapers supplied their readers with divergent accounts. The *Daily Austin Republican* claimed that whites had been fired upon, and in self-defense, under the authority of the sheriff, they had retaliated; no whites were reported killed or injured. "This is certainly conclusive proof that the negroes began the difficulty!" the paper confidently stated. The *San Antonio Express* blamed unrepentant Southerners. The whites engaged in the affair were "rebels," the paper contended. "All over the State," the paper argued, "the spirit of murder which has been awakened by 'my policy' [referring to Andrew Johnson's Reconstruction plan] and the Bryan convention [where the Conservatives had convened], is terrible."[68]

Millican's mayor, G. A. Wheat, gave his own account in a letter to the editor of the *Houston Telegraph*. Widely published, it subsequently appeared in the *New York Times* and other newspapers. Wheat's recollection had some element of truth, but the mayor carefully selected what he wanted known. He failed to mention the Ku Klux Klan and its extralegal activities, and he viewed the freedmen as the instigators of all the trouble. He ignored the fact that a majority of the events leading to the racial clash were a response by blacks to protect themselves against white incursions, and he did not discuss the refusal of civil officials to enforce federal law.

The mayor's evidence made blacks appear unduly aggressive. Wheat emphasized the formation of Millican blacks into a "military"-type organization that practiced military drills. Wheat characterized this action as "unpleasant in the sight of the [white] citizens." The mayor said that he had complained to Randlett that blacks who acted in a military manner could not produce "amicable relations between the races." The Bureau agent ordered the drilling to cease. What Wheat failed to mention was that whites were also included in the decree. The mayor contended the black community disobeyed the order once the Bureau agent left the scene.[69] There is no supporting evidence for this latter charge.

The remaining details in Wheat's open letter also appear questionable. Wheat stated that during the meetings with the black leader, Brooks, Wheat's life was openly threatened. He also said that those who supported the black community chief were "rabble, who were clamorous for war." He blamed the freedmen for firing the first shot. Randlett (thorough in relating almost all other aspects of the Millican riot) mentioned nothing in his report about this type of atmosphere surrounding the meeting, although he often suggested how excitable whites became at the wildest rumors. (It is indeed possible such an incident happened as tensions between the two races were at a feverish pitch.) Although Randlett had not yet arrived in Millican when these conversations occurred, he was very thorough in obtaining information for his report.

Wheat accused Brooks of breaking an agreement whereby blacks agreed to lay down their arms and desist from wearing them in town; nothing is said about the same restriction being placed upon whites. When Brooks failed to appear for a second session (he may have been dead), Wheat declared that the earlier agreement had been violated. Once Bryan and Millican whites banded together, the mayor wrote, the "negroes saw the utter impracticability of success and desisted." Ever since the incident, Wheat stated, blacks had returned to work and "say that from this time out they have no desire to do military duty." Wheat, uncertain how many blacks had been killed, said nothing about white deaths and injuries.[70]

An interesting sidelight on what happened is that a letter signed, "A Colored Man," appeared in the *Daily Austin Republican* not long after the culmination of the Millican riot. The writer attempted to explain the character of the slain black leader, Brooks. In 1867, when yellow fever raged through Texas, wrote the anonymous individual, Millican blacks attended to many of the whites "who have been murdering them in return." One of the "chief nurses and faithful servants" who provided assistance was Brooks, who proved worthy of his occupation. "What few of these poor, abused, and wronged people remain in that little city," the freedman concluded, "will not forget this wickedness and inhumanity which has been returned for their faithfulness."[71]

Randlett wrote that "there was no just cause for the riot." The confrontation, he believed, was "founded, and based upon the excitability of the people and aggravated by foolish rumors afloat in the vicinity and in the press of the country."[72] The underlying causes went much deeper than excitable people and foolish rumors. The state was so large that the Bureau simply did not have the manpower to keep abreast of every situation that arose. Many whites in small, relatively isolated communities believed they could treat blacks in ways that differed little from the antebellum years. They ignored black pleas for justice and refused to listen to any grievances that freedpeople might have.

Politics played a significant role in bringing about the confrontation between the two races. As blacks gained some political awareness, they saw an opportunity to elevate themselves and to protect their community. This new self-image, along with the continuing struggle in the economic arena, where two entirely disparate views existed, disturbed whites. The blacks, on the other hand, struggled to establish a viable community identity, organization, and independence. They believed that freedom conferred certain basic rights, such as self-protection, and they attempted to put into practice all the privileges that it supposedly brought.

Freedom brought responsibilities and also conveyed new rights. Leaders emerged and political organizations began to appear. Economic relationships were transformed. The right to bear arms without interference and to protect their village against depredations by masked raiders was unquestionably every citizen's prerogative under the Constitution. The exercise of specific civil rights became of paramount importance for stabilizing any type of unity among the blacks. Maintaining a cohesive, organized, and safe community required numerous skills. Freedom, leadership, politics, economics, and the Ku Klux Klan helped to spur the Millican black community in its organizational process.

The sight of blacks drilling and bearing arms in some kind of military formation, no matter how justifiable, whites found abhorrent. When groups of blacks gathered for church functions or political gatherings, whites became uneasy. These demonstrations of black solidarity, particularly driving the Klan out of their village, suggested to whites that no longer could blacks be easily controlled. The white community was not prepared to accept such concerted social, economic, and political activity on the part of Millican blacks. Foolish rumors adrift in the town and the deep-seated bitterness of the area newspapers fueled human emotions and led to an increasing distrust between the two races.[73]

Unquestionably, whites, frightened by the assertiveness, aggressiveness, and politicization of the Millican black community, responded negatively. Blacks, no matter what new rights they had been endowed with, had to be made aware of their proper rung on the social ladder. Their status on this scale did not allow for any armed "show" of independence. Black leaders knew that without a recognizable community solidarity the former slaves would continue to be pawns of the white establishment. With the two races composing nearly equal portions of Brazos County population, it became imperative to maintain the status quo: white supremacy should be demonstrated at the outset, or race relations would deteriorate beyond any recognition of the antebellum years.

By killing the black leaders, Thomas and, especially, Brooks, and by attempting to destroy a burgeoning black community organization, whites left the freedmen in a disorganized condition. With these two important individuals out of the way, blacks would not be the ominous threat they had been when directed by effective leadership, nor would their institutions be as secure. "The opportunity to silence the leaders of the Millican black community, proved irresistible to Brazos County whites." Across the South, as occurred in Millican, "other black leaders suffered fates in later turmoil in which whites used the excuse of the riots to kill black community and political leaders," writes Hennessey.[74]

For Millican blacks the immediate and long-range cost of losing its two main leaders is difficult to imagine. Brooks, whom we know too little about, was clearly attuned to the purposes and principles of Reconstruction. Although characterized by a Hempstead newspaper as a "negro demagogue," this black minister certainly galvanized local blacks and was clearly aware of the possibilities of freedom, change, and organization.[75] His many social and political activities suggest that Brooks was a dynamic leader, and through his ministry he had connections to other state black leaders. He was intimately involved with the rise and development of the Millican black community, and his death had incalculable ramifications.

The withdrawal of the Freedmen's Bureau, which occurred within three months after the riot, assured local whites that there would be a minimum of outside interference. The Bureau attempted to moderate and mediate differences between Brazos County whites and blacks. But with limited manpower and almost no military support, the representatives of the agency could not prevent the recurring violence. In a sense, the situation in Millican is a key to the Texas Reconstruction experience because it suggests the almost insurmountable obstacles the Bureau and local blacks had to overcome in a constant struggle to survive in an atmosphere poisoned by racism, the loss of the war, economic change, and new black assertiveness.

Conclusion

WILLIAM MANCHESTER recently wrote that in current literature many "are practicing what might be described as generational chauvinism—judging past eras by the standards of the present. The passing of such ex post facto judgments seems to be increasingly popular."[1] This theme runs through many of the studies of the Freedmen's Bureau. Whether in Texas, or in other Southern states, the Bureau has been judged by a standard that would be impossible for most current or past organizations to attain. For all the limitations that surrounded it, and the extent of them cannot be exaggerated, the Texas Freedmen's Bureau, on the whole, performed rather well. Indeed, black Texans would have been much worse off without its presence.

After much wrangling, Congress established the Freedmen's Bureau in March 1865. The country (at least a reluctant North) assumed "charge of the emancipated Negro as the ward of the nation." Vast "responsibilities, indefinite powers, and limited resources" faced the organization. The Bureau, wrote W. E. B. Du Bois at the turn of the century, executed laws and "interpreted them; it laid and collected taxes, defined and punished crime, maintained and used military force, and dictated such measures as it thought necessary and proper for the accomplishment of its varied ends." It became a "vast labor bureau," exercised judicial functions, and attempted to guard its work against "paternalistic methods."[2]

Until the 1970s, the Texas Freedmen's Bureau generated such little interest that historians depended upon previous interpretations without investigating the large number of records it left behind. Even after material began to appear based upon the Bureau archives, the agency still only received piecemeal treatment. Various essays have appeared, of uneven quality, that continue to portray the Texas agency in a way that would be recognizable to past chroniclers of the Bureau. Historians, by barely scratching the surface, have distorted the Bureau's image and misunderstood its functions. A clearer

picture begins to emerge when the intentions of the agency are defined and explained instead of the Bureau being seen as a hindrance
or an interference.

The leaders of the Texas Bureau had to confront a state whose vast
distances hampered communication, prevented rapid military de-
ployment to protect the freedpeople, and left the agents, blacks, and
Unionists with little support. Favoring a free labor concept, although their methods of achieving this status for the black worker
varied, Bureau agents attempted to implement some type of contract
system. To them, it gave the former slave some kind of bargaining
power and legal protection in relation to his or her new employer.
Using the resources at their means, the Texas assistant commissioners probably could not have done much more than they did.
Those blacks reached by the Bureau, limited to be sure, did gain
some leverage in the economic sphere.

Interest in education fluctuated among the Texas Bureau agents,
but whenever they received extra money they generally devoted it to
the furtherance of black literacy. Allocations varied, but through the
determined commitment of black Texans and the Bureau's "on
again, off again" assistance, the beginnings of a black educational
system became a reality. Two setbacks retarded its development:
whenever blacks had to pay tuition to support a school, attendance
faltered; and the 1867 yellow fever epidemic totally disrupted the
educational endeavor, leaving many schools without teachers. Nevertheless, the system recovered, and local agents continued to provide as much aid to black education as they could.

The twin facets of securing justice for and protecting the freedmen
from violence posed problems which the Texas assistant commissioners never resolved. They attempted a variety of means to safeguard the lives of the freedpeople, but manpower shortages and too
much territory to be policed prevented effective defense. The agents
carried out their responsibilities, provided limited security, and supported the black inhabitants within their range of effective control.
To their credit, the Texas Bureau leaders concerned themselves with
enforcing Congressional Reconstruction laws and demonstrated
through their aversion to what they considered new forms of bondage that white treatment of former slaves had to change as blacks
had been endowed with specific rights.

On the subdistrict level, the type of problems and difficulties with
which an agent had to contend becomes more evident. In the Thirtieth Subdistrict, a diverse set of Bureau agents generally perceived
their duties as a serious undertaking. A summary of their efforts
demonstrates that they made concerted efforts to assist the black

community whenever possible. Their conflicts with civil and judicial officials suggests the nature of their activities. Whether it be in attempting to stabilize labor relations and ensure some independence for blacks or in attempting to protect black rights before a hostile white community, local agents found themselves in a situation that can only be described as unstable.

Although the Boston agent, William G. Kirkman, may have been an atypical Bureau agent in the sense that he was assassinated, he nonetheless provides a contrast for the generally negative view of the agency in past writings. It is difficult to fault Kirkman for what he attempted and for what he achieved as a Bureau agent. Considering the little support he received, Kirkman performed rather incredibly. Active as a field agent, sensitive to the grievances of the black community, and a quiet but firm proponent of Reconstruction, he gave his life to further the principles in which he believed. More than anything else, the Kirkman story shows that the past portrayal of how a Bureau agent functioned is in need of revision.

At the core of much of what the Freedmen's Bureau had to contend with between whites and blacks were their relations with each other. To maintain harmony between those who had been in total control and those who had been freed from the shackles of slavery was a task that no one could achieve. The Freedmen's Bureau tried. At the same time that they attempted to be sensitive about the perceptions of the white community, they also were aware of protecting the new rights of blacks. They encouraged the freedmen to participate politically and vote their beliefs. This tightrope could not be walked for long. In Millican, white fears met black aggression, and the Bureau could do nothing to stop the confrontation.

Willie Lee Rose wrote that "surely the difference between slavery and freedom is about the greatest difference in status we can imagine, no matter how kindly a view some historians might want to take of slavery, no matter how limited and curtailed freedom may have turned out to be."[3] In Texas the Freedmen's Bureau enhanced the opportunities for blacks to experience the full realities of freedom, no matter how harsh the lessons might have been. Within the boundaries established by Congress, working in a hostile environment, and receiving little financial assistance, the Texas Bureau was neither as dismal as past historians have pictured it nor as successful as it might have been. It did make a difference for the freedpeople.

Du Bois concluded that the Bureau's "successes were the result of hard work, supplemented by the aid of philanthropists and the eager striving of black men." Its "failures were the result of bad local agents, inherent difficulties of the work, and national neglect." In

Texas many factors limited the Bureau's success, but it was "committed to the independence of the freedmen in a way that former masters and most white southerners were not," writes Herman Belz.[4] This rings true of the Texas Freedmen's Bureau throughout its existence. From a modern perspective, the quality of freedom and independence may not be what was envisioned for black Texans, but the Texas Freedmen's Bureau did what was humanly possible.

Notes

Introduction

1. *The War of the Rebellion: A Compilation of the Official Records of the Union and Confederate Armies,* 128 vols. (Washington, D.C.: Government Printing Office, 1880–1901), series III, vol. IV, 381–382.

2. J. G. de Roulhac Hamilton, "The Freedmen's Bureau in North Carolina," *South Atlantic Quarterly* 8 (April 1909): 158.

3. W. E. Burghardt Du Bois, "The Freedmen's Bureau," *Atlantic Monthly* 87 (March 1901): 354, 365, 357–358.

4. Du Bois, "The Freedmen's Bureau," 362; idem, "Reconstruction and Its Benefits," *American Historical Review* 15 (July 1910): 783.

5. Nora Estelle Owens, "Presidential Reconstruction in Texas: A Case Study," (Ph.D. diss., Auburn University, 1983), 350–351. For Texas Reconstruction historiography, see Barry A. Crouch, "'Unmanacling' Texas Reconstruction: A Twenty-Year Perspective," *Southwestern Historical Quarterly* 93 (January 1990): 275–302. For the Bureau records, see Crouch, "Hidden Sources of Black History: The Texas Freedmen's Bureau Records as a Case Study," *Southwestern Historical Quarterly* 83 (January 1980): 211–226; idem, "Freedmen's Bureau Records: Texas, a Case Study," in *Afro-American History: Sources for Research,* ed. Robert L. Clarke (Washington, D.C.: Howard University Press, 1981), 764–794; Barry A. Crouch and Larry Madaras, "Reconstructing Black Families: Perspectives from the Texas Freedmen's Bureau Records," *Prologue* 18 (Summer 1986): 109–122.

6. William S. McFeely, *Yankee Stepfather: General O. O. Howard and the Freedmen* (New Haven: Yale University Press, 1968), 1; Diane Neal and Thomas W. Kremm, "'What Shall We Do with the Negro?': The Freedmen's Bureau in Texas," *East Texas Historical Journal* 27 (Fall 1989): 23; Du Bois, "The Freedmen's Bureau," 360 (italics mine). The two most recent national studies of Reconstruction are Michael Perman, *Emancipation and Reconstruction, 1862–1879* (Arlington Heights, Ill.: Harlan Davidson, 1987); Eric Foner, *Reconstruction: America's Unfinished Revolution, 1863–1877* (New York: Harper and Row, 1988).

1. The Freedmen's Bureau in Texas

1. *Congressional Globe,* 37th Cong., 3d Sess. (January 19, 1863), 381; 38th Cong., 1st Sess. (February 10, 1864), 566–573.

2. John G. Sproat, "Blueprint for Radical Reconstruction," *Journal of Southern History* 23 (February 1957): 33–44; David Donald, *Charles Sumner and the Rights of Man* (New York: Knopf, 1970), 120, 173–178; Herman Belz, *Reconstructing the Union: Theory and Policy during the Civil War* (Ithaca: Cornell University Press, 1969), 245, 296; Richard B. Drake, "Freedmen's Aid Societies and Sectional Compromise," *Journal of Southern History* 29 (May 1963): 175–186. The Senate Committee on Emancipation replaced the Senate Committee on Slavery and Freedmen. "In effect," Sproat writes, "this committee became the legislative counterpart of the administration's Inquiry Commission" (38).

3. Herman Belz, "The Freedmen's Bureau Act of 1865 and the Principle of No Discrimination According to Color," *Civil War History* 21 (September 1975): 200–201; idem, "Origins of Negro Suffrage during the Civil War," *Southern Studies* 17 (Summer 1978): 115–130; idem, *A New Birth of Freedom: The Republican Party and Freedmen's Rights, 1861 to 1866* (Westport, Conn.: Greenwood Press, 1976), 35–91. For governmental action, Northern racial attitudes, and Union occupation policy, see V. Jacque Voegeli, *Free but Not Equal: The Midwest and the Negro during the Civil War* (Chicago: University of Chicago Press, 1967), 3–72; Forrest G. Wood, *Black Scare: The Racist Response to Emancipation and Reconstruction* (Berkeley and Los Angeles: University of California Press, 1968), 21–43; Louis S. Gerteis, *From Contraband to Freedmen: Federal Policy toward Southern Blacks, 1861–1865* (Westport, Conn.: Greenwood Press, 1973), 183–194; Philip Shaw Paludan, *"A People's Contest": The Union and the Civil War, 1861–1865* (New York: Harper and Row, 1988), 198–230.

4. A good introduction is Harold M. Hyman, "The Freedmen's Bureau: Self-Help versus Paternalism," in *The Radical Republicans and Reconstruction, 1861–1870,* ed. Harold M. Hyman (Indianapolis: Bobbs-Merrill, 1967), 189–229. For background on the AFIC and its reports, see *The War of the Rebellion: A Compilation of the Official Records of the Union and Confederate Armies,* 128 vols. (Washington, D.C.: Government Printing Office, 1880–1901), series 3, vol. III, 73–74; 430–454 (preliminary report); series 3, vol. IV, 289–382 (final report); Sproat, "Blueprint for Radical Reconstruction," 37, 41; Eric Foner, *Reconstruction: America's Unfinished Revolution, 1863–1877* (New York: Harper and Row, 1988), 68–69 (1st quotation); Herman Belz, *Emancipation and Equal Rights: Politics and Constitutionalism in the Civil War Era* (New York: Norton, 1978), 71 (2d quotation); idem, "The Freedmen's Bureau Act of 1865," 198; James M. McPherson, *The Struggle for Equality: Abolitionists and the Negro in the Civil War and Reconstruction* (Princeton: Princeton University Press, 1964), 178–191. Foner points out the "tension between the laissez-faire and interventionist approaches" over which the AFIC split. Belz notes the contradiction between "paternalistic supervision or guardianship and genuine

civil liberty." Gerteis, in *From Contraband to Freedman,* believes the AFIC "reflected the paternalism and condescension that characterized the Union's best wartime programs involving freedmen," 34.

5. Foner, *Reconstruction,* 68. On the still-controversial land question, see LaWanda Cox, "The Promise of Land for the Freedmen," *Mississippi Valley Historical Review* 45 (December 1958): 413–440; Herman Belz, "The New Orthodoxy in Reconstruction Historiography," *Reviews in American History* 1 (March 1973): 106–113; Robert F. Horowitz, "Land to the Freedmen: A Vision of Reconstruction," *Ohio History* 86 (Summer 1977): 187–199; Claude F. Oubre, *Forty Acres and a Mule: The Freedmen's Bureau and Black Land Ownership* (Baton Rouge: Louisiana State University Press, 1978); Michael L. Lanza, *Agrarianism and Reconstruction Politics: The Southern Homestead Act* (Baton Rouge: Louisiana State University Press, 1990). For what might have happened had blacks been granted land, see C. Vann Woodward, "Reconstruction: A Counterfactual Playback," in *The Future of the Past* (New York: Oxford University Press, 1989), 183–202. On confiscation, see John Syrett, "The Confiscation Acts: Efforts at Reconstruction during the Civil War" (Ph.D. diss., University of Wisconsin, 1971); Patricia M. L. Lucie, "Confiscation: Constitutional Crossroads," *Civil War History* 23 (December 1977): 307–321.

6. *Congressional Globe,* 38th Cong., 2d Sess. (February 9, 1865), 691. See also Herman Belz, "Protection of Personal Liberty in Republican Emancipation Legislation of 1862," *Journal of Southern History* 42 (August 1976): 385–400.

7. *Statutes at Large (SAL),* XIII, 507–509; Donald G. Nieman, *To Set the Law in Motion: The Freedmen's Bureau and the Legal Rights of Blacks, 1865–1868* (Millwood, N.Y.: KTO Press, 1979), xiv–xv; idem, "Andrew Johnson, the Freedmen's Bureau, and the Problem of Equal Rights, 1865–1866," *Journal of Southern History* 44 (August 1978): 399–420. An excellent introduction to the Bureau's background and beginnings is Cox, "Promise of Land," 413–440. See also George R. Bentley, *A History of the Freedmen's Bureau* (Philadelphia: University of Pennsylvania Press, 1955), 1–49; Victoria Marcus Olds, "The Freedmen's Bureau as a Social Agency" (D. S. W. diss., Columbia University, 1966); Louis Henry Bronson, "The Freedmen's Bureau: A Public Policy Analysis" (D. S. W. diss., University of Southern California, 1970). On the same day, Congress also passed the Enrollment Act, giving back pay to black troops who had served in South Carolina; Herman Belz, "Law, Politics, and Race in the Struggle for Equal Pay during the Civil War," *Civil War History* 22 (September 1976): 197–213, esp. 213.

8. *SAL,* XIV, 173–177; XV, 83–84, 193–194; Nieman, *To Set the Law in Motion,* 106–109; John and LaWanda Cox, "Andrew Johnson and His Ghost Writers: An Analysis of the Freedmen's Bureau and Civil Rights Veto Messages," *Mississippi Valley Historical Review* 48 (December 1961): 460–479; Hans L. Trefousse, *The Radical Republicans: Lincoln's Vanguard for Racial Justice* (New York: Knopf, 1969), 330–331, 345. On civil rights the most recent and balanced accounts are Robert L. Kohl, "The Civil Rights Act of 1866, Its Hour Come Round at Last: *Jones v. Alfred H. Mayer Co.,*" *Virginia*

Law Review 55 (March 1969): 272–300; Robert J. Kaczorowski, "The Nationalization of Civil Rights: Constitutional Theory and Practice in a Racist Society, 1866–1883" (Ph.D. diss., University of Minnesota, 1971); idem, "Revolutionary Constitutionalism in the Era of the Civil War and Reconstruction," *New York University Law Review* 61 (1986): 863–940; idem, "To Begin the Nation Anew: Congress, Citizenship, and Civil Rights after the Civil War," *American Historical Review* 92 (February 1987): 45–68.

9. Foner, *Reconstruction*, 168. Considerable debate has arisen about whether the Civil War actually benefited the former slaves. This controversy can be followed in John S. Rosenberg, "Toward a New Civil War Revisionism," *American Scholar* 38 (Spring 1969): 250–272; idem, "The Reader Replies," *American Scholar* 38 (Autumn 1969), 731–732; Philip S. Paludan, "The American Civil War Considered as a Crisis in Law and Order," *American Historical Review* 77 (October 1972): 1013–1034; idem, "The American Civil War: Triumph through Tragedy," *Civil War History* 20 (September 1974): 239–250; John H. Rosenberg, "The American Civil War and the Problem of 'Presentism': A Reply to Philip S. Paludan," *Civil War History* 21 (September 1975): 242–253; Philip S. Paludan, "Taking the Benefits of the Civil War Seriously: A Rejoinder to John S. Rosenberg," *Civil War History* 21 (September 1975): 254–260. The argument is presented in different terms in Michael P. Johnson, "Battle Cry of Freedom?" *Reviews in American History* 17 (June 1989): 214–218.

10. Willie Lee Rose, *Slavery and Freedom*, ed. William W. Freehling (New York: Oxford University Press, 1982), 96; Foner, *Reconstruction*, 243. Works that are important for probing postwar Southern psychology include the following: Eric L. McKitrick, *Andrew Johnson and Reconstruction* (Chicago: University of Chicago Press, 1960); Michael Perman, *Reunion without Compromise: The South and Reconstruction, 1865–1868* (Cambridge: Cambridge University Press, 1973); Dan T. Carter, *When the War Was Over: The Failure of Self-Reconstruction in the South, 1865–1867* (Baton Rouge: Louisiana State University Press, 1985); idem, "'Fateful Legacy': White Southerners and the Dilemma of Emancipation," *Proceedings of the South Carolina Historical Association* (1977): 49–63. What the Bureau had to endure on the contemporary scene is judiciously delineated in Thomas W. Conway (assistant commissioner, Louisiana) to Oliver Otis Howard (commissioner), August 12, 1865, Louisiana, Assistant Commissioner, Letters Sent, Vol. 15, 250–251, Bureau of Refugees, Freedmen, and Abandoned Lands, Record Group 105 (National Archives).

11. Bentley, *A History of the Freedmen's Bureau*, 214. His ideas, applied to one state, are expressed in "The Political Activity of the Freedmen's Bureau in Florida," *Florida Historical Quarterly* 28 (July 1949): 28–37. Bentley's interpretation is not far removed from that of Paul Skeels Peirce (although their books appeared five decades apart), who wrote in the first general account of the Bureau in 1904, that the "authority of the bureau was widely exercised for political profit, that it served as a convenient political machine for the organization and management of the negroes, that it was an important factor in maintaining republican principles at a time most trying

in the history of that party, and that it was made a prominent political issue by the democrats of the north." Moreover, it was "largely attributable" to the Bureau that in the early twentieth century "political lines and race lines [were] so nearly coincident in the south" (Peirce, *The Freedmen's Bureau: A Chapter in the History of Reconstruction*, Studies in Sociology, Economics, Politics, and History, vol. III, no. 1 [Iowa City: State University of Iowa, 1904], 170, 171); Vernon L. Wharton, "Reconstruction," in *Writing Southern History: Essays in Historiography in Honor of Fletcher M. Green*, ed. Arthur S. Link and Rembert W. Patrick (Baton Rouge: Louisiana State University Press, 1965), 312–313. The change in Freedmen's Bureau historiography between the 1940s and the 1950s is readily apparent when E. Merton Coulter's *The South during Reconstruction, 1865–1877* (Baton Rouge: Louisiana State University Press, 1947) is compared with Kenneth M. Stampp, *The Era of Reconstruction, 1865–1877* (New York: Knopf, 1965). Coulter's views were the pinnacle of the Dunning tradition.

12. LaWanda Cox, "From Emancipation to Segregation: National Policy and Southern Blacks," in *Interpreting Southern History: Historiographical Essays in Honor of Sanford W. Higginbotham*, ed. John B. Boles and Evelyn Thomas Nolen (Baton Rouge: Louisiana State University Press, 1987), 226; William S. McFeely, *Yankee Stepfather: O. O. Howard and the Freedmen* (New Haven: Yale University Press, 1968), 8–9. See also McFeely, "Unfinished Business: The Freedmen's Bureau and Federal Action in Race Relations," in *Key Issues in the Afro-American Experience*, ed. Nathan I. Huggins, Martin Kilson, and Daniel M. Fox, 2 vols. (New York: Harcourt Brace Jovanovich, 1971), II, 5–25. Woolfolk finds, like Cox, that McFeely's thesis is flawed through misplaced morality. "Disenchantment with the morality of men and agencies of the nation's past may deserve a new iconoclasm," Woolfolk concludes, "but that judgment must focus upon the morality of their day, not of ours; the morality of the total milieu, not the individual" (Review of *Yankee Stepfather, Journal of Negro History* 54 [April 1969]: 200).

13. John A. Carpenter, *Sword and Olive Branch: Oliver Otis Howard* (Pittsburgh: University of Pittsburgh Press, 1964), 156; John Cox and LaWanda Cox, "General O. O. Howard and the 'Misrepresented Bureau,'" *Journal of Southern History* 19 (November 1953), 428–429; W. E. B. Du Bois, *The Souls of Black Folk: Essays and Sketches* (Chicago: McClure, 1903), 38; Foner, *Reconstruction*, 170; Belz, "The Freedmen's Bureau Act of 1865," 217. In another analogy, Guion Griffis Johnson, "Southern Paternalism toward Negroes after Emancipation," *Journal of Southern History* 23 (November 1957): 507, writes that "instead of the Freedmen's Bureau and Northern missionaries, the scapegoats are now the National Association for the Advancement of Colored People and the Communists." Cox, in "From Emancipation to Segregation," summarizing the 1970s and 1980s literature, remarks that the "stern and sweeping judgments pronounced against army, Freedmen's Bureau, and national policy have evoked reappraisals more subtle and more charitable than those conditioned by the temper of the 1960s. Although these voices are not dominant, there is a growing recognition that even as the immediate aims of the bureau and of Southern planters

coincided, their long-range goals in respect to the status of the freedmen fundamentally differed," 227.

14. Martin Abbott, *The Freedmen's Bureau in South Carolina, 1865–1872* (Chapel Hill: University of North Carolina Press, 1967), 131–133. The older work, not based on primary sources, is Laura Josephine Webster, *The Operations of the Freedmen's Bureau in South Carolina,* Studies in History, vol. 1, no. 1 (Northampton, Mass.: Smith College, 1916). Perhaps the best recent study of the Bureau is Paul A. Cimbala, "The Terms of Freedom: The Freedmen's Bureau and Reconstruction in Georgia, 1865–1870" (Ph.D. diss., Emory University, 1983).

15. Howard A. White, *The Freedmen's Bureau in Louisiana* (Baton Rouge: Louisiana State University Press, 1970), 165. For a critical evaluation, see Barry A. Crouch's review in *Societas* 1 (Autumn 1971): 317–318. The previous evaluation of the Louisiana Bureau was done by John Cornelius Engelsman, "The Freedmen's Bureau in Louisiana" (M.A. thesis, Louisiana State A&M, 1937), reprinted in *Louisiana Historical Quarterly* 32 (January 1949): 145–224. A good account of a Louisiana agent is J. Thomas May, "The Freedmen's Bureau at the Local Level: A Study of a Louisiana Agent," *Louisiana History* 9 (Winter 1968): 5–19.

16. Nieman, *To Set the Law in Motion,* 222.

17. Ibid., pp. 221, ix.

18. O. M. Roberts, "The Political, Legislative, and Judicial History of Texas for Its Fifty Years of Statehood, 1845–1895," in *A Comprehensive History of Texas, 1685 to 1897,* ed. Dudley G. Wooten, 2 vols. (Dallas: Scarff, 1898), II, 169–170. Similar viewpoints are expressed in Rev. Homer S. Thrall, *A Pictorial History of Texas, from the Earliest Visits of European Adventurers, to A.D. 1879* (St. Louis: Thompson, 1879), 409–428; Hubert Howe Bancroft, *History of the North Mexican States and Texas,* 2 vols. (San Francisco: History Company Publishers, 1889), II, 478–500; John Henry Brown, *History of Texas, from 1685 to 1892,* 2 vols. (St. Louis: L. E. Daniell, 1893), II, 444–455; W. D. Wood, "The Ku Klux Klan," *Quarterly of the Texas State Historical Association* 9 (April 1906): 262–263; Louis J. Wortham, *A History of Texas: From Wilderness to Commonwealth,* 5 vols. (Fort Worth: Wortham-Molyneaux, 1924), V, 4. See also Lawrence Edward Honig, "John Henry Brown, Texian Journalist" (M.A. thesis, University of Texas, Austin, 1972); Mary Beth Fleischer, ed., "Dudley G. Wooten's Comment on Texas Histories and Historians of the Nineteenth Century," *Southwestern Historical Quarterly* 73 (October 1969): 235–242.

19. Charles William Ramsdell, *Reconstruction in Texas* (New York: Columbia University Press, 1910), 76–77, 134, 140; idem, "Presidential Reconstruction in Texas," *Quarterly of the Texas State Historical Association* 11 (April 1908): 288–294. On Ramsdell, see James Payne Sutton, "Texas Historiography in the Twentieth Century: A Study of Eugene C. Barker, Charles W. Ramsdell, and Walter P. Webb" (Ph.D. diss., University of Denver, 1972). For the man and milieu under which Ramsdell studied, see Alan D. Harper, "William A. Dunning: The Historian as Nemesis," *Civil War History* 10 (March 1964): 54–66; Philip R. Muller, "Look Back without Anger: A Reap-

praisal of William A. Dunning," *Journal of American History* 61 (September 1974): 325–338; John Harelson Homer, "William A. Dunning: 'The Greatest Historian,'" *Mid-America* 68 (April–July 1986): 57–78.

20. S. S. McKay, "Social Conditions in Texas in the Eighteen Seventies," *West Texas Historical Association Year Book* 15 (1939): 34.

21. Claude Elliott, "The Freedmen's Bureau in Texas," *Southwestern Historical Quarterly* 61 (July 1952): 1–24. In fact, Elliott barely skimmed the tremendous amount of manuscripts available for writing a balanced history of the Texas Bureau. He has only twenty references to material in the National Archives, and several of these citations are to Bureau circulars, which only suggest what policy the Bureau attempted to implement, not what the field agents did. For an overview of the Texas records, see Barry A. Crouch, "Hidden Sources of Black History: The Texas Freedmen's Bureau Records as a Case Study," *Southwestern Historical Quarterly* 83 (January 1980): 211–226; idem, "Freedmen's Bureau Records: Texas, a Case Study," *Afro-American History: Sources for Research*, ed. Robert L. Clarke (Washington, D.C.: 1981), 764–794.

22. Elliott, "The Freedmen's Bureau in Texas," 2–3, 6 n. 14, 7–9, 10, 11–13, 21. Elliott seems to be arguing that white violence directed at blacks was either grossly exaggerated or being used as a propaganda device to enhance the Bureau's power. Even Andrew Johnson could be accused of being "pathetically ignorant" of the Texas situation. In particular, see James E. Sefton, *Andrew Johnson and the Uses of Constitutional Power* (Boston: Little, Brown, 1980); David W. Bowen, *Andrew Johnson and the Negro* (Knoxville: University of Tennessee Press, 1989); Hans L. Trefousse, *Andrew Johnson. A Biography* (New York: Norton, 1989).

23. W. C. Nunn, *Texas under the Carpetbaggers* (Austin: University of Texas Press, 1962), 5, 135–136, 246. Foner, in *Reconstruction*, points out that in states like Texas, with a small black population and few native white Republicans, carpetbaggers had little influence but "this did not prevent historians from inventing a myth of carpetbagger control." Nunn thus incorrectly titled his book "despite the fact that virtually every important leader of Texas Reconstruction was Southern-born," 349 n. 6. Nunn took his thesis from Bancroft.

24. Ernest Wallace, *Texas in Turmoil, 1849–1875* (Austin: Steck-Vaughn, 1965), 153–154, 155–159, 186, 197, 207–210, 229–230, 252. See also his *The Howling of the Coyotes: Reconstruction Efforts to Divide Texas* (College Station: Texas A&M University Press, 1979), 25–28.

25. T. R. Fehrenbach, *Lone Star: A History of Texas and the Texans* (New York: Macmillan, 1968), 396, 402–403, 410; Lawrence D. Rice, *The Negro in Texas, 1874–1900* (Baton Rouge: Louisiana State University Press, 1971), 153–156, 165. Fehrenbach's book is evidently highly considered as it is a selection of the nationally known History Book Club. He exaggerates and misinterprets the celebrated clash between the Bureau and the governor over pardoning blacks incarcerated in the state penitentiary. The prison case is much more complicated than Fehrenbach relates. The Bureau did not recommend the pardoning of all 227 black inmates, only the most grievous cases.

26. Edgar P. Sneed, "A Historiography of Reconstruction in Texas: Some Myths and Problems," *Southwestern Historical Quarterly* 72 (April 1969): 443–444. For a more positive approach, see Barry A. Crouch, "'Unmanacling' Texas Reconstruction: A Twenty-Year Perspective," *Southwestern Historical Quarterly* 93 (January 1990): 277–282; Ralph A. Wooster, "The Civil War and Reconstruction in Texas," in *A Guide to the History of Texas,* ed. Light Townsend Cummins and Alvin R. Bailey, Jr. (New York: Greenwood Press, 1988), 37–50.

27. Robert W. Shook, "Federal Occupation and Administration of Texas, 1865–1870" (Ph.D. diss., North Texas State University, 1970), 240 (1st quote), 244 (2d quote), 262 (4th quote), 486 (5th quote); idem, "The Federal Military in Texas," *Texas Military History* 4 (Spring 1967): 21 (3d quote).

28. William L. Richter, *The Army in Texas during Reconstruction, 1865–1870* (College Station: Texas A&M University Press, 1987), 32–46. His articles include "Spread-Eagle Eccentricities: Military-Civilian Relations in Reconstruction Texas," *Texana* 8 (1970): 311–327; "Outside My Profession: The Army and Civil Affairs in Texas Reconstruction," *Military History of Texas and the Southwest* 9 (1970): 5–21; "Texas Politics and the United States Army, 1866–1867," *Military History of Texas and the Southwest* 10 (1972): 159–186; "The Army and the Negro during Texas Reconstruction, 1865–1870," *East Texas Historical Journal* 10 (Spring 1972): 7–19; "'We Must Rubb Out and Begin Anew': The Army and the Republican Party in Texas Reconstruction, 1867–1870," *Civil War History* 19 (December 1973): 334–352; "The Brenham Fire of 1866: A Texas Reconstruction Atrocity," *Louisiana Studies* 14 (Fall 1975): 287–314; "Tyrant and Reformer: General Griffin Reconstructs Texas, 1865–1866," *Prologue* 10 (Winter 1978): 225–241; "'It Is Best to Go in Strong Handed': Army Occupations of Texas, 1865–1866," *Arizona and the West* 27 (Summer 1985): 113–142; "'Devil Take Them All': Military Rule in Texas, 1862–1870," *Southern Studies* 25 (Spring 1986): 5–30; "General Phil Sheridan, the Historians, and Reconstruction," *Civil War History* 33 (June 1987): 131–154; and what started it all, "The Army in Texas during Reconstruction, 1865–1870" (Ph.D. diss., Louisiana State University, 1970).

29. Richter, *The Army in Texas,* 39, 40, 43. Part of this analysis is based upon a reading of all of Richter's writings. Because Richter's work is the most recent (last publication 1990), he can be criticized for not using more effectively the newer published work on the Bureau. Instead, he relies heavily upon Elliott and an unpublished paper for his perceptions. Richter has begun to study the Bureau. His articles are cited where relevant.

30. Ross Nathaniel Dudney, Jr., "Texas Reconstruction: The Role of the Bureau of Refugees, Freedmen, and Abandoned Lands, 1865–1870, Smith County (Tyler) Texas" (M.A. thesis, Texas A&I University, 1986), iii, 3–4, 13, 18–20, 23–24, 36–37, 44, 46, 48–49, 56, 71–75. Dudney cites none of the recent literature on the Bureau in Smith County or the black family.

31. James M. Smallwood, "The Freedmen's Bureau Reconsidered: Local Agents and the Black Community," *Texana* 11 (1973): 309–312, 317–318;

idem, "Charles E. Culver, a Reconstruction Agent in Texas: The Work of Local Freedmen's Bureau Agents and the Black Community," *Civil War History* 27 (December 1981): 350–361. Smallwood's account of William G. Kirkman's death in "The Freedmen's Bureau Reconsidered" is erroneous (see chapter 4). Both these articles are similar, only the names have been changed, and Smallwood makes the same case for Culver that he did for Kirkman. Smallwood is wrong about the size of Kirkman's subdistrict and also alludes to him as a "Congregationalist." There is no evidence to indicate his religious affiliation. Moreover, there are nagging mistakes throughout the essay and many printing errors. Kirkman is often referred to as "Kirkland." Barry A. Crouch, "The Freedmen's Bureau and the 30th Sub-District in Texas: Smith County and Its Environs During Reconstruction," *Chronicles of Smith County, Texas* 11 (Spring 1972): 15–30; Barry A. Crouch, ed., "View from Within: Letters of Gregory Barrett, Freedmen's Bureau Agent," *Chronicles of Smith County, Texas* 12 (Winter 1973): 13–28.

32. William L. Richter, "'The Revolver Rules the Day!' Colonel DeWitt C. Brown and the Freedmen's Bureau in Paris, Texas, 1867–1868," *Southwestern Historical Quarterly* 93 (January 1990): 304–306, 320, 332. Richter seems to be altering his interpretation about the army presented in *The Army in Reconstruction Texas.* One of the problems with Richter's essay is that he has not kept abreast of recent Reconstruction scholarship, and he continues to cite Elliott and an unpublished seminar paper as the authorities on the Texas Bureau. Brown's subdistrict comprised Red River, Fannin, and Lamar counties in northeastern Texas.

33. Cecil Harper, Jr., "Freedmen's Bureau Agents in Texas: A Profile" (Paper presented at the Texas State Historical Association Convention, Galveston, 1987), 2 13; Carpenter, *Sword and Olive Branch,* 99; Shook, "Federal Occupation and Administration of Texas," 247. The dishonesty of one Texas agent is poorly and not convincingly chronicled in Thomas H. Smith, "Conflict and Corruption: The Dallas Establishment vs. the Freedmen's Bureau Agent," *Legacies* 1 (Fall 1989): 24–30. See also Joseph T. Glatthaar, *Forged in Battle: The Civil War Alliance of Black Soldiers and White Officers* (New York: Free Press, 1990). Across the region generally, Foner writes in *Reconstruction,* because of underfinancing, the Bureau employed "at its peak, no more than 900 agents in the entire South," 143. Carpenter identified 2,441 Bureau agents who served during the agency's Southern existence; LaWanda Cox, "From Emancipation to Segregation," 228 n. 50. Although he does not identify them as former Bureau agents, those who did enter state politics and secured various positions of influence are discussed in James A. Baggett, "The Rise and Fall of the Texas Radicals, 1867–1883" (Ph.D. diss., North Texas State University, 1972), and Carl M. Moneyhon, *Republicanism in Reconstruction Texas* (Austin: University of Texas Press, 1980), has material on some Bureau officials who became state officials under the Republicans.

34. James M. Smallwood, "Perpetuation of Caste: Black Agricultural Workers in Reconstruction Texas," *Mid-America* 61 (January 1979): 10.

35. Ibid., 13–14, 23; James M. Smallwood, *Time of Hope, Time of Despair: Black Texans during Reconstruction* (Port Washington, N.Y.: Kennekat Press, 1981), 68–95; Rice, *The Negro in Texas*, 209–215.

36. Randolph B. Campbell, *A Southern Community in Crisis: Harrison County, Texas, 1850–1880* (Austin: Texas State Historical Association, 1983), 47, 295; Smallwood, "Perpetuation of Caste," 10, 13–14, 23; Nora Estelle Owens, "Presidential Reconstruction in Texas: A Case Study" (Ph.D. diss., Auburn University, 1983), 382–383, 385. See also Allan Coleman Ashcraft, "Texas, 1860–1866: The Lone Star State in the Civil War" (Ph.D. diss., Columbia University, 1960), 260–305; idem, "Texas in Defeat: The Early Phase of A. J. Hamilton's Provisional Governorship of Texas, June 17, 1865, to February 7, 1866," *Texas Military History* 8 (1970): 208–209.

37. Ira C. Colby, "The Freedmen's Bureau in Texas and Its Impact on the Emerging Social Welfare System and Black-White Social Relations, 1865–1885" (D.S.W. diss., University of Pennsylvania, 1984), 10–11, 14, 16, 64–65, 68, 75, 111–112, 205, 207–209, 211. A summary of Colby's ideas is contained in "The Freedmen's Bureau: From Social Welfare to Segregation," *Phylon* 46 (September 1985): 219–230. By my count, Colby's dissertation includes a total of 333 notes but only 31 of them (29 of them appearing in chapter 2) are citations to primary Texas Bureau materials. Moreover, he cites none of the recent literature on the Texas Bureau, and his conception of the agency is simply wrong. He approaches it from the perspective that the agency was empowered to promote a full-scale Southern social revolution, including integration of services and institutions, which it was never designed to implement. For a different interpretation of these kinds of activities, see John Hope Franklin, "Public Welfare in the South during the Reconstruction Era, 1865–80," *Social Service Review* 44 (December 1970): 379–392; Howard N. Rabinowitz, "From Exclusion to Segregation: Health and Welfare Services for Southern Blacks, 1865–1890," *Social Service Review* 48 (September 1974): 327–354. For state developments, see Debbie Mauldin Cottrell, "The County Poor Farm System in Texas," *Southwestern Historical Quarterly* 93 (October 1989): 169–173.

38. Alton Hornsby, Jr., "The Freedmen's Bureau Schools in Texas, 1865–1870," *Southwestern Historical Quarterly* 76 (April 1973): 399–404, 406, 406 n. 26, 27, 408–412, 414; idem, "Negro Education in Texas, 1865–1917" (M.A. thesis, University of Texas, Austin, 1962), chap. 1, 166–170; Colby, "The Freedmen's Bureau in Texas and Its Impact," 91, 93–94, 97–98. Colby's interpretation is much like that of James D. Anderson, *The Education of Blacks in the South, 1860–1935* (Chapel Hill: University of North Carolina Press, 1988), who generally denigrates white efforts in behalf of black education. No industrial schools were established in Texas. It should be noted that Hornsby's conclusions are not based upon Texas Bureau archival material (which is fairly extensive) but on published Bureau reports. Elliott, "The Freedmen's Bureau in Texas," 7–9, 24; Rice, *The Negro in Texas*, 211–212, 230; Dudney, "Texas Reconstruction," 74–75; Alwyn Barr, *Black Texans: A History of Negroes in Texas, 1528–1971* (Austin: Pemberton Press, 1973), 60–64, 69; Campbell, *A Southern Community in*

Crisis, 261, 295, 297–298. Elliott is mistaken when he states that the AMA did not provide teachers for the Texas freedpeople's schools. Also worth consulting are Henry Allen Bullock, *A History of Negro Education in the South from 1619 to the Present* (Cambridge: Harvard University Press, 1967); William Preston Vaughn, *Schools For All: The Blacks and Public Education in the South, 1865–1877* (Lexington: University of Kentucky Press, 1974); Ronald E. Butchart, *Northern Schools, Southern Blacks, and Reconstruction: Freedmen's Education, 1862–1875* (Westport, Conn.: Greenwood Press, 1980); Robert C. Morris, *Reading, 'Riting, and Reconstruction: The Education of the Freedmen in the South, 1861–1870* (Chicago: University of Chicago Press, 1981). For a comparison with Georgia, see Jacqueline Jones, *Soldiers of Light and Love: Northern Teachers and Georgia Blacks, 1865–1873* (Chapel Hill: University of North Carolina Press, 1980). For a comparison with another oppressed Texas class, see Kenneth L. Stewart and Arnoldo De León, "Literacy among *Inmigrantes* in Texas, 1850–1890," *Latin American Research Review* 20 (1985): 180–187. For the development of higher education during this era, see Michael R. Heintze, *Private Black Colleges in Texas, 1865–1954* (College Station: Texas A&M University Press, 1985), 3–46; Lloyd K. Thompson, "The Origins and Development of Black Religious Colleges in East Texas" (Ph.D. diss., North Texas State University, 1976); Alton S. Hornsby, "The 'Colored Branch University' Issue in Texas—Prelude to *Sweatt* vs. *Painter,*" *Journal of Negro History* 61 (January 1976): 51–60; Merline Pitre, "The Evolution of a Black University in Texas," *Western Journal of Black Studies* 3 (Fall 1979): 216–223.

39. Crouch, "The Freedmen's Bureau and the 30th Sub-District in Texas," 20; James M. Smallwood, "Early 'Freedom Schools': Black Self-Help and Education in Reconstruction Texas: A Case Study," *Negro History Bulletin:* 41 (January–February 1978), 790; idem, "Black Education in Reconstruction Texas: The Contributions of the Freedmen's Bureau and Benevolent Societies," *East Texas Historical Journal* 19 (1981): 17; idem, *Time of Hope, Time of Despair,* 71–72. Chapter 4 in *Time of Hope, Time of Despair* and Smallwood's *ETHJ* article are essentially the same. It is interesting to note that Smallwood fails to cite Hornsby's piece on Bureau education.

40. Diane Neal and Thomas W. Kremm, "'What Shall We Do with the Negro?' The Freedmen's Bureau in Texas," *East Texas Historical Journal* 27 (Fall 1989): 24–26, 28–30, 32. Although this essay is an improvement over Elliott's older piece, and is based upon more Bureau archival material, it still allows past interpretations to dictate its framework. In addition, almost none of the newer literature on the Bureau is cited. The reason agents and civil officials frequently clashed is not because the Bureau agents did not understand the technicalities of the law but because civil authorities denied blacks their legal and constitutional rights.

41. Rupert Norval Richardson, Ernest Wallace, and Adrian N. Anderson, *Texas: The Lone Star State,* 3d ed. (Englewood Cliffs, N.J.: Prentice-Hall, 1970), 210–211, 221; 4th ed. (1981), 250–251; 5th ed. (1988), 233–234. In the 1981 edition, the authors relate the penitentiary episode in much the same manner as Fehrenbach, 252–253. In a very garbled account, Seymour V.

Connor, *Texas, a History* (New York: Crowell, 1971), states that the Bureau "sought to influence the erstwhile slaves" to vote Republican. Its "political stepchild," the "Loyal Union League, was designed to spread political propaganda among untutored Negro voters," 219, 228–230. It should be pointed out that the Union League was established long before Congress created the Bureau.

42. Robert A. Calvert and Arnoldo De Leon, *The History of Texas* (Arlington Heights, Ill.: Harlan Davidson, 1990), 133–134. Another new textbook does not mention the Bureau (David G. McComb, *Texas, a Modern History* [Austin: University of Texas Press, 1989]).

43. Owens, "Presidential Reconstruction in Texas," 382–383. Owens is clearly sympathetic to the Bureau's purposes and what it attempted to accomplish.

2. The Texas Assistant Commissioners

1. Thomas North, *Five Years in Texas; or, What You Did Not Hear during the War from January 1861 to January 1866: A Narrative of His Travels, Experiences, and Observations, in Texas and Mexico* (Cincinnati: Elm Street, 1871), 102–103; William L. Richter, "'It Is Best to Go in Strong-Handed': Army Occupation of Texas, 1865–1866," *Arizona and the West* 27 (Summer 1985): 114; Randolph B. Campbell, *An Empire for Slavery: The Peculiar Institution in Texas, 1821–1865* (Baton Rouge: Louisiana State University Press, 1989), 257; D. W. Meinig, *Imperial Texas: An Interpretive Essay in Cultural Geography* (Austin: University of Texas Press, 1969), 63–78; Terry G. Jordan, with John L. Bean, Jr., and William M. Holmes, *Texas, a Geography* (Boulder: University of Colorado Press, 1984), 48–79.

2. E. R. S. Canby to Ulysses S. Grant, May 26, 1865, p. 95; Assistant Adjutant General to N. P. Banks, May 26, 1865, p. 94; Canby to E. Kirby Smith, May 27, 1865, p. 101; C. T. Barrett (captain and aide de camp) to Dr. T. E. Hughes (New Orleans), May 31, 1865, pp. 130–131, Letters Sent (LS), Department of the Gulf (DG), all in vol. 61, Records of the United States Army Continental Commands, 1821–1920, Record Group (RG) 393 (National Archives); Joseph Howard Parks, *General Edmund Kirby Smith, C.S.A.* (Baton Rouge: Louisiana State University Press, 1954), 456–480; Robert L. Kerby, *Kirby Smith's Confederacy: The Trans-Mississippi South, 1863–1865* (New York: Columbia University Press, 1972), 377–434; Steven E. Woodworth, *Jefferson Davis and His Generals: The Failure of Confederate Command in the West* (Lawrence: University Press of Kansas, 1990), 305–316.

3. Canby to Grant, May 31, 1865, pp. 134–135; Canby to Ashbel Smith and W. P. Ballinger, May 29, 1865, pp. 115–116, DG, LS, all in vol. 61, RG 393; John C. Walker, "Reconstruction in Texas," *Southern Historical Society Papers* 24 (1896): 41–57; Charles W. Ramsdell, *Reconstruction in Texas* (New York: Columbia University Press, 1910), 36. On military operations in Texas, see Robert W. Shook, "Federal Occupation and Administration of Texas, 1865–1870" (Ph.D. diss., North Texas State University, 1970); idem, "The Federal Military in Texas, 1865–1870," *Texas Military History*

6 (Spring 1967): 3–53; William L. Richter, "The Army in Texas during Reconstruction, 1865–1870" (Ph.D. diss., Louisiana State University, 1970); idem, *The Army in Texas during Reconstruction, 1865–1870* (College Station: Texas A&M University Press, 1987); James E. Sefton, *The United States Army and Reconstruction, 1865–1877* (Baton Rouge: Louisiana State University Press, 1967).

4. *The War of the Rebellion: A Compilation of the Official Records of the Union and Confederate Armies,* 128 vols. (Washington, D.C.: Government Printing Office, 1880–1901), series I, vol. 48, pt. 2, p. 929 (hereafter *OR*); Randolph B. Campbell, "The End of Slavery in Texas: A Research Note," *Southwestern Historical Quarterly* 88 (July 1984): 71; *Flake's Daily Bulletin* (Galveston), June 29, 1865.

5. *Flake's Daily Bulletin,* June 29, 1865; William L. Richter, "The Army and the Negro during Texas Reconstruction, 1865–1870," *East Texas Historical Journal* 10 (Spring 1972): 7.

6. Thomas W. Conway (assistant commissioner [AC], Louisiana) to Oliver Otis Howard, June 5, 1865, p. 53; Conway to Howard, June 9, 1865, pp. 57–58; Conway to Francis George Shaw (president, National Freedmen's Relief Association), July 1, 1865, pp. 107–108, all in Louisiana, AC, LS, vol. 15, Records of the Bureau of Refugees, Freedmen, and Abandoned Lands, RG 105 (National Archives); William S. McFeely, *Yankee Stepfather: General O. O. Howard and the Freedmen* (New Haven: Yale University Press, 1968), 166–189. (Unless otherwise indicated all citations will be to the Louisiana or Texas Bureau records in RG 105.)

7. Conway to Howard, July 14, 1865, vol. 15, p. 150 (telegram); Howard to Conway, July 17, 1865, T-11, Box 7 (telegram); Howard to Conway, July 15, 1865, Louisiana, AC, Letters Received (LR), vol. 1, p. 566, all RG 105.

8. M. P. Hanson to Conway, September 18, 1865, p. 178; Benjamin L. Brisbane to Conway, September 27, 1865, p. 38, both in AC, LR, vol. 1; R. K. Diossy to Conway, September 8, 1865, AC, LR, D-48, Box 2, all in Louisiana, RG 105.

9. W. B. Stickney to Conway, July 2, 1865, S-28; August 1, 26, 1865, S-68, both in Louisiana, AC, LR, Box 6; Edgar M. Gregory to Howard, January 31, 1866, vol. 4, p. 23, Texas, AC, LS, all in RG 105; U.S. Bureau of the Census, Ninth Census (1870), *Population* (Washington, D.C.: Government Printing Office, 1872), I, 65.

10. Conway to Howard, September 2, 1865, p. 314; D. G. Fenno to Thomas Callahan, September 19, 1865, p. 348; Fenno to Willson Millar (Corpus Christi), September 6, 1865, pp. 319–320, Louisiana, AC, LS, vol. 15; Gregory to Howard, September 21, 1865, Texas, vol. 4, p. 6, all in RG 105.

11. *Houston Daily Telegraph,* June 15, 22, 1865. A study needs to be made of Texas attitudes at the close of the Civil War and continuing through the end of Reconstruction. This subject deserves special consideration for two reasons. First, because Texas was imbued with the Old South philosophy and all that implied for class and race relationships, it was little different from any other Deep South state whose culture was based upon slavery.

Second, and what makes the Lone Star State unusual, is that the area was also infused with a western perspective, where individuality, the law, and violence frequently came into conflict. All these aspects, which are intimately bound to the concept of honor, became prime elements in the violence committed upon blacks in the early years after the war. For an outstanding beginning, see Nancy Cohen-Lack, "'An Irresistible Power to Which All Must Bow': Emancipation, Free Labor, and National Sovereignty in Texas, 1865" (Seminar paper, Columbia University, 1990).

12. [Oliver Otis Howard], *The Autobiography of Oliver Otis Howard*, 2 vols. (New York: Baker and Taylor, 1908), II, 217–218; McFeely, *Yankee Stepfather*, 60–61, 68; Richter, "The Army and the Negro during Texas Reconstruction," 7.

13. Mark Mayo Boatner III, *The Civil War Dictionary* (New York: David McKay, 1959), 358; Francis B. Heitman, *Historical Register and Dictionary of the United States Army*, 2 vols. (Washington, D.C.: 1903), I, 477; Walter Prescott Webb and H. Bailey Carroll, eds., "Edgar M. Gregory," *The Handbook of Texas*, 2 vols. (Austin: Texas State Historical Association, 1952), I, 734; Richter, *The Army in Texas*, 35; George R. Bentley, *A History of the Freedmen's Bureau* (Philadelphia: University of Pennsylvania Press, 1955), 60, 121. Gregory died in 1871.

14. Gregory to Benjamin G. Harris, January 20, 1866, vol. 4, pp. 109–113.

15. Gregory to Howard, September 21, 1865, p. 6; Gregory to W. J. Jones, September 30, 1865, p. 8, both in vol. 4.

16. Gregory to Harris, January 20, 1866, vol. 4, pp. 105–113.

17. Circular no. 1, October 12, 1865, vol. 1, pp. 301–303; Gregory to Howard, October 31, 1865, pp. 37–38; Chauncey C. Morse to James L. Greene, October 25, 1865, p. 30; Morse to J. W. McConoughey, January 19, 1866, p. 98; Morse to B. J. Arnold, January 25, 1866, p. 106, all in vol. 4; Richter, "The Army and the Negro during Texas Reconstruction," 11.

18. Thomas Callahan (assistant superintendent of Freedmen's Bureau, Shreveport) to Conway, September 6, 1865, Louisiana, AC, LR, C-19, Box 7, RG 105.

19. Calahan to Conway, October 2, 1865, C-70, Box 2; September 6, 1865, C-19, Box 7, both in Louisiana, AC, LR, RG 105. On race and class, see Armstead L. Robinson, "Beyond the Realm of Social Consensus: New Meanings of Reconstruction for American History," *Journal of American History* 68 (September 1981): 276–297; Barbara Jeanne Fields, "The Nineteenth-Century American South: History and Theory," *Plantation Society in the Americas* 2 (April 1983): 7–27; idem, "Ideology and Race in American History," *Race and Reconstruction: Essays in Honor of C. Vann Woodward*, ed. J. Morgan Kousser and James M. McPherson (New York: Oxford University Press, 1982), 143–177, where Fields asserts that "class is a concept that we can locate both at the level of objective reality and at the level of social appearances. Race is a concept that we can locate at the level of appearances only," 151. She underestimates the impact of race, however.

20. Andrew J. Hamilton to Andrew Johnson, July 24, 1865, Andrew

Johnson Papers (Manuscript Division, Library of Congress); Gregory to Howard, December 9, 1865, vol. 4, pp. 65–70. Into 1866 and beyond, some Texas planters were still discussing a gradual emancipation of three to five years; Thomas P. Collins (Crockett, Texas) to Thaddeus Stevens, February 19, 1866, Container 6, Thaddeus Stevens Papers (Manuscript Division, Library of Congress).

21. Gregory to Howard, December 9, 1865, vol. 4, pp. 65–70; Claude Elliott, "The Freedmen's Bureau in Texas," *Southwestern Historical Quarterly* 56 (July 1952): 3.

22. Gregory to Howard, October 31, 1865, pp. 37–38; December 9, 1865, pp. 65–70; April 18, 1866, 192–195; William H. Sinclair to John F. Brown, March 8, 1866, p. 156, all in vol. 4; Bentley, *A History of the Freedmen's Bureau*, 82. For Gregory's trouble with the *Telegraph*, see Morse to Byron Porter, January 26, 1866, vol. 4, p. 107.

23. Gregory to Harris, January 20, 1866, vol. 4, pp. 109–113.

24. Ibid.

25. Gregory to Howard, January 31, 1866, vol. 4, pp. 122–125. Gregory defined "social disruptions" as theft, idleness, and vagrancy.

26. Gregory to Howard, April 18, 1866, vol. 4, pp. 192–195. See note 3 for the military and the number of troops stationed in Texas during this period.

27. Gregory to Howard, April 18, 1866, vol. 4, pp. 192–195.

28. Circular no. 2, December 5, 1865, pp. 304–305; Circular no. 4, December 27, 1865, p. 307; Circular no. 5, February 1, 1866, p. 308; Circular no. 6, March 3, 1866, p. 309, all in vol. 1; Gregory to Howard, January 31, 1866, p. 124; William H. Sinclair to William Baxter, March 9, 1866, p. 158; Sinclair to Philip Howard, April 17, 1866, p. 189; Joseph B. Kiddoo to Howard, June 26, 1866, pp. 259–260; June 26, 1866, pp. 264–265; Kiddoo to Fullerton and Steedman, July 11, 1866, pp. 271–272, all in vol. 4; Bentley, *A History of the Freedmen's Bureau*, 131, 137; John A. Carpenter, *Sword and Olive Branch: Oliver Otis Howard* (Pittsburgh: University of Pittsburgh Press, 1964), 99.

29. Cyrus B. Comstock Diary, February 11, 1866, Cyrus B. Comstock Papers (Manuscript Division, Library of Congress); P. H. Sheridan to Howard, December 20, 1865; H. G. Wright to Sheridan, December 18, 1865, vol. 2, both in Commissioner's Files, Letters Received; Sinclair to William Longworth, March 23, 1866, vol. 4, p. 176. For his own defense, see Gregory to Howard, March 17, 1866, vol. 4, p. 169; McFeely, *Yankee Stepfather*, 247, 292. See also Brooks D. Simpson, "Grant's Tour of the South Revisited," *Journal of Southern History* 54 (August 1988): 425–448; Howard K. Beale, *The Critical Year: A Study of Andrew Johnson and Reconstruction* (New York: Harcourt Brace Jovanovich, 1930), 157.

30. Although I am not citing all the correspondence, there are letters in the Commissioner's Files, RG 105, and the Andrew Johnson Papers (Library of Congress) that clearly delineate the opposition to Gregory and agitation for his dismissal. See also Bentley, *A History of the Freedmen's Bureau*, 121; McFeely, *Yankee Stepfather*, 68–69. Gregory believed that the "re-

spectable gentlemen" belonged "to that class of our people who do not readily understand the rights of others, until their eyes are opened by the discipline of the law. Hence these tears."

31. Bentley, *A History of the Freedmen's Bureau*, 131, 137; Carpenter, *Sword and Olive Branch*, 99.

32. Richter, "The Army and the Negro during Texas Reconstruction," 7.

33. Ibid., 7–8. Gregory's efforts in behalf of free labor and his abilities can be compared with what occurred in Alabama, Mississippi, and Georgia in Kenneth B. White, "Wager Swayne: Racist or Realist?" *Alabama Review* 31 (April 1978): 92–109; Paul A. Cimbala, "The 'Talisman Power': Davis Tillson, the Freedmen's Bureau, and Free Labor in Reconstruction Georgia, 1865–1866," *Civil War History* 28 (June 1982): 153–171; George D. Humphrey, "The Failure of the Mississippi Freedmen's Bureau in Black Labor Relations, 1865–1867," *Journal of Mississippi History* 45 (February 1983): 23–37.

34. Kiddoo to Howard, May 14, 1866, pp. 219–220; May 28, 1866, p. 229, both in vol. 4. Kiddoo requested that twenty-five men from a black regiment be detailed for duty at headquarters; Kiddoo to C. H. Whittelsey, May 14, 1866, vol. 4, p. 220.

35. Boatner, *The Civil War Dictionary*, 458–459; Heitman, *Historical Register and Dictionary of the United States Army*, I, 477; Richter, *The Army in Texas*, 40; Bentley, *A History of the Freedmen's Bureau*, 121, 216; "Joseph B. Kiddoo," in *Appleton's Cyclopaedia of American Biography*, ed. James Grant Wilson and John Fiske (New York: Appleton, 1887), III, 532–533. Kiddoo is not mentioned in *The Handbook of Texas*.

36. Kiddoo to Howard, June 26, 1866, pp. 259–260; June 28, 1866, pp. 264–265, both in vol. 4.

37. Kiddoo to Generals Fullerton and Steedman, July 11, 1866, vol. 4, pp. 271–272. Joseph Scott Fullerton, a confidant of Howard's, and James B. Steedman, a Democratic general hostile to blacks, were chosen by Johnson to "investigate the Bureau and to expose the members who reportedly mistreated Negroes in order to convince the nation that there were justifiable reasons for terminating the agency" (McFeely, *Yankee Stepfather*, 247).

38. Kiddoo to Howard, July 23, 1866, vol. 4, pp. 288–294.

39. Kiddoo to Howard, August 8, 1866, pp. 303–305; July 23, 1866, pp. 288–294, both in vol. 4.

40. Kiddoo to Howard, July 23, 1866, vol. 4, pp. 293–294.

41. Ibid., 288–294.

42. Ibid.

43. Ibid., May 14, 1866, p. 220; August 20, 1866, p. 318; October 23, 1866, pp. 361–362; December 24, 1866, p. 436; December 26, 1866, pp. 441–442; January 5, 1867, p. 468, all in vol. 4; Bentley, *A History of the Freedmen's Bureau*, 158; Theodore Brantner Wilson, *The Black Codes of the South* (University: University of Alabama Press, 1965), 109–110; Claude H. Nolen, *The Negroes Image in the South: The Anatomy of White Supremacy* (Lexington: University of Kentucky Press, 1967), 158. For a comparison of

codes, see Donald G. Nieman, "The Freedmen's Bureau and the Mississippi Black Code," *Journal of Mississippi History* 40 (May 1978): 91–118.

44. Kiddoo to Howard, July 23, 1866, vol. 4, p. 293.

45. Kiddoo to Howard, January 5, 1867, pp. 467–468; January 7, 1867, pp. 475–476; Kiddoo to Reverend Bishop Simpson, January 7, 1867, pp. 472–473, all in vol. 4.

46. Kiddoo to Howard, July 23, 1866, vol. 4, p. 294. Kiddoo also believed that education would influence blacks to attribute more sacredness to marriage. Their domestic relations "should be more carefully guarded" and "ties of consanguinity made more affectionate." Planters claimed that the former slaves had "no family relation manifesting itself" when it came to the care of the sick and suffering. Slavery, the assistant commissioner wrote, "blunted the moral and better instincts of negroes socially and intellectually." On Wheelock, see Charles Kassel, "Educating the Slave—A Forgotten Chapter of Civil War History," *Open Court* 31 (April 1927): 239–256; idem, "Edwin Miller Wheelock," *Open Court* 34 (September 1930): 564–569.

47. Kiddoo to Howard, August 20, 1866, vol. 4, pp. 318–319.

48. For the general state of the educational program and its advancement in Texas, see volumes 14–17, 19–23, and boxes 22–33.

49. Kiddoo to Howard, August 8, 1866, pp. 303–305; August 20, 1866, pp. 318–319; January 2, 1867, p. 456, all in vol. 4.

50. Kiddoo to Governor James W. Throckmorton, September 13, 1866, pp. 335–336; January 3, 1867, pp. 461–462; January 17, 1867, p. 495; Kiddoo to Howard, October 30, 1866, pp. 364–365, all in vol. 4. There were also tensions over the torching of Brenham (see William L. Richter, "The Brenham Fire of 1866: A Texas Reconstruction Atrocity," *Louisiana Studies* 14 [Fall 1975]: 287–314).

51. S. H. Lathrop (acting AC) to Howard, December 17, 1866 (telegram), p. 416; Kiddoo to Howard, December 19, 1866 (telegram), p. 420; December 21, 1866, pp. 430–432; December 24, 1866, pp. 435–436; Kiddoo to Mr. Richardson (editor, *Galveston News*), December 19, 1866, p. 421; Kiddoo to Charles Griffin (commander, District of Texas), December 19, 1866, p. 422, all in vol. 4.

52. Kiddoo to Griffin, January 25, 1867, p. 506; Kiddoo to Howard, January 25, 1867, pp. 506–507, January 28, 1867 (telegram), p. 508, all in vol. 4.

53. Byron Porter to John Scott, December 9, 1865, p. 65; Morse to Stanton Weaver, January 15, 1866, p. 92; February 12, 1866, p. 135; Morse to O. M. Swingley, January 16, 1866, p. 95; Morse to Samuel C. Sloan, January 22, 1866, p. 103; Gregory to Howard, January 31, 1866, pp. 122–125; Kiddoo to Howard, May 28, 1866, p. 229, all in vol. 4; Bentley, *A History of the Freedmen's Bureau*, 148, 150; McFeely, *Yankee Stepfather*, 207.

54. Carpenter, *Sword and Olive Branch*, 98; John and LaWanda Cox, "General O. O. Howard and the 'Misrepresented Bureau,'" *Journal of Southern History* 19 (November 1953): 428.

55. Boatner, *The Civil War Dictionary*, 361.

56. Ezra J. Warner, *Generals in Blue: Lives of the Union Commanders* (Baton Rouge: Louisiana State University Press, 1964), 190–191; Boatner, *The Civil War Dictionary*, 361; Heitman, *Historical Register and Dictionary of the United States Army*, I, 478; Hugo Ellis, "Charles Griffin," *The Handbook of Texas*, I, 736; William L. Richter, "Tyrant and Reformer: General Griffin Reconstructs Texas, 1865–1866," *Prologue* 10 (Winter 1978): 225–241; Richter, *The Army in Texas*, 79–115.

57. Griffin to Howard, July 1, 1867, vol. 5, pp. 104–109.

58. Ibid.

59. Griffin to Howard, July 1, 1867, vol. 5, pp. 104–109. For an explanation of this system, which is indeed confusing, see John David Smith, "More than Slaves, Less than Freedmen: The 'Share Wages' Labor System during Reconstruction," *Civil War History* 26 (September 1980): 256–266. Blacks also favored the share system, as it gave them more independence and decision-making power but not as much as sharecropping.

60. Griffin to Howard, July 1, 1867, vol. 5, pp. 104–109.

61. Griffin to Howard, July 11, 1867, vol. 4, pp. 101–102.

62. Ibid.

63. Griffin to Howard, July 1, 1867, vol. 5, pp. 104–109.

64. Ibid.

65. Ibid., 107.

66. Ibid.

67. Griffin to Howard, February 12, 1867, vol. 4, p. 519; July 1, 1867, vol. 5, p. 107.

68. Griffin to Howard, July 1, 1867, p. 109; J. T. Kirkman to Abert, July 23, 1867, pp. 124–125, both in vol. 5.

69. Griffin to Howard, July 1, 1867, vol. 5, pp. 107–108.

70. Griffin to Howard, May 1, 1867, pp. 34–36; July 1, 1867, p. 108, both in vol. 5.

71. Griffin to Mr. Yard (president, Howard Association), August 23, 1867, p. 140; Griffin to Howard, August 26, 1867, p. 142; Charles Garretson to Howard, September 13, 1867, p. 145; September 15, 1867, p. 145; Garretson to T. M. K. Smith (agent, Nacogdoches), October 15, 1867, pp. 156–157, all in vol. 5.

72. Joseph J. Reynolds to Howard, November 20, 1867, vol. 5, pp. 183–184.

73. Boatner, *The Civil War Dictionary*, 694–695; Louise Kelly, "Joseph Jones Reynolds," *The Handbook of Texas*, II, 466; Heitman, *Historical Register and Dictionary of the United States Army*, I, 825; Warner, *Generals in Blue*, 397–398; Zenobia Self, "Court-Martial of J. J. Reynolds," *Military Affairs* 37 (April 1973): 52–56; Richter, *The Army in Texas*, 119–196. Richter writes extensively and very negatively about Reynolds as a military commander and politician in his numerous works on the U.S. army in Reconstruction Texas.

74. Reynolds to Howard, November 20, 1867, vol. 5, pp. 183–184, 190–191.

75. Ibid., 190–192; Roger L. Ransom and Richard Sutch, *One Kind of*

Freedom: The Economic Consequences of Emancipation (New York: Cambridge University Press, 1977), 56; Smith, "More than Slaves, Less than Freedmen," 256–257. Under the share wages system, blacks did not control the land as they did with sharecropping. Thus, they generally opposed share wages.

76. Reynolds to Howard, November 20, 1867, vol. 5, p. 191. Reynolds' statement about gang labor on the farms is interesting because many historians believe that by this time it had been done away with due to vehement opposition by the freedmen. It may have been slower to disappear in Texas because of the state's large area and isolation.

77. Reynolds to Howard, November 20, 1867, vol. 5, p. 191.

78. Richardson to Howard, March 21, 1868, vol. 5, pp. 279–280.

79. Ibid.

80. Ibid.

81. Joseph Welch (superintendent of education) to Reynolds, October 17, 1868, vol. 5, p. 439.

82. Reynolds to Howard, November 20, 1867, p. 192; April 14, 1868, pp. 291–292, both in vol. 5.

83. Ibid.; Richardson to Nesbit B. Jenkins (agent, Wharton), February 19, 1868, p. 252; Reynolds to George S. Startsuff (AAAG, Fifth Military District, New Orleans), February 20, 1868, pp. 254–255; Richardson to R. Chandler (assistant secretary for civil affairs, New Orleans), March 11, 1868, pp. 271–272, all in vol. 5. A "representation of the condition of affairs" had been made to Governor Throckmorton, but it had "failed to impress upon him the fact that any wrong was being done to this unfortunate race of people."

84. Reynolds to Howard, September 19, 1868, p. 408; C. S. Roberts (AAAG) to Henry C. Lacey (agent, Crockett), September 25, 1868, p 416, both in vol. 5; Richter, *The Army in Texas*, 139–171. Much better on politics is Carl M. Moneyhon, *Republicanism in Reconstruction Texas* (Austin: University of Texas Press, 1980).

85. Reynolds to Howard, October 20, 1868, vol. 5, pp. 435–436.

86. Ibid.

87. Ibid.

88. W. H. Sinclair to Governor E. M. Pease, November 15, 1868, Pease-Graham-Niles Family Papers, Austin–Travis County Collection (Austin Public Library, Austin). Richter posits the idea in a very strained argument that Sinclair "was the man who ran the show in the name of the assistant commissioners, established a crucial link between the men at headquarters and the men in the field, and, after his Bureau service ended, became a selfless contributor to the improvement and development of his adopted southern home" (William L. Richter, "Who Was the Real Head of the Texas Freedmen's Bureau? The Role of Brevet Colonel William H. Sinclair as Acting Assistant Inspector General," *Military History of the Southwest* 20 [Fall 1990]: 121–156).

89. Gregory to Howard, October 31, 1865, vol. 4, pp. 37–38; and generally volumes 1, 4, and 5 for the policies of the other assistant commissioners. General E. R. S. Canby served very briefly in 1869 as assistant com-

missioner but the Bureau had essentially completed its work (see Max L. Heyman, *Prudent Soldier: A Biography of Major General E. R. S. Canby, 1817–1873* [Glendale, Calif.: Clark, 1959], 333–339).

90. Reynolds to Howard, April 14, 1868, vol. 5, p. 293. See also volumes 4 and 5, letters sent by the assistant commissioners for their complaints; Bentley, *A History of the Freedmen's Bureau*, 161, 167; Carpenter, *Sword and Olive Branch*, 128, 134; McFeely, *Yankee Stepfather*, 271; Paul Skeels Peirce, *The Freedmen's Bureau: A Chapter in the History of Reconstruction*, Studies in Sociology, Economics, Politics, and History, vol. III, no. 1 (Iowa City: University of Iowa, 1904), 144; Cox and Cox, "General O. O. Howard and the 'Misrepresented Bureau,'" 455; Sefton, *The United States Army and Reconstruction*, 90, 147, 191–192, 221.

91. Edgar M. Sneed, "A Historiography of Reconstruction in Texas: Some Myths and Problems," *Southwestern Historical Quarterly* 72 (April 1969): 445; Criminal Offences Committed in the State of Texas, AC, Austin, vols. 11–13; Barry A. Crouch, "A Spirit of Lawlessness: White Violence, Texas Blacks, 1865–1868," *Journal of Social History* 18 (Winter 1984): 217–232; *New York Times*, November 7, 1868, p. 1; Michael Wallace, "The Uses of Violence in American History," *American Scholar* 40 (Winter 1970–1971): 86. In addition, see George A. Custer to Zachariah Chandler, January 8, 14, 1866, vol. 3; James S. Brisbin to Chandler, October 5, 1866, vol. 4, both in Zachariah Chandler Papers (Manuscript Division, Library of Congress); William Alexander (attorney general, Texas) to Salmon P. Chase, December 21, 1865, vol. 96; July 17, 1866; December 17, 1866, both in vol. 97, all in Salmon P. Chase Papers (Manuscript Division, Library of Congress); John A. Carpenter, "Atrocities in the Reconstruction Period," *Journal of Negro History* 47 (October 1962): 234–247.

92. The writer found only one instance of a subassistant commissioner forming a Union League, although there were undoubtedly more; Edward Miller (agent, Millican) to Kirkman, July 29, 1867, AC, Operations Reports, Box 14. For a comparison, see George R. Bentley, "The Political Activity of the Freedmen's Bureau in Florida," *Florida Historical Quarterly* 28 (July 1949): 28–37.

3. The Texas Bureau in Microcosm

1. Chauncey C. Morse (acting assistant adjutant general [AAAG]) to H. Seymour Hall (agent, Marshall), December 20, 1865, vol. 4, p. 75, Bureau of Refugees, Freedmen, and Abandoned Lands, Texas, Record Group (RG) 105 (National Archives). Marshall was some seventy miles distant from Tyler, the county seat of Smith County. An unsatisfactory overview is Ross Nathaniel Dudney, Jr., "Texas Reconstruction: The Role of the Bureau of Refugees, Freedmen, and Abandoned Lands, 1865–1870, Smith County (Tyler), Texas" (M.A. thesis, Texas A&I University, 1986). Unless otherwise noted, all references will be to the Texas Bureau records in RG 105.

2. See chapter 2.

3. U.S. Bureau of the Census, *Compendium to the Population Census*

Schedule, 1870 (Washington, D.C.: Government Printing Office, 1872), 65–66; General and Special Orders, Circulars and Rosters of Officers, 1865–1868, vol. 9, pp. 376–377; David L. Montgomery (agent, Tyler) to J. T. Kirkman (AAAG), April 24, 1867, vol. 162, p. 12. County ranking for 1870 by black and white population and black percentage of total inhabitants: Smith, 5/12/43%; Henderson, 56/43/24%; Wood, 62/35/18%; Van Zandt, 77/34/11%; and Cherokee, 31/21/30%. For a comparison, Charles E. Culver, headquartered at Cotton Gin, supervised the Thirty-eighth Subdistrict, which included Freestone, Limestone, and Navarro counties, an area covering 2,800 square miles. County ranking for 1870 by black and white population and black percentage of total inhabitants: Freestone, 29/49/41%; Limestone, 51/25/22%; and Navarro, 45/27/25%; totals; 18,067 whites, 7,532 blacks, who composed 29%; James M. Smallwood, "Charles E. Culver, a Reconstruction Agent in Texas: The Work of Local Freedmen's Bureau Agents and the Black Community," *Civil War History* 27 (December 1981): 350–361. My figures do not agree with Smallwood's.

4. The late John A. Carpenter shared his extensive notes on the backgrounds of the various Texas agents. The material is from the pension files, the compiled military service records of the individuals, and the appointments, commissions, and personnel branch files. The first is in the Records of the Veterans' Administration, RG 15; and the latter two are in the Records of the Adjutant General's Office, RG 94, all in the National Archives. See also vol. 9 of the Texas Bureau records for the rosters of the Texas agents and when they served. (In the following citations, the agents of the Thirtieth Subdistrict will be abbreviated by their initials; DLM, GB, LCB, HJ, and DCB.) Brown later served as a Bureau agent at Paris; see William L. Richter, "'The Revolver Rules the Day!' Colonel DeWitt C. Brown and the Freedmen's Bureau in Paris, Texas, 1867–1868," *Southwestern Historical Quarterly* 93 (January 1990): 303–332.

5. DLM to Kirkman, April 24, 1867, vol. 162, pp. 11–12.

6. Ibid.

7. Ibid. For the precincts established and the men selected, see DLM to Kirkman, April 25, 1867, vol. 162, pp. 12–14.

8. DLM to A. H. M. Taylor (AAAG, District of Texas), July 1, 1867, p. 25; July 8, 1867, p. 26; July 15, 1867, pp. 31–32, all in vol. 162. For the political background, see Charles W. Ramsdell, *Reconstruction in Texas* (New York: Columbia University Press, 1910), 161–163; John Pressley Carrier, "A Political History of Texas during the Reconstruction, 1865–1874" (Ph.D. diss., Vanderbilt University, 1971), 156–248; Carl M. Moneyhon, *Republicanism in Reconstruction Texas* (Austin: University of Texas Press, 1980), 3–81.

9. DLM to Kirkman, April 30, 1867, vol. 162, pp. 14–15.

10. DLM to Kirkman, July 9, 1867, vol. 162, p. 29 (also in AC, Operations Report (OR), M-426, Box 13).

11. LCB to Kirkman, July 31, 1867, pp. 36–37 (also, AC, OR, B-243, Box 14); DLM to Kirkman, September 4, 1867, p. 44; DLM to Charles Garretson (AAAG), October 31, 1867, p. 71 (also, AC, OR, M-71, Box 15); DLM to J. P. Richardson (AAAG), November 28, 1867, p. 81; DLM to Richardson, De-

cember 31, 1867, pp. 94–95 (also AC, OR, M-126, Box 16); DLM to Richardson, February 5, 1868, pp. 108–109 (also AC, OR, M-150, Box 16); DLM to Richardson, February 29, 1868, pp. 113–114 (also AC, OR, M-168, Box 17), all, except where noted, in vol. 162.

12. GB to Richardson, March 31, 1868, pp. 127–128 (also AC, OR, B-116, Box 17); GB to Richardson, April 30, 1868, p. 141 (also AC, OR, B-123, Box 17), in vol. 162, except where noted. For an intensive look at Barrett, see Barry A. Crouch, "View from Within: Letters of Gregory Barrett, Freedmen's Bureau Agent," *Chronicles of Smith County, Texas* 12 (Winter 1973): 13–26.

13. GB to Charles A. Vernou (AAAG), June 1, 1868, p. 156 (also AC, OR, B-161, Box 18); June 30, 1868, pp. 187–188 (also AC, OR, B-176, Box 18); August 1, 1868, pp. 208–209 (also AC, OR, Box 18); August 31, 1868, p. 219 (also AC, OR, B-218, Box 18); September 30, 1868, pp. 232–233 (also AC, OR, B-233, Box 19), all in vol. 162, except where noted.

14. Eric Foner, *Reconstruction: America's Unfinished Revolution, 1863–1877* (New York: Harper and Row, 1988), 168. See also his *Nothing but Freedom: Emancipation and Its Legacy* (Baton Rouge: Louisiana State University Press, 1983); idem, "Reconstruction and the Crisis of Free Labor," in *Politics and Ideology in the Age of the Civil War* (New York: Oxford University Press, 1980), 97–127; Gerald David Jaynes, *Branches without Roots: Genesis of the Black Working Class in the American South, 1862–1882* (New York: Oxford University Press, 1986). The literature on the economic aspects of Southern Reconstruction is vast and confusing. Foner analyzes, interprets, and synthesizes it as well as anyone.

15. DLM to Richardson, November 16, 1867, p. 77; DLM to Willis Jones (justice of the peace [JP], Flora), October 14, 1867, p. 66, both in vol. 162; DCB to [Garretson?], August 23, 1867, vol. 161, pp. 22–23.

16. DLM to Kirkman, April 30, 1867, p. 14; July 8, 1867, p. 26; July 9, 1867, p. 29; DCB to John H. Morrison (agent, Palestine), August 31, 1867, p. 41; DCB to Edward Collins (agent, Brenham), September 5, 1867, p. 47; DLM to A. G. Malloy (agent, Marshall), September 9, 1867, p. 48; DLM to Anthony M. Bryant (agent, Sherman), November 27, 1867, p. 78; DLM to Malloy, November 25, 1867, pp. 78–79; GB to Vernou, June 30, 1868, p. 186; August 31, 1868, pp. 219–220, all in vol. 162.

17. GB to Agent, Marshall, June 24, 1868, p. 179; GB to Vernou, June 30, 1868, p. 186; August 31, 1868, pp. 219–220, all in vol. 162. For the many complaints that blacks brought to the agents about not getting paid for their labor, see volumes 163 and 164, which deal specifically with this type of complaint.

18. DLM to Mr. Stevenson (Henderson County), March 31, 1868, vol. 162, p. 124.

19. GB to Agent, Marshall, June 24, 1868, p. 179; GB to Vernou, June 30, 1868, p. 186; August 31, 1868, pp. 219–220, all in vol. 162.

20. LCB to Kirkman, July 12, 1867, p. 31; DLM to Garretson, October 8, 1867, pp. 53–54; GB to Richardson, April 30, 1868, pp. 138–139, all in vol. 162; Richardson to GB, May 12, 1868, vol. 161, pp. 32–33. The agents also encountered rather unusual circumstances as when Montgomery met a

man who claimed to be a Bureau agent but turned out to be an imposter. He was either cheating blacks out of their profits or was allied with the planters in enforcing strict labor laws. Montgomery informed another agent that the imposter should be arrested; DLM to Morrison, June 14, 1867, vol. 162, pp. 18–19.

21. DLM to Kirkman, August 9, 1867, p. 39; DLM to Garretson, October 9, 1867, pp. 54–56; GB to Roberts, April 30, 1868, p. 143, all in vol. 162.

22. DLM to Taylor, June 21, 1867, vol. 162, pp. 23–24.

23. Ibid.

24. Ibid.

25. GB to Vernou, July 18, 1868, vol. 162, pp. 192, 195; Vernou to GB, July 28, 1868, p. 40; Endorsement, GB, p. 41, both in vol. 161.

26. DLM to Kirkman, July 9, 1867, p. 29 (also AC, OR, M-426, Box 13); DLM to Taylor, May 31, 1867, p. 17, both in vol. 162.

27. A case in point is J. M. Hoge to GB, April 28, 1868, Box 44.

28. DLM to Kirkman, July 9, 1867, pp. 28–29 (also AC, OR, M-426, Box 13); DLM to Taylor, May 31, 1867, p. 17, both in vol. 162. Cases were also referred to other agents; DLM to Morrison, July 9, 1867, vol. 162, p. 30.

29. DLM to Kirkman, July 9, 1867, vol. 162, p. 28; James Pinkston (JP, Henderson County) to GB, May 5, 1868, Box 44. The tally of total cases is my own.

30. DLM to Kirkman, September 4, 1867, p. 44; DLM to Garretson, October 31, 1867, p. 72; November 4, 1867, pp. 72–73; DLM to Richardson, November 28, 1867, p. 79; LCB to Malloy, August 6, 1867, p. 38; LCB to Kirkman, July 31, 1867, p. 36, all in vol. 162. In the last letter cited, a man threatened to shoot Bootes if he delivered the summons.

31. DLM to Richardson, January 7, 1868, pp. 95–96; DLM to J. P. Ewing (JP, Cherokee County), January 10, 1868, p. 100, both in vol. 162; Sam L. Earle (judge, Ninth Judicial District) to DLM, December 30, 1867, Box 44; David M. Jordan, *Winfield Scott Hancock: A Soldier's Life* (Bloomington: Indiana University Press, 1988), 200–212.

32. GB to Richardson, March 31, 1868, vol. 162, pp. 128–129. Under state law the defendant's lawyer was allowed to choose the jurors.

33. GB to Richardson, March 31, 1868, p. 130; GB to Malloy, April 7, 1868, p. 132, both in vol. 162.

34. GB to Richardson, March 31, 1868, p. 130; GB to Malloy, April 7, 1868, p. 132; GB to Squire Shuford (JP, Quitman), April 21, 1868, p. 136, all in vol. 162.

35. GB to Richardson, April 21, 1868, vol. 162, pp. 137–138.

36. Ibid.

37. Ibid., April 30, 1868, vol. 162, p. 142.

38. GB to the Sheriffs of Van Zandt, Henderson, Wood, and Rusk Counties, April 23, 1868, p. 138; GB to Richardson, April 30, 1868, p. 142, both in vol. 162.

39. GB to Thomas Clairbourne (sheriff, Cherokee County), June 16, 1868, vol. 162, p. 175; Clairbourne to GB, June 10, 1868, Box 44.

40. Ibid.

41. GB to the Sheriffs of Van Zandt, Henderson, Wood, and Rusk Counties, April 23, 1868, p. 138; GB to Richardson, April 30, 1868, p. 142, both in vol. 162.

42. GB to the Sheriff of Cherokee County, May 6, 1868, p. 147; May 25, 1868, p. 151; GB to Vernou, June 1, 1868, pp. 157–158; June 6, 1868, p. 164; GB to the Sheriff of Wood County, June 12, 1868, p. 171, all in vol. 162.

43. GB to William Davis (sheriff, Henderson County), June 10, 1868, pp. 170–171; GB to Thomas Clairbourne (sheriff, Cherokee County), June 16, 1868, p. 175, both in vol. 162.

44. GB to Vernou, June 27, 1868, p. 189; July 25, 1868, pp. 200–201, both in vol. 162.

45. GB to Vernou, June 6, 1868, vol. 162, pp. 165–167; Statement of Ann Doomis, June 6, 1868, B-160, AC, LR, Box 6. On the development of black juries, see the significant essay by Donald G. Nieman, "Black Political Power and Criminal Justice: Washington County, Texas, 1868–1884," *Journal of Southern History* 55 (August 1989): 391–420.

46. GB to Vernou, June 8, 1868, vol. 162, pp. 167–169.

47. Ibid.

48. Ibid. See also Barry A. Crouch and L. J. Schultz, "Crisis in Color: Racial Separation in Texas during Reconstruction," *Civil War History* 16 (March 1970): 37–49. A study of Texas blacks and the legal system during Reconstruction would begin to clarify many misperceptions.

49. John C. Hendrick (agent, Montgomery, Ala.) to DLM, December 9, 1867, Box 44. There are also numerous letters in volume 162 that deal with the problems of reuniting black families. For background on the slave family, see Randolph B. Campbell, "The Slave Family in Antebellum Texas," Social Sciences Symposium, 1988, *The American Family* (Victoria: Victoria College, 1988), 1–28; idem, *An Empire for Slavery: The Peculiar Institution in Texas, 1821–1865* (Baton Rouge: Louisiana State University Press, 1989), 153–169.

50. Barry A. Crouch and Larry Madaras, "Reconstructing Black Families: Perspectives from the Texas Freedmen's Bureau Records," *Prologue* 18 (Summer 1986): 109–122; reprinted in *Our Family, Our Town: Essays on Family and Local History Sources in the National Archives*, comp. Timothy Walch (Washington, D.C.: 1987), 156–167; James M. Smallwood, "Emancipation and the Black Family: A Case Study in Texas," *Social Science Quarterly* 57 (March 1977): 849–857; idem, "From Slavery to Freedom: Smith County's Black Community in 1870, a Statistical Overview," *Chronicles of Smith County, Texas* 18 (Summer 1979): 58–61; idem, *Time of Hope, Time of Despair,* 111–117. Black families may not have been as stable as many have suggested. See Barry A. Crouch, "The Struggle for Stability: The Texas Black Family, the Freedmen's Bureau, and the Law" (MS, 1991).

51. DLM to Matthew and Samuel Rogers (Kaufman County), March 30, 1867, p. 9; DLM to Kirkman, April 10, 1867, pp. 9–10, both in vol. 162; John T. Carrier, "The Era of Reconstruction, 1865–1875," in *Tyler and Smith*

County, Texas: An Historical Survey, ed. Robert W. Glover (Tyler: Walsworth, 1976), 57–79.

52. DLM to Kirkman, July 9, 1867, p. 29; July 23, 1867, pp. 33–34; DLM to Anthony M. Bryant (agent, Sherman), July 9, 1867, p. 30, all in vol. 162; DLM to AAAG, July 1, 1867, pp. 18–19; Kirkman, Endorsement, p. 19, both in vol. 161.

53. DLM to Kirkman, April 10, 1867, pp. 9–10; July 9, 1867, p. 29; July 23, 1867, pp. 33–34; DLM to Matthew and Samuel Rogers (Kaufman County), March 30, 1867, p. 9; DLM to Bryant (agent, Sherman), July 9, 1867, p. 30, all in vol. 162; DLM to Headquarters, July 1, 1867, pp. 18–19; Kirkman, Endorsement, p. 19, both in vol. 161.

54. Ibid.

55. DLM to Kirkman, July 8, 1867, p. 26; DLM to Jess Rasbury (county judge, Smith County), January 8, 1868, p. 99; DLM to Richardson, January 10, 1868, p. 100; GB to Vernou, July 30, 1868, p. 205, all in vol. 162; Roberts to GB, August 13, 1868, vol. 161, p. 42. For a weak and flawed analysis of the Bureau's social services, see Ira C. Colby, "The Freedmen's Bureau in Texas and Its Impact on the Emerging Social Welfare System and Black-White Social Relations, 1865–1885" (D.S.W. diss., University of Pennsylvania, 1984); idem, "The Freedmen's Bureau: From Social Welfare to Segregation," *Phylon* 46 (September 1985): 219–230.

56. DLM to Superintendent of Education (SOE), July 1, 1867, vol. 14; Office of SOE, School Houses Rented and Repaired, 1867, Cherokee County, vol. 17, pp. 22–23; Smith County, vol. 17, pp. 186–187.

57. DLM to Kirkman, July 9, 1867, p. 29; LCB to Kirkman, July 31, 1867, p. 37; DLM to DCB, September 13, 1867, p. 42; DLM to Garretson, October 31, 1867, p. 72, all in vol. 162.

58. DLM to Kirkman, September 4, 1867, p. 44; DLM to Garretson, October 1, 1867, p. 52; DCB to Miss Lizzie Gladey (New Orleans), October 8, 1867, p. 54; DLM to Garretson, October 14, 1867, p. 65; DLM to Garretson, October 31, 1867, p. 71; DLM to E. M. Wheelock (SOE), November 14, 1867, p. 75; DLM to Richardson, November 15, 1867, p. 76, all in vol. 162; DLM to SOE, September 30, October 31, 1867, vol. 14; DLM to [SOE], October 31, 1867, vol. 16, p. 114.

59. DLM to Richardson, November 30, 1867, p. 81; December 12, 1867, p. 88; December 31, 1867, p. 94, all in vol. 162.

60. DLM to Richardson, February 29, 1868, p. 113; GB to C. S. Roberts (AAAG), March 31, 1868, p. 125; GB to Richardson, April 30, 1868, p. 141; GB to Vernou, June 1, 1868, p. 156, all in vol. 162; Office of SOE, Record of Schools, 1867–1869, vol. 23, pp. 6, 86, 89, 90; Richardson to DLM, January 24, 1868, Box 44.

61. GB to Richardson, March 31, 1868, vol. 162, pp. 127–128; Richardson to GB, May 6, 1868, Box 44.

62. GB to Roberts, May 30, 1868, p. 154; GB to Vernou, June 1, 1868, p. 156, both in vol. 162.

63. GB to Vernou, June 6, 1868, vol. 162, pp. 163–165.

64. Ibid.

65. Ibid.

66. GB to Vernou, June 27, 1868, p. 187; July 30, 1868, p. 208; August 31, 1868, p. 219; September 30, 1868, pp. 232–233; DLM to Richardson, December 12, 1867, p. 88; GB to Roberts, August 3, 1868, p. 211 (Roberts endorsement, August 14, 1868, Box 44); August 28, 1868, pp. 217–218, all in vol. 162; Office of SOE, Record of Schools, 1867–1869, vol. 23, pp. 92–93, 95–96, 98, 100.

67. Mary Stripling to GB, July 2, 1868, Box 44; GB to Vernou, June 27, 1868, p. 187; July 30, 1868, p. 208; DLM to Richardson, December 12, 1867, p. 88; GB to Roberts, August 3, 1868, p. 211; August 28, 1868, pp. 217–218, all in vol. 162; Office of SOE, Record of Schools, 1867–1869, vol. 23, pp. 92–93, 95–96. Stripling did receive her pay and wrote that she had at last begun to eat well and had clothes to wear. It is quite possible that Barrett and Stripling were smitten with each other.

68. GB to Vernou, June 27, 1868, p. 187; July 10, 1868, p. 191, both in vol. 162.

69. GB to Vernou, June 27, 1868, p. 187; July 10, 1868, p. 191, both in vol. 162.

70. W. H. Hartz (acting agent) to Disbursing Officer, November 10, 1868, vol. 162, p. 242; Hartz, Monthly Report, November 10, 1868, Box 44.

71. DLM to Kirkman, April 30, 1867, pp. 14–15; DLM to J. J. McDonald (JP, Henderson County), September 23, 1867, p. 49; October 3, 1867, p. 50; DLM to Thomas Hutchings (JP, Winsborough), October 14, 1867, p. 56, all in vol. 162. For all the recorded violence committed in the Thirtieth Subdistrict during this era, see "Criminal Offenses Committed in the State of Texas," Assistant Commissioner, Austin, vols. 11–13.

72. DLM to A. P. Shuford (district attorney, Ointueau, Texas), December 27, 1867, p. 91; GB to Malloy, March 30, 1868, pp. 123–124; GB to N. H. Faine (Larissa), April 11, 1868, p. 136; GB to Morrison, May 6, 1868, pp. 145–146; GB to the Sheriff of Henderson County, May 6, 1868, p. 146; GB to the Sheriff of Cherokee County, May 6, 1868, p. 147; May 25, 1868, p. 151; GB to Vernou, June 1, 1868, p. 156; August 1, 1868, p. 209; August 14, 1868, pp. 214–215; August 31, 1868, p. 220, all in vol. 162.

73. GB to Vernou, June 6, 1868, pp. 160, 163; August 31, 1868, p. 220; GB to T. M. K. Smith (commander, Post of Marshall), June 13, 1868, pp. 174–175, all in vol. 162; Allen W. Trelease, *White Terror: The Ku Klux Klan Conspiracy and Southern Reconstruction* (New York: Harper and Row, 1971), 137–148; Richter, *The Army in Texas during Reconstruction,* 32–38, 58–59, 143–145, 177–178; James M. Smallwood, "When the Klan Rode: White Terror in Reconstruction Texas," *Journal of the West* 25 (October 1986): 4–13.

74. GB to Vernou, June 6, 1868, Vol. 162, pp. 164–165.

75. Ibid., June 1, 1868, p. 157; June 6, 1868, p. 164, both in vol. 162. In a freak office accident, an individual dropped a derringer which discharged, the bullet lodging in Barrett's thigh. A painful wound, it severely limited his mobility.

76. GB to Vernou, June 24, 1868, vol. 162, pp. 177–178; Vernou to GB, July 8, 1868, Box 44.

77. GB to Vernou, July 21, 1868, pp. 195–197; September 8, 1868, pp. 228–230, both in vol. 162; Statement of GB, July 12, 1869, Box 2, Post of Jefferson, Texas, Records of the U.S. Army Continental Commands, 1821–1920, Record Group 393 (National Archives).

78. GB to Vernou, July 27, 1868, vol. 162, pp. 202–203. Barrett did attempt an early form of gun control by requesting authority from headquarters to prevent the carrying of weapons in Tyler, but his request was denied.

79. DLM to Garretson, October 14, 1867, p. 65; DLM to T. D. Eliot (chairman, Committee on Freedmen's Affairs, House of Representatives), January 22, 1868, pp. 103–104, both in vol. 162.

4. To Die in Boston (Texas, That Is)

1. W. E. Burghardt Du Bois, "The Freedmen's Bureau," *Atlantic Monthly* 87 (March 1901): 360; John and LaWanda Cox, "General O. O. Howard and the 'Misrepresented Bureau,'" *Journal of Southern History* 19 (November 1953): 427–456; J. Thomas May, "The Freedmen's Bureau at the Local Level: A Study of a Louisiana Agent," *Louisiana History* 9 (Winter 1968): 5–19. The experience of Texas agents is recounted in James M. Smallwood, "The Freedmen's Bureau Reconsidered: Local Agents and the Black Community," *Texana* 11 (1973): 309–320; idem, "Charles E. Culver, a Reconstruction Agent in Texas: The Work of Local Freedmen's Bureau Agents and the Black Community," *Civil War History* 27 (December 1981): 350–361; William L. Richter, "'The Revolver Rules the Day!' Colonel DeWitt C. Brown and the Freedmen's Bureau in Paris, Texas, 1867–1868," *Southwestern Historical Quarterly* 93 (January 1990): 303–332.

2. Eric Foner, *Reconstruction: America's Unfinished Revolution, 1863–1877* (New York: Harper and Row, 1988), 142–143.

3. George Shorkley (agent, Clarksville), to C. S. Roberts (acting assistant adjutant general [AAAG]), October 9, 1868, p. 1; October 9, 1868, pp. 4–5; October 15, 1868, pp. 9–13, all in vol. 83; Joseph J. Reynolds (assistant commissioner [AC], Texas) to Oliver Otis Howard (commissioner), October 20, 1868, vol. 5, p. 437; October 24, 1868 (telegram), vol. 5, p. 445; William G. Kirkman (WGK) (agent, Boston) to Roberts September 24, 1868, vol. 68, p. 131; WGK to Reynolds, December 4, 1867, vol. 67, pp. 134–135. In his last report, Kirkman stated that the only government property he possessed was two revolvers; WGK to Roberts, September 9, 1868, vol. 68, p. 122, Records of the Bureau of Refugees, Freedmen, and Abandoned Lands, Texas, Record Group 105 (National Archives); T. U. Taylor, "Swamp Fox of the Sulphur, or Life and Times of Cullen Montgomery Baker" (typescript), 86–87, T. U. Taylor Papers (Eugene C. Barker Texas History Center [ECBTHC], University of Texas, Austin). Unless otherwise indicated, all references are to the Texas Bureau records in RG 105.

4. Shorkley to Roberts, October 15, 1868, vol. 83, pp. 10, 13; Shorkley

to William A. Payne, November 10, 1868, vol. 83, pp. 26–27; Charles A. Vernou (AAAG) to Shorkley, October 28, 1868, vol. 83, p. 4; Reynolds to Howard, October 29, 1868, vol. 5, p. 450; Taylor, "Swamp Fox of the Sulphur," 87.

5. Shorkley to Roberts, October 9, 1868, p. 1; October 9, 1868, pp. 4–5; October 15, 1868, pp. 9–13, all in vol. 83.

6. Shorkley to Roberts, October 15, 1868, vol. 83, pp. 9–13.

7. Shorkley to Roberts, October 9, 1868, vol. 83, p. 1; R. H. Watlington, "Memoirs" (typescript), 84–85, R. H. Watlington Papers (ECBTHC).

8. Shorkley to Roberts, October 9, 1868, vol. 83, p. 1; Shorkley to Payne, November 10, 1868, vol. 83, pp. 26–27; Reynolds to Shorkley, October 28, 1868, vol. 5, p. 449. Copies of the reports of the events surrounding the agent's murder were sent to his brothers, Joel and Marshall; Vernou to Shorkley, October 28, 1868, vol. 83, p. 4; Vernou to M. M. Kirkman (Chicago), November 5, 1868, vol. 5, p. 456; Shorkley to M. M. Kirkman, November 29, 1868, vol. 83, p. 29; Reynolds to Howard, October 27, 1868, vol. 5, p. 447.

9. Finding reliable information on Kirkman's background has been frustrating. Even the genealogists of the Kirkman family know little about him. Kirkman is listed in the 1850 census as Gilbert, age seven (Gilbert was probably his middle name). His father, Thomas, killed his mother, Catherine, in 1850, and was subsequently committed to the Illinois state mental hospital. No one seems to know what happened to the children after this, but apparently they were raised by relatives (Terence S. Tarr to the writer, [June 1989]).

10. William G. Kirkman, Compiled Military Service Record, Records of the Adjutant General's Office, Record Group 94 (National Archives); Regimental Descriptive Book, Thirty-ninth Infantry, Companies F to K, Illinois, ibid.

11. WGK to Charles Griffin (AC, Texas), September 25, 1867, vol. 67, p. 63; WGK to S. H. Starr (commander, Mount Pleasant), February 22, 1868, p. 37; WGK to J. P. Richardson (AAAG), February 29, 1868, pp. 48–50, both in vol. 68; Roberts to WGK, September 22, 1868, vol. 5, p. 414. This chapter explores in greater depth Kirkman's activities and beliefs than was possible in Smallwood's essay. It also corrects several erroneous statements made by him in "The Freedmen's Bureau Reconsidered," 309–320. This article is ostensibly about Kirkman, but too often its focus becomes blurred, and Kirkman disappears altogether.

12. WGK to Roberts, September 18, 1868, p. 130; September 24, 1868, p. 131; Receipt, B. W. Gray (attorney), September 26, 1868, p. 134, all in vol. 68; Roberts to WGK, September 22, 1868, vol. 5, p. 414; "Boston," *The Handbook of Texas*, I, 471; U.S. Bureau of the Census, *Compendium to the Population Census Schedule, 1870* (Washington, D.C.: Government Printing Office, 1872), 63–66. In white population, Davis ranked thirty-seventh and Bowie eighty-third among Texas counties. Blacks comprised 48 percent of the total inhabitants in Bowie County and 38 percent in Davis.

13. General Orders, Special Orders, Circulars, and Rosters, AC, Texas,

1865–1869, June 22, 1867, vol. 9, pp. 172–173; Griffin to Howard, June 3, 1867, p. 69; J. T. Kirkman ([JTK], AAAG) to A. H. M. Taylor (AAAG, District of Texas), June 23, 1868, p. 87, both in vol. 5; WGK to Griffin, July 8, 1867, p. 1; WGK to JTK, July 9, 1867, p. 6; July 11, 1867, p. 7; WGK to Thomas Latchford (commander, Jefferson), August 1, 1867, p. 19, all in vol. 67. It should be noted that Kirkman's brother (Joel T.) was employed as acting assistant adjutant general by the Texas Bureau headquarters for approximately one year. See also, Kathleen Davis, "Year of Crucifixion: Galveston, Texas," *Texana* 8 (1970): 140–153.

14. WGK to Griffin, July 9, 1867, vol. 67, pp. 1–5; WGK to Griffin, July 31, 1867, AC, LR, K-54, Box 14; Taylor, "Swamp Fox," 86.

15. Thomas T. Abel (agent, Fort Smith, Ark.) to J. W. Sprague (AC, Ark.), May 4, 1866, Arkansas, Narrative Reports, AC, Letters Received, Box 9, RG 105.

16. Sprague to Howard, July 11, 1866, Arkansas, Operation Reports Retained, AC, Letters Sent, Box 12, RG 105.

17. WGK to Richardson, April 30, 1868, pp. 79–81; WGK to Vernou, May 30, 1868, pp. 91–93; June 30, 1868, p. 99; August 4, 1868, pp. 112–114, all in vol. 68.

18. WGK to Vernou, May 30, 1868, vol. 68, p. 92.

19. WGK to C. Jeans (Order no. 15), July 22, 1867, p. 2; WGK to Planters and Plantations in Bowie County (Order no. 30), November 5, 1867, pp. 5–6, both in vol. 69. Two copies of the contract were deposited with the agent, and each laborer received one.

20. WGK to Richardson, October 31, 1867, vol. 67, pp. 93–97; Theodore Brantner Wilson, *The Black Codes of the South* (University: University of Alabama Press, 1965), 108–111, 118, 142; John Conger McGraw, "The Texas Constitution of 1866" (Ph.D. diss., Texas Technological College, 1959), 156–196.

21. WGK to Planters and Plantations in Bowie County (Order no. 30), November 5, 1867, vol. 69, pp. 5–6.

22. WGK to Richardson, November 14, 1867, vol. 67, pp. 111–113.

23. WGK to Richardson, October 31, 1867, vol. 67, pp. 93–97; WGK to Richardson, January 31, 1868, pp. 20–24; February 29, 1868, 68, pp. 48–50, all in vol. 68.

24. WGK to Richardson, March 31, 1868, pp. 62–68; April 30, 1868, p. 80; WGK to Vernou, May 30, 1868, p. 92; June 30, 1868, p. 99; August 4, 1868, p. 114, all in vol. 68.

25. WGK to Spencer Lewis (freedman) (Order no. 62), December 28, 1867, p. 19; WGK to W. C. Nixon (Circular no. ?), March 13, 1868, p. 41; March 16, 1868, p. 41; WGK to E. R. Fort (Circular no. ?), March 27, 1868, p. 44; WGK to Scipio Peters (freedman), July 3, 1868, p. 66, all in vol. 69; *R. F. Peters* vs. *Daniel Richardson (freedman)*, [August 1867], p. 7; *G. W. Morrow* vs. *A. McFarland and Nicholas Dorsey (freedman)*, February 19, 1868, p. 19, both in vol. 70.

26. *Mrs. M. A. Paxton* vs. *Eli Ball (freedman)*, March 23, 1868, vol. 70, p. 21; Endorsement, Willis, May 12, 1868, vol. 66, p. 175.

27. WGK to Willis, November 28, 1867, vol. 67, pp. 128–129; WGK to Richardson, February 29, 1868, pp. 49–50; March 31, 1868, pp. 62–68, in vol. 68; *H. R. Runnels* vs. *Malinda Walters (freedwoman)*, June 27, 1868, vol. 70, p. 40. Walters lived in Arkansas.

28. WGK to Garretson, October 31, 1867, vol. 67, pp. 93–97.

29. B. W. Teller (Spring Hill) to WGK, July 11, 1868, vol. 66, p. 188; WGK to Garretson, October 31, 1867, vol. 67, pp. 93–97; WGK to Richardson, April 4, 1868, pp. 70–71; WGK to Dr. T. M. Fort (Paris), August 8, 1868, p. 115; WGK to DeWitt C. Brown (agent, Paris), August 8, 1868, p. 115, all in vol. 68; WGK to Mrs. Mary S. Boyce (Order no. 61), December 28, 1867, p. 19; WGK to Hiram F. Willis (agent, Rockey Comfort, Ark.), June 26, 1868, p. 64; WGK to W. S. Coleman (Order no. 40), December 3, 1867, p. 10, all in vol. 69; *U.S.* vs. *R. F. Weatherly*, March 2, 1868, p. 22; *Edmond Smith (freedman)* vs. *Zac Garret*, October 29, 1867, p. 11; *William Haskins and Wife (freedpeople)* vs. *S. B. McDaniel*, September 21, 1867, p. 9, all in vol. 70. See also the numerous settlements that Kirkman made in vol. 70, pp. 55–56.

30. WGK to Griffin, September 16, 1867, vol. 67, pp. 54–58.

31. A. R. Moores to WGK, April 7, 1868, p. 134; Endorsement, WGK, April 9, 1868, p. 135; Richardson to WGK, April 24, 1868, p. 146, all in vol. 66; WGK to Garretson, October 31, 1867, vol. 67, pp. 93–97; WGK to Richardson, May 13, 1868, p. 85; WGK to Vernou, June 30, 1868, p. 98, both in vol. 68; David M. Jordan, *Winfield Scott Hancock: A Soldier's Life* (Bloomington: Indiana University Press, 1988), 200–212.

32. WGK to Richardson, January 31, 1868, vol. 68, pp. 20–24; WGK to J. E. Rosser, May 16, 1868, p. 60; WGK to M. L. Ingram (Order no. 32), November 7, 1867, p. 7, both in vol. 69.

33. WGK to Richardson, January 31, 1868, vol. 68, p. 23; *Ben Tickle (freedman)* vs. *S. A. Owen*, [December 1867], vol. 70, p. 16.

34. WGK to William Leigh (Jefferson), October 4, 1867, p. 75; November 12, 1867, pp. 105–106; WGK to Willis, September 5, 1867, pp. 44–45, all in vol. 67; WGK to Richardson, December 31, 1867, 68, pp. 5–7; January 31, 1868, p. 24; WGK to Brown, January 8, 1868, p. 11, all in vol. 68; WGK to Uriah Cole (Order no. 52), December 20, 1867, vol. 69, p. 15; *James Smith (freedman)* vs. *Estate of W. Smith and William Lee*, September 11, 1867, p. 8; *Lewis Granderson (freedman)* vs. *Judge John Leigh*, November 27, 1867, p. 10, both in vol. 70.

35. WGK to Edward P. Burnett, March 5, 1868, p. 36; WGK to V. M. Lassiter, April 24, 1868, p. 54; WGK to George W. Morrow, June 1, 1868, p. 62, all in vol. 69; *Preston W. Roberts (freedman)* vs. *V. M. Lassiter*, April 24, 1868, p. 28; *Susan Sherrell (freedwoman)* vs. *Anderson Sherrell*, May 21, 1868, p. 32; *Rachel Ellis (freedwoman)* vs. *John King*, August 2, 1867, p. 6; *Clarissa and Violet (freedwomen)* vs. *William Moores*, August 3, 1867, p. 6; *Joiner Smith (freedman)* vs. *Edward P. Burnett*, March 20, 1868, p. 20, all in vol. 70.

36. "Note," WGK, June 15, 1868, vol. 69, p. 63; *Mary Ann Jeanes (freedwoman)*, vs. *W. Johnson* [September 1867], p. 8; *T. W. Wammock* vs. *Simeon Terry (freedman)*, April 1, 1868, p. 21, both in vol. 70; Bertram Wilbur

Doyle, *The Etiquette of Race Relations in the South: A Study in Social Control* (Chicago: University of Chicago Press, 1937), 109–135.

37. George R. Bentley, *A History of the Freedmen's Bureau* (Philadelphia: University of Pennsylvania Press, 1955), 159.

38. WGK to Garretson, October 31, 1867, vol. 67, pp. 93–97; WGK to Richardson, January 31, 1868, vol. 68, p. 23; WGK to W. H. Tilson (Order no. 69), December 20, 1867, vol. 69, p. 20; *Sally Criner (freedwoman)* vs. *Thomas Bennett,* December 27, 1867, p. 18; *Henry Ivey (freedman)* vs. *John King and Thacker,* October 1, 1867, p. 9; *Coleman Jones et. al. (freedpeople)* vs. *J. Tobert* (Harrison County), August 26, 1867, p. 5; *Sam Dixon, Jessie English, and T. Burroughs (freedmen)* vs. *Ellis Dandridge,* August 27, 1867, p. 8; *Polly Davis (freedwoman)* vs. *James T. Roseborough,* November 28, 1867, p. 15; *Ely Dickson, Frank Rochelle, and Carter Copeland (freedmen)* vs. *John Rochelle,* November 8, 1867, p. 11; *Nelson Eiceland (freedman)* vs. *Jessie D. Duke,* May 6, 1868, pp. 26–27; *George Jackson (freedman)* vs. *Lewis Daniel (freedman),* April 9, 1868, p. 22, all in vol. 70.

39. WGK to JTK, July 19, 1867, pp. 11–12; WGK to Garretson, September 30, 1867, p. 71, both in vol. 67; WGK to Spencer, Lewis, Boyd, and Whittaker (Temporary Committee of the Colored School), (Order no. 22), August 27, 1867, p. 2; WGK, Circular no. ?, March 4, 1868, p. 39, both in vol. 69.

40. WGK to Garretson, October 31, 1867, pp. 93–97; WGK to Richardson, November 30, 1867, pp. 130–131, both in vol. 67; January 31, 1868, vol. 68, pp. 20–24.

41. WGK to Garretson, October 31, 1867, vol. 67, pp. 93–97; WGK to Richardson, January 31, 1868, pp. 20–24; February 29, 1868, pp. 48–50; March 31, 1868, pp. 62–68; April 30, 1868, pp. 79–81; WGK to Vernou, May 30, 1868, p. 91; June 30, 1868, p. 99; August 4, 1868, pp. 112–114, all in vol. 68.

42. WGK to Richardson, March 31, 1868, pp. 62–68; WGK to Joseph Welch (superintendent of education [SOE]), May 2, 1868, p. 83, both in vol. 68.

43. Roberts to WGK, May 28, 1868, p. 160; Endorsement, WGK, June 13, 1868, p. 165; Welch to WGK, June 8, 1868, pp. 176, 178; June 28, 1868, p. 178; John M. Carch (chief clerk, District of Texas) to WGK, June 29, 1868, p. 186. Roberts to WGK, August 26, 1868, p. 198; Memoranda, WGK, [June 15, 1868], p. 175, all in vol. 66; WGK to E. M. Wheelock (SOE), March 4, 1868, p. 53; WGK to Forrest Hooks, March 4, 1868, p. 55; September 30, 1868, p. 135; Receipt, Hooks, September 26, 1868, p. 134; WGK to Roberts, April 17, 1868, p. 72; July 22, 1868, pp. 104–105; August 15, 1868, p. 116; October 4, 1868, pp. 138–139; Contract, United States of America, April 1868, pp. 73–75, all in vol. 68; Office of SOE, Record of Schools, 1867–1869, vol. 23, p. 21. In the contract, Hooks agreed, within sixty days, to complete the Myrtle Springs school and church by adding twelve seats and desks, finish the ceiling, purchase window sashes for two windows (eighteen panes in each window), and erect a split board fence around the two acres of land. Hooks was to pay $148 still due on the building, and the remaining $102 was pay for his work. In addition, the freedpeople spent about $150 on the building besides doing most of the work. Although it was

completed in "quite a neat manner," an extension of the original time had to be made because Hooks became ill. The black teacher was also "disappointed" in the men who had agreed to assist him with the carpentry work and splitting the rails for the fence. Kirkman believed that Hooks would have finished the work within the time restraints "if it had been possible to have done so."

44. Welch to WGK, August 22, 1868, p. 194; School Report, Hooks, August 1868, p. 194, both in vol. 66; WGK to Welch, September 3, 1868, p. 119; WGK to Hooks, September 5, 1868, p. 120; WGK to Richardson, April 30, 1868, pp. 79–81; WGK to Vernou, May 30, 1868, p. 91, all in vol. 68; WGK to Hooks (Circular no. ?), March 4, 1868, p. 39; Endorsement, Wheelock, April 4, 1868, p. 39, both in vol. 69; Office of SOE, List of Houses Rented and Teachers Employed, 1869–1870, vol. 20, pp. 24–26; Office of SOE, Record of Schools, 1867–1869, vol. 23, pp. 41–42, 86, 89, 91–92, 94, 96, 98, 100.

45. WGK to Richardson, December 31, 1867, pp. 5–7; April 30, 1868, pp. 79–81; WGK to Vernou, May 30, 1868, p. 92; June 30, 1868, p. 99; August 4, 1868, pp. 112–114, all in vol. 68.

46. WGK to Anthony M. Bryant (agent, Sherman), August 3, 1867, vol. 67, pp. 22–23; WGK to Richardson, March 23, 1868, p. 68; March 31, 1868; pp. 62–68; WGK to Welch, June 30, 1868, p. 97; WGK to (agent, Sherman), January 18, 1868, p. 17; WGK to Vernou, May 30, 1868, pp. 92–93, all in vol. 68; WGK to Judge A. G. Haskins, March 3, 1868, vol. 69, p. 36; *Squire Belle (freedman)* vs. *Crecy Belle and Others (colored)*, July 26, 1867, vol. 70, p. 5.

47. WGK to Anthony M. Bryant (agent, Sherman), August 3, 1867, vol. 67, pp. 22–23; WGK to Richardson, March 23, 1868, p. 68; March 31, 1868; pp. 62–68; WGK to Welch, June 30, 1868, p. 97; WGK to (agent, Sherman), January 18, 1868, p. 17; WGK to Vernou, May 30, 1868, pp. 92–93, all in vol. 68; WGK to Judge A. G. Haskins, March 3, 1868, vol. 69, p. 36; *Squire Belle (freedman)* vs. *Crecy Belle and Others (colored)*, July 26, 1867, vol. 70, p. 5. See also Barry A. Crouch, "The Struggle for Stability: The Texas Black Family, the Freedmen's Bureau, and the Law" (MS, 1991).

48. WGK to Vernou, May 30, 1868, pp. 92–93; June 30, 1868, p. 98; August 4, 1868, p. 114, all in vol. 68; WGK to Richardson, November 30, 1867, pp. 130–131; *Peggy Barksman (freedwoman)* vs. *Anderson Moores*, December 3, 1867, p. 16, both in vol. 70.

49. WGK to JTK, July 19, 1867, pp. 11–12; August 15, 1867, pp. 24–25; August 17, 1867, pp. 26–27; September 4, 1867, pp. 43–44; WGK to Griffin, August 22, 1867, pp. 33–35; August 26, 1867, p. 36; September 2, 1867, pp. 38–39, all in vol. 67.

50. WGK to W. A. Shaw, September 23, 1867, vol. 67, p. 59; WGK to Richardson, February 29, 1868, vol. 68, pp. 48–50.

51. WGK to Vernou, May 30, 1868, vol. 68, p. 92.

52. WGK to Garretson, October 31, 1867, vol. 67, pp. 93–97; WGK to C. E. Morse (AAAG), February 23, 1868, vol. 68, p. 38.

53. WGK to JTK, September 4, 1867, vol. 67, pp. 43–44; WGK to Morse,

February 23, 1868, p. 38; WGK to Richardson, February 26, 1868, pp. 43–44, both in vol. 68.

54. WGK to Vernou, June 13, 1868, pp. 94–95; WGK to Richardson, March 23, 1868, p. 67, both in vol. 68; WGK to the Sheriff of Bowie County, May 11, 1868, vol. 69, p. 57; *Dennis Burns (freedman)* vs. *Sheriff of Bowie County,* [April 1868], vol. 70, p. 24. It was WGK that ordered the arrest of the individual the sheriff failed to take into custody; WGK to Sheriff of Bowie County or any Constable of Bowie County, May 11, 1868, vol. 69, pp. 57–58. When the sheriff failed to post the necessary additional bond, the county would be without a law officer, as the constable position was also vacant, and so no officers would be available to execute the process of the courts. WGK recommended, "as a reliable man" and the "choice of a number of citizens," Thomas A. Morrow. T. M. C. Yates (brother of former governor Yates of Illinois) could also qualify and would accept the position. Immediately after the problems with the circus, Kirkman recommended that James Smeltzer be appointed sheriff in place of Duke "with as little delay as possible." The agent thought Smeltzer "maintained Union principals [sic]," but whatever his background, he was a "good man" and would "execute his duties" more promptly than Duke; WGK to Richardson, November 22, 1867, vol. 67, pp. 119–120; WGK to Vernou, June 13, 1868, pp. 94–95; WGK to Richardson, February 26, 1868, pp. 43–44, both in vol. 68.

55. Endorsement, Richardson, November 25, 1867, vol. 66, p. 80; WGK to Hooks, July 26, 1868, vol. 68, p. 106.

56. WGK to Richardson, November 30, 1867, vol. 67, p. 130; WGK to Vernou, August 4, 1868, vol. 68, p. 114.

57. Endorsement, Vernou, May 18, 1868, p. 153; May 27, 1868, p. 159, both in vol. 66; WGK to Roberts, May 1, 1868, p. 82; WGK to Vernou, May 27, 1868, p. 89; WGK to Richardson, May 9, 1868, p. 84; March 23, 1868, p. 68, all in vol. 68. Kirkman also asked numerous questions about how costs and fees were to be paid in civil and criminal cases.

58. WGK to Richardson, January 31, 1868, p. 21; April 30, 1868, p. 81; March 23, 1868, pp. 66–67, all in vol. 68.

59. N. B. McLaughlin (commander, Mount Pleasant) to WGK, January 20, 1868, p. 120; Endorsement, Roberts, March 18, 1868, p. 126, both in vol. 66; WGK to Ira W. Claflin, September 2, 1867, pp. 40–41; WGK to Starr, November 23, 1867, pp. 121–122; November 14, 1867, p. 114; WGK to Richardson, December 22, 1867, p. 143; WGK to Latchford, September 30, 1867, pp. 70–71; WGK to Garretson, October 31, 1867, pp. 93–97, all in vol. 67; WGK to McLaughlin, December 31, 1867, p. 5; WGK to Starr, January 15, 1868, p. 14, both in vol. 68. In May 1868 the soldiers were removed because the commander of the Fifth Military District had forbidden soldiers be detailed to citizen agents.

60. Starr to WGK, February 8, 1868, p. 108; February 21, 1868, p. 112, both in vol. 66; WGK to Garretson, October 31, 1867, pp. 93–97; WGK to Richardson, December 31, 1867, pp. 5–7, both in vol. 67; WGK to Starr, January 15, 1868, p. 14; February 6, 1868, pp. 28–29; February 19, 1868,

p. 35; February 22, 1868, p. 37; WGK to Morse, February 25, 1868, p. 40; February 23, 1868, p. 38; February 29, 1868, pp. 48–50; March 23, 1868, p. 60; March 31, 1868, pp. 62–68; WGK to Roberts, April 1, 1868, p. 69, all in vol. 68. For a corporal of the Sixth Cavalry, who had been stationed with Kirkman at Boston, then deserted when relieved of duty, and who apparently tried to con some freedpeople, see WGK to Starr, December 21, 1867, vol. 67, pp. 141–142.

61. C. Vann Woodward, "Birth of a Nation," *New York Review of Books*, November 20, 1980, p. 49; idem, *Origins of the New South, 1877–1913* (Baton Rouge: Louisiana State University Press, 1951), 159; Herbert Shapiro, "Afro-American Response to Race Violence during Reconstruction," *Science and Society* 36 (Summer 1972): 158.

62. WGK to Reynolds, November 22, 1867, pp. 115–120; WGK to Starr, December 21, 1867, pp. 141–142; WGK to Richardson, November 23, 1867, p. 121; November 30, 1867, p. 130; WGK to Reynolds, December 18, 1867, pp. 138–140, all in vol. 67; Allanson to WGK, November 28, 1867, vol. 66, p. 88. One of the horses that Kirkman captured was allegedly a race horse valued at $500 specie; WGK to Richardson, December 3, 1867, vol. 67, p. 132. Johnson's bond was not canceled until September 1868; WGK to Roberts, August 21, 1868, p. 204; Endorsement, Roberts, September 1, 1868, p. 205, both in vol. 66.

63. WGK to Richardson, November 27, 1867, vol. 67, pp. 124–126.

64. WGK to Starr, December 8, 1867, pp. 137–138; December 18, 1867, pp. 140–141; December 21, 1867, pp. 141–142; WGK to Reynolds, December 18, 1867, pp. 138–140, all in vol. 67.

65. WGK to Roberts, August 21, 1868, p. 204; Endorsement, Roberts, September 1, 1868, p. 205, both in vol. 66; WGK to Starr, February 18, 1868, p. 34; WGK to Reynolds, February 24, 1868, p. 39; March 18, 1868, p. 58; WGK to Richardson, March 23, 1868, pp. 66–67; WGK to Vernou, August 21, 1868, p. 118; WGK to Roberts, September 26, 1868, pp. 133–134, all in vol. 68; WGK, "Order for Tiller to Report," June 2, 1868, vol. 69, p. 63. Tiller also shot a freedman, intending to kill him but instead broke his arm; WGK to Starr, December 21, 1867, vol. 67, pp. 141–142.

66. J. B. Scott (clerk, District Court, Hopkins County) to Starr, October 8, 1867, pp. 47–49; Endorsement, WGK, October 16, 1867, p. 47; Endorsement, Duke, December 4, 1867, p. 47; Endorsement, WGK, December 6, 1867, p. 47; Endorsement, Moses Wiley (AAQM, Sixth Cavalry), April 28, 1868, pp. 169, 171; Garretson to WGK, October 17, 1867, p. 64, all in vol. 66; WGK to Griffin, August 22, 1867, p. 35; September 5, 1867, pp. 45–47; September 12, 1867, pp. 51–53; September 16, 1867, p. 54; WGK to Ira Claflin, September 6, 1867, pp. 47–48; WGK to W. E. Duke (sheriff, Bowie County), September 9, 1867, p. 48; WGK to JTK, September 2, 1867, pp. 39–40; WGK to Starr, September 27, 1867, pp. 67–68; WGK to Garretson, September 30, 1867, pp. 69–70; WGK to Richardson, November 12, 1867, pp. 106–107, all in vol. 67; WGK to Charles Rand (agent, Clarksville), January 9, 1868, p. 13; WGK to Starr, January 15, 1868, pp. 14–16; July 29, 1868, pp. 107–109, all in vol. 68. For a summary of the violence and black

depositions, see WGK, "Reports of Assaults and Other Outrages," April 10, 14, 1868, pp. 86–90; Deposition of Hooks, April 4, 1868, pp. 84–86, both in vol. 70.

67. Rollins, Kirkman wrote, was reported to be the "chief man" in Baker's "clan." He allegedly had been involved in "certain robberies" and with "associating" and "aiding" Baker. He had twice saved Baker from military arrest through timely information. A "large number" of Davis County citizens had presented Kirkman with a petition in support of Rollins. If Rollins would come forward, the Boston agent stated to the petitioners, give a $500 bond with two good securities, and report to him every twenty days, he would refer the matter to headquarters but thought the case "could be investigated before some civil officer." The friends of Rollins believed he would appear under this kind of arrangement. The case should be investigated and tried, Kirkman suggested to headquarters, without "too much of an opinion being formed before." The Boston agent hinted, however, that Rollins' neighbors were ignorant or hiding knowledge of his extensive activities. After all, Kirkman concluded, Rollins lived near Baker; he at least assisted Baker in hauling cattle; and Baker certainly had "associates" when he robbed and killed the freedpeople. He would have to give bond in Marshall; WGK to Adam C. Malloy (agent, Marshall), September 26, 1867, vol. 67, pp. 63–65.

68. Latchford to WGK, August 4, 1867, pp. 14–15; Allanson to WGK, August 5, 1867, p. 12; Adam Kramer to WGK, August 11, 1867, pp. 16–19; September 18, 1867, pp. 20–21, all in vol. 66; WGK to Claflin, July 25, 1867, pp. 13–14; WGK to JTK, July 25, 1867, pp. 14–16; September 4, 1867, pp. 43–44; WGK to Latchford, July 26, 1867, pp. 16–18; August 20, 1867, pp. 32–33; WGK to Richardson, November 13, 1867, pp. 108–111; WGK to Kramer, August 1, 1867, p. 18, all in vol. 67. Another soldier was wounded in the affray, but Kirkman deeply felt the loss of Titus, who was buried on July 26, calling him a "good and brave soldier." The Boston agent now needed two men: one to replace Titus and the other to relieve a corporal who had been observed "under the influence of liquor several times" and whom Kirkman did not think he could depend on. For his praise of another soldier who acquitted himself well when attacked by Baker, see WGK to Ira C. Clapp, August 20, 1867, vol. 67, pp. 30–31.

69. WGK to Ira C. Clapp, August 20, 1867, vol. 67, pp. 30–31; V. V. Smith (agent, Lewisville, Ark.) to Jonathan E. Bennett (AAAG), November 30, 1867, AC, Arkansas, Narrative Reports, LR-1593, Box 11.

70. Louis L'Amour, *The First Fast Draw* (New York: Bantam, 1959). Taylor, "Swamp Fox of the Sulphur," 1–13; Thomas Orr, ed., *Life of the Notorious Desperado Cullen Baker from His Childhood to His Death with a Full Account of All the Murders He Committed* (Little Rock: Price and Barton, 1875). The only scholarly treatment, which is incredibly weak, is Boyd W. Johnson, "Cullen Montgomery Baker, the Arkansas-Texas Desperado," *Arkansas Historical Quarterly* 25 (Autumn 1966): 229–239. My son, "Bear," brought the L'Amour book to my attention.

71. R. H. Watlington, "Memoirs," 83–84, ECBTHC.

72. V. V. Smith (agent, Lewisville, Ark.) to Jonathan E. Bennett (AAAG), November 30, 1867, Narrative Reports, AC, LR-1593, Box 11, Arkansas, RG 105; WGK to JTK, July 25, 1867, pp. 14–16; WGK to Latchford, July 26, 1867, pp. 16–18, both in vol. 67.

73. WGK to Griffin, August 22, 1867, pp. 34–35; WGK to Roberts, September 27, 1867, p. 67, both in vol. 67; Allanson to WGK, August 5, 1867, p. 12; Thad McRae (private secretary to Governor Pease) to Roberts, September 13, 1867, pp. 28, 30, both in vol. 66; Smith to Bennett, November 30, 1867, Narrative Reports, AC, LR-1593, Box 11, Arkansas, RG 105.

74. Willis to WGK, October 4, 1867, vol. 66, pp. 60, 62; WGK to Allanson, October 8, 1867, pp. 76–77; WGK to Garretson, October 4, 1867, pp. 81–82; October 8, 1867, pp. 77–78; WGK to Starr, October 7, 1867, p. 80, all in vol. 67.

75. Willis to WGK, October 4, 1867, pp. 60, 62; Brown to WGK, November 25, 1867, p. 84, both in vol. 66; WGK to Willis, October 22, 1867, p. 85; WGK to Brown, November 27, 1867, p. 128; December 22, 1867, p. 142, all in vol. 67; Willis to Samuel M. Mills (AAAG), July 31, 1868, Narrative Reports, AC, LR-871, Box 12, Arkansas, RG 105; Barry A. Crouch, "A Spirit of Lawlessness: White Violence, Texas Blacks, 1865–1868," *Journal of Social History* 18 (Winter 1984): 226.

76. Taylor, "Swamp Fox of the Sulphur," 88–92.

77. *Texarkana Gazette,* November 4, 1981, p. 3A.

78. Ibid.; Taylor, "Swamp Fox of the Sulphur," 148; Orr, *Life of the Notorious Desperado,* 131–132. Problems about compiling reliable information on Baker is evident in WGK to Starr, October 26, 1867, vol. 67, p. 90.

79. WGK to Richardson, February 29, 1868, vol. 68, pp. 48–50.

80. WGK to Reynolds, May 16, 1868, vol. 68, pp. 85–86.

81. WGK to Richardson, January 31, 1868, p. 21; December 31, 1867, pp. 5–7; WGK to Morse, February 23, 1868, p. 38, all in vol. 68.

82. WGK to Reynolds, May 27, 1868, vol. 68, pp. 88–89. Kirkman did not explain the necessity of why he had to break up an assembly of Davis County blacks, and the writer could find no answer in the Bureau or other records.

83. WGK to McLaughlin, December 23, 1867, vol. 67, pp. 143–144; WGK to Roberts, September 18, 1868, p. 130; September 24, 1868, p. 131; Receipt, Gray, September 26, 1868, p. 134, all in vol. 68.

84. N. B. Anderson (county clerk, Bowie County) to J. J. Reynolds (commander, Fifth Military District), September 13, 1868, Texas, AC, LR, A-38, RG 105.

85. Ibid.

86. WGK to McLaughlin, December 23, 1867, vol. 67, pp. 143–144; WGK to Roberts, September 18, 1868, p. 130; September 24, 1868, p. 131; Receipt, Gray, September 26, 1868, p. 134, all in vol. 68.

87. Anderson to Shorkley, November 4, 1868, p. 8; Endorsement, Shorkley, November 27, 1868, p. 7; Shorkley to M. M. Kirkman (Chicago), November 29, 1868, p. 29, all in vol. 83.

88. Robert J. Kaczorowski, *The Politics of Judicial Interpretation: The*

Federal Courts, Department of Justice and Civil Rights, 1866–1876, New York University School of Law Linden Studies in Legal History (New York: Oceana, 1985), 27.

5. Reconstructing Brazos County

1. S. L. Love to Mrs. S. V. Young (Concord, N.C.), August 9, 1868, Burton and Young Family Papers (Southern Historical Collection, University of North Carolina, Chapel Hill).

2. Ibid. The tactic of holding "barbecues" to placate disgruntled blacks was often used by the Democrats (see Barry A. Crouch, "Self-Determination and Local Black Leaders in Texas," *Phylon* 29 [December 1978]: 353). For a similar situation which occurred later in the century, see Lawrence C. Goodwyn, "Populist Dreams and Negro Rights: East Texas as a Case Study," *American Historical Review* 76 (December 1971): 1435–1456.

3. The most recent works on Reconstruction violence include Gilles Vandal, "The New Orleans Riot: The Anatomy of a Tragedy" (Ph.D. diss., College of William and Mary, 1978); idem, "The Origins of the New Orleans Riot of 1866, Revisited," *Louisiana History* 22 (Spring 1981): 135–165; Bobby L. Lovett, "Memphis Riots: White Reaction to Blacks in Memphis, May 1865–July 1866," *Tennessee Historical Quarterly* 38 (Spring 1979): 9–33; Altina L. Waller, "Community, Class, and Race in the Memphis Riot of 1866," *Journal of Social History* 18 (Winter 1984): 233–246; Allen W. Trelease, *White Terror: The Ku Klux Klan Conspiracy and Southern Reconstruction* (New York: Harper and Row, 1971), xliv, 137–148; Barry A. Crouch, "Postbellum Violence, 1871," in *Congress Investigates: A Documentary History, 1794–1974,* ed. Arthur M. Schlesinger, Jr., and Roger Bruns, 5 vols. (New York: Chelsea House, 1975), III, 1689–1846; George C. Rable, *But There Was No Peace: The Role of Violence in the Politics of Reconstruction* (Athens: University of Georgia Press, 1984); Herbert Shapiro, *White Violence and Black Response: From Reconstruction to Montgomery* (Amherst: University of Massachusetts Press, 1988), 5–29. On Texas specifically, see Barry A. Crouch, "A Spirit of Lawlessness: White Violence; Texas Blacks, 1865–1868," *Journal of Social History* 18 (Winter 1984): 217–232.

4. Charles William Ramsdell, *Reconstruction in Texas* (New York: Columbia University Press, 1910), 230. In the "abstract" the assertion by blacks of their "new rights" might "seem just enough," Ramsdell wrote, but their "manner of assertion" often brought "them into immediate collision with the whites." For criticism, see Stephen Stagner, "Epics, Science, and the Lost Frontier: Texas Historical Writing, 1836–1936," *Western Historical Quarterly* 12 (April 1981): 165–181.

5. Elmer Grady Marshall, "The History of Brazos County, Texas" (M.A. thesis, University of Texas, Austin, 1937), 88–89. Marshall did not cite Ramsdell.

6. Ibid. In all my work on the Millican riot, this is the only reference to Meyers that I have encountered.

7. Ibid., 86–87. In addition, "no contract could be made with a Negro

without the consent of those [Bureau agents] who were appointed to look after his welfare."

8. Michael Wallace, "The Uses of Violence in American History," *American Scholar* 40 (Winter 1970–1971): 86. Ramsdell cites two sources for his account of the Millican affair, both newspapers, only one of which is applicable. Wallace cites no references.

9. Melinda Meek Hennessey, "To Live and Die in Dixie: Reconstruction Race Riots in the South" (Ph.D. diss., Kent State University, 1978), 77.

10. Marshall, "The History of Brazos County, Texas," 1–2, 126–128; Randolph B. Campbell, *An Empire for Slavery: The Peculiar Institution in Texas, 1821–1865* (Baton Rouge: Louisiana State University Press, 1989), 264.

11. William H. Sinclair (Bureau inspector) to J. B. Kiddoo (assistant commissioner [AC], Texas), December 23, 1866, AC, Letters Received (LR), S-136, Box 4; Sinclair to Henry A. Ellis (acting assistant adjutant general [AAAG]), December 2, 1866, AC, LR, S-98, Box 4; Edward Miller (agent, Millican) to J. T. Kirkman (AAAG), May 31, 1867, AC, LR, M-377, Box 3; Miller to Kirkman, July 1, 1867, AC, Operations Reports (OR), Box 13, Records of the Bureau of Refugees, Freedmen, and Abandoned Lands, Texas, Record Group 105 (National Archives); Marshall, "The History of Brazos County, Texas," 69–70, 110; "Brazos County," *The Handbook of Texas*, II, 199; *Lippincott's Gazetteer of the World*, 2 vols. (Philadelphia: Lippincott, 1883), II, 1422. (Unless otherwise noted all references will be to the Texas Freedmen's Bureau records).

12. Miller to Kirkman, May 31, 1867, AC, LR, M-377, Box 3; Miller to Kirkman, July 1, 1867, AC, OR, Box 13. Conditions in Millican were probably not much different from those surrounding Kansas cattle towns during the same era, the exception being the black citizens; Robert R. Dykstra, *The Cattle Towns* (New York: Knopf, 1968).

13. Marshall, "A History of Brazos County, Texas," 85a, 85b, 85c.

14. Captain L. H. Sanger to Kiddoo, July 23, 1866 (telegram), AC, LR, S-71, Box 4; Sinclair to Kiddoo, December 23, 1866, AC, LR, S-136, Box 4; Sinclair to Ellis, December 2, 1866, AC, LR, S-98, Box 4; Miller to Kirkman, May 31, 1867, AC, LR, M-377, Box 3; Miller to Kirkman, July 1, 1867, AC, OR, Box 13.

15. William L. Richter, "Tyrant and Reformer: General Griffin Reconstructs Texas, 1865–66," *Prologue* 10 (Winter 1978): 225–241. Hereafter initials of the three agents will be used in citations: Sloan (SCS), Edward Miller (EM), and Nathan H. Randlett (NHR).

16. U.S. Bureau of the Census, *Compendium to the Federal Population Census Schedule, 1870* (Washington, D.C.: Government Printing Office, 1872), 65; *Statistics of Population*, Ninth Census [1870] (Washington, D.C.: Government Printing Office, 1872), 63–67. It is impossible to determine the precise population and racial composition of Millican, as the 1870 census taker did not delineate towns, but precincts, in Brazos County. He simply included everyone without town distinction. In terms of county ranking by

whites and black percentage of total inhabitants: Brazos, 39/41 percent; Grimes, 40/60 percent; and Burleson, 45/37 percent.

17. See volume 9 of the Texas Bureau records for the organization and tenure of the agents. The background material on the agents comes from their pension files, compiled military service records, and their appointments, commissions, and personnel branch papers. The first is in the Records of the Veterans' Administration, RG 15, and the latter two are in the Records of the Adjutant General's Office, RG 94, all in the National Archives. The author is indebted to the late John A. Carpenter and to Cecil Harper, Jr., for allowing him use of their extensive files on the Texas agents. All three agents had Bureau experience before being assigned to the Twentieth Subdistrict.

18. Sinclair to Kiddoo, December 23, 1866, AC, LR, S-136, Box 4; Sinclair to Ellis, December 2, 1866, AC, LR, S-98, Box 4. On Sinclair, see William L. Richter, "Who Was the Real Head of the Texas Freedmen's Bureau? The Role of Brevet Colonel William H. Sinclair as Acting Assistant Inspector General," *Military History of the Southwest* 20 (Fall 1990): 121–156.

19. SCS to Kiddoo, August 9, 1866, AC, LR, S-71, Box 4; Sloan to AC, January 1, 1867, AC, OR, Box 13.

20. SCS to Kiddoo, August 9, 1866, AC, LR, S-71, Box 4; SCS to AC, January 1, 1867, AC, OR, Box 13; Sinclair to Kiddoo, December 23, 1866, AC, LR, S-136, Box 4; Sinclair to Ellis, December 2, 1866, AC, LR, S-98, Box 4.

21. Sinclair to Kiddoo, December 23, 1866, AC, LR, S-136, Box 4; Sinclair to Ellis, December 2, 1866, AC, LR, S-98, Box 4.

22. EM to Kirkman, March 31, 1867, AC, OR, Box 13.

23. Ibid.

24. EM to Kirkman, May 31, July 1, 1867, AC, OR, Box 13; July 29, 1867, AC, OR, Box 14.

25. EM to Charles Garretson (AAAG), October 31, November 30, 1867, AC, OR, Box 15; SCS to AC, January 1, 1867, AC, OR, Box 13. For the type of justice the blacks received under Miller, see EM to Kirkman, April 30, May 31, 1867, AC, OR, Box 13.

26. EM to Kirkman, May 31, July 1, 1867, AC, OR, Box 13; EM to Kirkman, July 29, August 31, 1867, AC, OR, Box 14; EM to Garretson, October 5, 1867, AC, OR, Box 14; EM to Richardson, October 31, 1867, AC, OR, Box 15.

27. EM to Kirkman, May 31, 1867, AC, OR, Box 13.

28. EM to Kirkman, April 30, 1867, AC, OR, Box 13.

29. EM to Kirkman, July 29, 1867, AC, OR, Box 14; Marshall, "The History of Brazos County, Texas," 87.

30. EM to Kirkman, July 29, 1867, AC, OR, Box 14.

31. G. T. Ruby (Bureau inspector) to Kirkman, June 23, 1867, AC, LR, R-186, Box 4; Miller to Kirkman, July 12, 1867, AC, LR, M-492, Box 3.

32. G. T. Ruby (Bureau inspector) to Kirkman, June 23, 1867, AC, LR, R-186, Box 4; EM to Kirkman, July 12, 1867, AC, LR, M-492, Box 3.

33. SCS to AC, January 1, 1867, AC, OR, Box 13.

34. EM to Kirkman, March 2, 31, 1867, AC, OR, Box 13; SCS to AC, January 1, 1867, AC, OR, Box 13.

35. Ibid.

36. EM to Kirkman, March 31, 1867, AC, OR, Box 13. Volume 9 contains all the circulars and orders pertaining to the signing of contracts.

37. EM to Kirkman, May 31, July 1, 1867, AC, OR, Box 13; July 29, August 31, 1867, AC, OR, Box 14.

38. Marshall, "The History of Brazos County, Texas," 87.

39. E. P. Thompson, "Time, Work-Discipline, and Industrial Capitalism," *Past and Present* 38 (December 1967): 59–60; Thomas F. Armstrong, "From Task Labor to Free Labor: The Transition along Georgia's Rice Coast, 1820–1880," *Georgia Historical Quarterly* 64 (Winter 1980): 432–447; Philip D. Morgan, "Work and Culture: The Task System and the World of Lowcountry Blacks, 1700 and 1880," *William and Mary Quarterly*, 3d series, 39 (October 1982): 563–599.

40. Ibid.

41. EM to Kirkman, July 1, 1867, AC, OR, Box 13; Thompson, "Time, Work-Discipline, and Industrial Capitalism," 61.

42. W. E. Burghardt Du Bois, ed., *The Negro American Family* (Atlanta: Atlanta University, 1908), 42; Thompson, "Time, Work-Discipline, and Industrial Capitalism," 62–63, 73, 90; Herbert G. Gutman, "Work, Culture, and Society in Industrializing America, 1815–1919," *American Historical Review* 78 (June 1973): 574, n. 41.

43. NHR to Richardson, December 31, 1867; February 6, 1868, AC, OR, Box 16.

44. Ibid.; March 9, April 4, 1868, AC, OR, Box 17; November 13, 1867, AC, LR, R-52, Box 9. Randlett was no casual observer inexperienced in Bureau work: he had served in Navasota from April to May 1866, in Courtney from June 1866 to January 1867, and in Anderson from April 1867 to January 1868. All three towns are in Grimes County (part of the Twentieth Subdistrict), which is adjacent to Brazos County.

45. NHR to Richardson, December 31, 1867; February 6, 1868, AC, OR, Box 16; NHR to Richardson, March 9, May 6, 1868, AC, OR, Box 17; NHR to Vernou, June 8, 1868, AC, OR, Box 18.

46. Randlett to Vernou, June 8, 1868, AC, OR, Box 18. Even in context, it is difficult to know precisely what Randlett meant by this comment.

47. NHR to Vernou, July 9, 1868, AC, OR, Box 18; July 23, 1868, AC, LR, R-178, Box 9; Hennessey, "To Live and Die in Dixie," 78, writes that the "Loyal, or Union, League especially angered whites throughout the South, for the League sought to organize blacks within the Republican party, but the effectiveness of this Republican tactic was never as complete as Democrats claimed. Democrats, however, used the Loyal League as a justification for their organizations such as the Klan." See also, Michael W. Fitzgerald, *The Union League Movement in the Deep South: Politics and Change during Reconstruction* (Baton Rouge: Louisiana State University Press, 1989). On the Texas Klan, see Trelease, *White Terror*, 93, 106, 137–148; William L. Richter, *The Army in Texas during Reconstruction, 1865–1870* (College

Station: Texas A&M University Press, 1987), 32, 34–35, 37–38, 43, 58–59, 81, 143–145, 165, 177–178. For the denial of its existence or the view that it was a "benevolent" organization that saved the state from the "horrors" of Reconstruction, see Guy M. Bryan to Rutherford B. Hayes, August 29, 1871, "The Bryan-Hayes Correspondence," IV, ed. E. W. Winkler, *Southwestern Historical Quarterly* 26 (July 1922): 61; Bryan to Hayes, December 8, 1880, XIV, *Southwestern Historical Quarterly* 28 (January 1925): 238; W. D. Wood, "The Ku Klux Klan," *Quarterly of the Texas State Historical Association* 9 (April 1906): 262–268.

48. NHR to Vernou, July 23, 1868, AC, LR, R-178, Box 9; Hennessey, "To Live and Die in Dixie," 78.

49. NHR to Vernou, July 23, 1868, AC, LR, R-178, Box 9; Hennessey, "To Live and Die in Dixie," 78. For a refutation of the myth that blacks were horrified by the Klan beyond reason, see Trelease, *White Terror.*

50. NHR to Vernou, July 23, 1868, AC, LR, R-178, Box 9; Hennessey, "To Live and Die in Dixie," 78–79. Randlett was not present at the initial stage of the confrontation between Millican blacks and whites, but his is the most reliable report available. Except for largely unreliable newspaper accounts, there is little information on the riot itself.

51. NHR to Vernou, July 23, 1868, AC, LR, R-178, Box 9; Hennessey, "To Live and Die in Dixie," 78–79; Crouch, "Self-Determination and Local Black Leaders in Texas," 344–355. For information on other black leaders and their backgrounds, see Eric Foner, *Reconstruction: America's Unfinished Revolution, 1863–1877* (New York: Harper and Row, 1988). Brooks was an ordained minister. In my files is a copy of a marriage license, which he signed, when he officiated at the ceremony of Stephen Curtis, a black state legislator, who represented Brazos County.

52. NHR to Vernou, July 23, 1868, AC, LR, R-178, Box 9; Hennessey, "To Live and Die in Dixie," 79.

53. NHR to Vernou, July 23, 1868, AC, LR, R-178, Box 9.

54. Ibid.; Hennessey, "To Live and Die in Dixie," 79–80.

55. Ibid.

56. NHR to Vernou, July 23, 1868, AC, LR, R-178, Box 9.

57. Ibid.

58. Ibid.; Hennessey, "To Live and Die in Dixie," 80.

59. Ibid. Randlett mentioned that Brooks might be guilty of some crime. Why he made this reference is not clear. Possibly he had heard some rumor. Through all the turmoil, there is no indication that Brooks had broken the law or committed a crime. If he had done anything wrong, it was in leading and advising the Millican black community, which made him the chief target for white criticism and action.

60. NHR to Vernou, July 23, 1868, AC, LR, R-178, Box 9; Hennessey, "To Live and Die in Dixie," 81.

61. NHR to Vernou, July 23, 1868, AC, LR, R-178, Box 9. Apparently Randlett was not able to substantiate the charge because I discovered no such documents. The state constitutional convention, which was then meeting, sent a three-man investigative team, whose authority in the mat-

ter was questionable. If they produced a report, it no longer seems to exist. To postulate that the blacks killed their own community leader is totally unbelievable. The same day that Randlett was informed of Brooks' death, he directed the deputy sheriff to summon a sufficient posse and to search the area for additional blacks who might have been killed or wounded. This ground had been covered previously by a white group. The deputy sheriff reported two cases of men wounded. Whether the wounds occurred during the search or during the confrontation on July 15 was not made clear. The casualties were both black.

62. NHR to Vernou, July 23, 1868, AC, LR, R-178, Box 9; "Criminal Offences Committed in the State of Texas," AC, Austin, vol. 13, p. 156, case nos. 1954–1961.

63. Oliver Otis Howard (commissioner) to J. J. Reynolds (AC, Texas), July 20, 1868 (telegram), AC, LR, H-235, Box 7; Reynolds to Howard, July 20, 1868 (telegram), p. 358; July 21, 1868 (telegram), p. 359, AC, Letters Sent, both in vol. 5.

64. NHR to Vernou, August 3, September 4, 1868, AC, OR, Box 18; NHR to C. S. Roberts (AAAG), October 2, 1868, AC, OR, Box 19.

65. NHR to Vernou, July 23, 1868, AC, LR, R-178, Box 9; August 4, 1868, AC, LR, R-191, Box 9. I was unable to find any affidavits by whites or blacks. For a biased account by one who was an eyewitness to some of the Millican events, see G. A. Wheat (Millican mayor) to the Editor of the *Houston Telegraph*, July 17, 1868, in the *New York Times*, July 30, 1868, p. 5.

66. NHR to Vernou, August 20, 1868, AC, LR, R-201, Box 9.

67. *New Orleans Daily Picayune*, July 18, 1868; *Austin Tri-Weekly State Gazette*, July 22, 1868; *Texas Countryman* (Hempstead), July 22, 1868; *Flake's Daily Bulletin* (Galveston), July 17, 18, 1868; *Daily Austin Republican*, July 20, 22, 1868; *San Antonio Express*, July 19, 24, 1868. Of all these newspapers, the most accurate reporting came from *Flake's* and the *Express*.

68. *Daily Austin Republican*, July 22, 1868; *San Antonio Express*, July 24, 1868.

69. Wheat to the Editor of the *Houston Telegraph*, July 17, 1868, in the *New York Times*, July 30, 1868, p. 5.

70. Ibid.

71. *Daily Austin Republican*, July 28, 1868. This was not an actual communication, or cited as such, but extracts were quoted from the letter.

72. Randlett to Vernou, July 23, 1868, AC, LR, R-178, Box 9.

73. Ibid.

74. Hennessey, "To Live and Die in Dixie," 81.

75. *Texas Country* (Hempstead), July 22, 1868.

Conclusion

1. William Manchester to the Editor, *New York Times Book Review*, February 4, 1990, p. 33.

2. W. E. Burghardt Du Bois, "The Freedmen's Bureau," *Atlantic Monthly* 87 (March 1901): 357, 359, 361, 362, 363.

3. Willie Lee Rose, "Blacks without Masters: Protagonists and Issue," in *Slavery and Freedom*, ed. William W. Freehling (New York: Oxford University Press, 1982), 93.

4. Du Bois, "The Freedmen's Bureau," 363; Herman Belz, *Emancipation and Equal Rights: Politics and Constitutionalism in the Civil War Era* (New York: Norton, 1978), 72.

Essay on Sources

UNFORTUNATELY, Texas has no modern history of Reconstruction and no major article or book-length study of the Freedmen's Bureau has been based upon the sizable resources in the National Archives. The most recent survey of the state of Texas Reconstruction historiography is Barry A. Crouch, "'Unmanacling' Texas Reconstruction: A Twenty-Year Perspective," *Southwestern Historical Quarterly* 93 (January 1990): 275–302. On the national scene are two superb works: Eric Foner's *Reconstruction: America's Unfinished Revolution, 1863–1877* (New York: Harper and Row, 1988), has an excellent bibliography and is one of the few studies that attempts to integrate Texas into the flow of national events, and Leon F. Litwack's *Been in the Storm So Long: The Aftermath of Slavery* (New York: Knopf, 1979), which has much information on black Texans and should be the starting place for any scholar.

The three major studies of the Bureau from a national perspective include George R. Bentley, *A History of the Freedmen's Bureau* (Philadelphia: University of Pennsylvania Press, 1955); John A. Carpenter, *Sword and Olive Branch: Oliver Otis Howard* (Pittsburgh: University of Pittsburgh Press, 1964); and William S. McFeely, *Yankee Stepfather: O. O. Howard and the Freedmen* (New Haven: Yale University Press, 1968). In specific ways I disagree with all three. Bentley's book, the only general history of the Bureau based upon the massive papers in the National Archives, finds the Bureau to be a baneful political influence and overly sympathetic to the freedmen at white expense. Its overall viewpoint is not much different than the one originally proposed in 1904. Carpenter is very favorable to Howard and the assistant commissioners but tends to see the field agents as being less able and dedicated. This was not true in Texas. McFeely disparages the efforts of the Bureau and finds Howard's actions detrimental to the agency as a whole. This negative interpretation has influenced many other Bureau studies, but I reject it, preferring to consider the Bureau on its own terms.

Because this book is based almost solely upon the Bureau manuscripts in Record Group 105, the Records of the Bureau of Refugees, Freedmen, and Abandoned Lands, in the National Archives, I have attempted to carve out a different perspective than have past historians of the Bureau. For what the papers contain and some of the topics that might be investigated, see my

"Hidden Sources of Black History: The Texas Freedmen's Bureau Records as a Case Study," *Southwestern Historical Quarterly* 83 (January 1980): 211–226, and "Freedmen's Bureau Records: Texas, a Case Study," in *Afro-American History: Sources for Research,* ed. Robert L. Clarke (Washington, D.C.: Howard University Press, 1981), 74–94.

Although the Texas Freedmen's Bureau records are not of a size comparable to those of South Carolina, Louisiana, or Mississippi, they do comprise approximately 174 bound volumes and 44 boxes of papers. This, of course, does not include all the material pertaining to Texas in the Commissioner's Files or the Education Superintendent's. The Texas records of the Assistant Commissioner (M821) and those of the Superintendent of Education (M822) have been microfilmed by the National Archives and embrace thirty-two reels and eighteen reels, respectively. These are important sources of information, but the local records of the agents or subassistant commissioners have not been microfilmed, and they must be consulted at the National Archives. They provide much additional information that is not duplicated in the microfilm edition.

The Texas Bureau papers have two forms of organization. At the level of the assistant commissioner there are letters sent, letters received, circulars, rosters of agents, endorsements, and reports of operations and conditions. The extent of records kept at the local level depended partially upon the whims of subassistant commissioners, who generally made copies of letters sent, filed letters received, and entered settlements and cases adjudicated in another volume. If the matter did not need the attention of headquarters, it never became part of the assistant commissioners' files. Thus, much local material such as letters to local officials, the freedpeople, other Bureau agents, and the large number of cases settled can only be examined in the materials from the field agents. Much of this is the heart and soul of the Bureau organization and is where the least research has been done.

How blacks responded to the Bureau and how they used it for specific ends is explored in my "Black Dreams and White Justice," *Prologue* 6 (Winter 1974): 255–265, and Crouch and Larry Madaras, "Reconstruction Black Families: Perspectives from the Texas Freedmen's Bureau Records," *Prologue* 18 (Summer 1986): 109–122; reprinted in *Our Family, Our Town: Essays on Family and Local History Sources in the National Archives,* comp. Timothy Walch (Washington, D.C.: National Archives and Records Administration, 1987), 156–167. A similar approach, using the Bureau records, is my "Seeking Equality: Houston Black Women during Reconstruction," in *Black Dixie: Essays on Afro-Texan History in Houston,* ed. Howard Beath and Cary Wintz (College Station: Texas A&M University Press, 1992).

Several historians have dabbled in the Bureau papers; most of them barely scratching the surface. The two who have used the papers most extensively are James M. Smallwood and William L. Richter. Smallwood, in a series of articles and his book *Time of Hope, Time of Despair: Black Texans during Reconstruction* (Port Washington, N.Y.: Kennekat Press, 1981), is generally sympathetic to the efforts of the agents and uses the Bureau archives to explore the activities of black Texans during Reconstruction. His articles that deal with agents are discussed in chapter 1. Richter's original focus was the United States army and his ideas are presented in numerous articles and *The Army in Texas during Reconstruction, 1865–1870* (College Station: Texas A&M University Press, 1987).

In his extensive work on the army, Richter has also written a great deal about the individuals who served as Bureau assistant commissioners. He does not have much good to say about them as he tends to see military occupation of the South after the war as an unmitigated disaster. Caught up in army and state politics, their relations with the Democrats generally could be described as stormy. Richter blames the army for much of the upheaval, tends to believe that the violence that occurred in the state was probably exaggerated or, at least, not as extensive as other writers have suggested, and finds the citizenry hostile to both the army and the Bureau. His political interpretations, especially of the role of Joseph J. Reynolds, are unsubstantiated. The reverse side of the coin to Richter's interpretation is that of Robert W. Shook, "Federal Occupation and Administration of Texas, 1865–1870" (Ph.D. diss., North Texas State University, 1970), who has considerable information about the Bureau and its relationship to the army. Shook finds the efforts of the Bureau rather remarkable, considering the hostile environment that was constantly encountered.

Richter now turns his attention to the Bureau and focuses upon one agent, "'The Revolver Rules the Day!' Colonel DeWitt C. Brown and the Freedmen's Bureau in Paris, Texas, 1867–1868," *Southwestern Historical Quarterly* 93 (January 1990): 303–332, and a headquarters official, "Who Was the Real Head of the Texas Freedmen's Bureau? The Role of Brevet Colonel William H. Sinclair as Acting Assistant Inspector General," *Military History of the Southwest* 20 (Fall 1990): 121–156. He concludes that field agents did not receive much support from the Bureau chiefs and that Sinclair probably should be credited with most of the successes achieved by the Texas Bureau. Brown, hardly a typical agent, was not a particularly successful one, and although Sinclair, surely one of the ablest of Texas Bureau officials, made many recommendations, to posit the fact he really administered the Bureau seems rather strained.

The older, standard version of the Texas Bureau is Claude Elliott's "The Freedmen's Bureau in Texas," *Southwestern Historical Quarterly* 61 (July 1952): 1–24, which is based upon very minimal research in the archives. A newer, but still scantily researched piece, is Diane Neal and Thomas W. Kremm, "'What Shall We Do with the Negro?' The Freedmen's Bureau in Texas," *East Texas Historical Journal* 27 (Fall 1989): 23–34, which portrays the agents at a disadvantage in relation to the legal workings of the system because they were not lawyers. This view is not sustained by the sources. A general history of the Texas Freedmen's Bureau is still necessary to understand its relationship with state officials and the ways they assisted or hindered its activities.

On the agents, besides the work of Smallwood on Culver and Kirkman and Richter on Brown and Sinclair, there is little material. A sampling of what an agent encountered is Crouch, ed., "View from Within: Letters of Gregory Barrett, Freedmen's Bureau Agent," *Chronicles of Smith County, Texas* 12 (Winter 1973): 13–26. Although unpublished, the best general examination of the subassistant commissioners is Cecil Harper, Jr., "Freedmen's Bureau Agents in Texas: A Profile" (Paper presented at the annual meeting of the Texas State Historical Association, Galveston, 1987). Harper's statistical and narrative analysis clearly demonstrates that the agents had considerable qualifications. Corruption did exist in the Texas Bureau but was minimal, particularly compared to Louisiana. One example, but his duties and exact crime are not especially clear, is Thomas H. Smith, "Conflict and Corruption: The Dallas Establishment vs. the Freedmen's Bureau Agent," *Legacies* 1 (Fall 1989): 24–30. Smith did not examine the local records of this particular agent, William H. Horton.

Much more work is necessary on the Bureau, black labor, and the economic system. Smallwood partially used the records for his "Perpetuation of Caste: Black Agricultural Workers in Reconstruction Texas," *Mid-America* 61 (January 1979): 5–23, but this is only a beginning. Randolph B. Campbell, in perhaps the finest study of a Texas county, *A Southern Community in Crisis: Harrison County, Texas, 1850–1880* (Austin: Texas State Historical Association, 1983), has excellent material on the labor scene and the Bureau's interaction, but it is necessarily limited because of his focus. Nora Estelle Owens, "Presidential Reconstruction in Texas: A Case Study" (Ph.D. diss., Auburn University, 1983), sees the Bureau's efforts in behalf of blacks in the agricultural arena more positively than most writers.

Education is one area of Bureau activity that has been written about extensively, but surprisingly little is based upon the large number of Bureau educational records. Unquestionably, the two major sources are Smallwood and Alton Hornsby, Jr.'s, "The Freedmen's Bureau Schools in Texas, 1865–1870," *Southwestern Historical Quarterly* 76 (April 1973): 397–417, but all is based upon published records. Smallwood, also using the American Missionary Association archives, emphasizes black self-help more than the role of the Bureau. A work that concludes that the Bureau's efforts were very negative is Ira C. Colby, "The Freedmen's Bureau in Texas and Its Impact on the Emerging Social Welfare System and Black-White Social Relations, 1865–1885" (D.S.W. diss., University of Pennsylvania, 1984). Colby barely skimmed the Bureau records, ignores recent publications, and fails to understand the Bureau's intended role. He follows the same tack in his discussion of the social-welfare activities of the agency.

Few subdistrict studies of the Bureau exist. The only one available, Ross Nathaniel Dudney, Jr., "Texas Reconstruction: The Role of the Bureau of Refugees, Freedmen, and Abandoned Lands, 1865–1870, Smith County (Tyler), Texas" (M.A. thesis, Texas A&I University, 1986), is disappointingly thin. It fails to take advantage of the more current publications concerning the Bureau and only briefly uses the agency's materials, especially pertaining to Smith County.

Almost every Bureau agent complained about the extensive amount of violence in postwar Texas. Contrary to Richter's argument, *The Army in*

Texas, the evidence suggests that it was pervasive and concentrated upon black Texans. An overview, based upon the three-volume Bureau compilation, is Crouch, "A Spirit of Lawlessness: White Violence, Texas Blacks, 1865–1868," *Journal of Social History* 18 (Winter 1984): 217–232. Crouch estimates that 1 percent of the black male population between fifteen and forty-nine years of age were killed during the first three years of Reconstruction. A useful corrective, but one that defines politics very broadly, is Greg Cantrell, "Racial Violence and Reconstruction Politics in Texas, 1867–1868," *Southwestern Historical Quarterly* 93 (January 1990): 333–355. Much more needs to be done in relation to violence, the Ku Klux Klan, and the Bureau.

The Bureau has been accused of being deeply involved in politics. By its very nature, it was indeed a political agency. There is little specific information on this phenomena, however. Unquestionably, the best book on Texas politics is Carl H. Moneyhon, *Republicanism in Reconstruction Texas* (Austin: University of Texas Press, 1981). He does not deal specifically with the Bureau but has much information about some Bureau officials who later entered the political arena. The writings of James Alex Baggett, especially his "The Rise and Fall of the Texas Radicals, 1867–1883" (Ph.D. diss., North Texas State University, 1972), also need to be consulted when considering the Bureau's relationship to the state political scene.

One of the most significant problems that the historian of Texas Reconstruction encounters is that no general history of Reconstruction in the Lone Star State has been published since 1910. As a result, many of the interpretations are outdated and based upon extremely limited research in manuscript sources. The last and to date the best synthesis of the post–Civil War era was John Pressley Carrier, "A Political History of Texas during the Reconstruction, 1865–1874" (Ph.D. diss., Vanderbilt University, 1971). But Carrier's work is now two decades old, and newer perceptions have begun to emerge and modify some of his viewpoints. Until a general overview is forthcoming, based upon more recent ideas in Texas Reconstruction historiography, it will be difficult for scholars to weave their own specialized work into a coherent framework.

There are many other subjects that have not been dealt with in relation to the Bureau. More work needs to be done on the individual agents, and essays on the assistant commissioners would be helpful. The Bureau's relationship with the various provisional and elected governors has been neglected and is open to further investigation. In addition, the Bureau courts require more examination, as it was to these tribunals that blacks brought many of their problems to be adjudicated and resolved. Indeed, as suggested earlier, a full-scale history of the Texas Bureau still needs to be written in order to understand precisely where the agency fits into the Lone Star State Reconstruction experience.

Index